My Mother Was Nuts

My Mother Was Nuts

Penny Marshall

A Memoir

New Harvest
Houghton Mifflin Harcourt
BOSTON   NEW YORK
2012

This edition published by special arrangement with Amazon Publishing

For information about permission to reproduce selections from this book,
write to Permissions, Houghton Mifflin Harcourt Publishing Company,
215 Park Avenue South, New York, New York 10003.

www.hmhbooks.com

Library of Congress Cataloging-in-Publication Data is available.
ISBN 978-0-547-89262-7

Printed in the United States of America
DOC 10 9 8 7 6 5 4 3 2 1

To my Mommy and Daddy,
who gave me their best;
my brother, who gave me a job; my sister,
who helped me cross the street; and
my daughter, Tracy, and my grandchildren,
Spencer, Bella, and Viva, who provided
me with the opportunity to love them forever.

Contents

INTRODUCTION *xi*

1. FIVE MORE MINUTES 1
2. WHAT DID'YA EXPECT —HEDY LAMARR? 8
3. THE GRAND CONCOURSE 14
4. DINNERTIME 20
5. STRICTLY BALLROOM 24
6. DEAR MOM & DAD 32
7. THE MARSHALL PLAN 39
8. MUCHO GRATH-E-ATH 46
9. THE FACTS OF LIFE 52
10. MRS. HENRY 57
11. FORGET THE GAS, I WANT THE JELL-O 64
12. TAKE EVERYTHING 70
13. A WORK IN PROGRESS 75
14. THANK GOD MY BROTHER HAD A JOB 81
15. THE MANSON MURDERS 87
16. I MADE HIM SICK 92
17. ALL IN THE FAMILY 98
18. FUNNY BUSINESS 106
19. OUT WITH A LAUGH 111
20. LIVE FROM NEW YORK 114
21. READY FOR PRIME TIME 118
22. CHICK FIGHT 125

23. FROM SUDS TO STARDOM   131

24. LIVE FROM NEW ORLEANS   135

25. WHERE'S MOM?   141

26. THE REMODEL   146

27. TRIPPING   154

28. DIRTY LAUNDRY   162

29. TAKING DIRECTION   170

30. OLD FRIENDS   176

31. GOOD-BYE SHIRL   182

32. IN THE EVENT OF MY DEATH   188

33. PEGGY SUE BLUES   193

34. JUMPIN' JACK FLASH   202

35. KEEPING THINGS IN PERSPECTIVE   209

36. GETTING STREET CRED   213

37. HEART AND SOUL   219

38. A MEDICAL MYSTERY TOUR   231

39. BATTER UP   247

40. ADDING WOOD   259

41. THE GOSPEL   269

42. THE LAST BULL RUN   280

43. RIDING IN CARS   290

44. MAKE IT FUNNY, HONEY   301

45. GET ME SOME WHITE CASTLES   306

46. FIVE MORE MINUTES   317

    ACKNOWLEDGMENTS   323

I've always been crazy
but it's kept me from going insane.

— WAYLON JENNINGS (framed in my bathroom)

Night of the Ninjas

I'M NOT SOMEONE who's had to deal with much personal drama outside of the usual: growing up with parents who hated each other, two marriages and divorces, the ups and downs of various relationships, raising a daughter, and watching friends crack up and overdose. There was the cancer thing, too. As you can see, though, there's nothing out of the ordinary, nothing that most people don't go through, nothing that says, "Penny, you were lucky to get through that one."

Oh, except for when I was robbed by the knife-wielding ninjas.

Let me explain. I had come home one night after watching dailies of myself, something I never do because I think I look terrible. I pulled on my favorite flannel nightgown, the one with a *New York Times* crossword puzzle pattern on it, and applied a facial mask, one of those thick pastes. As it began to harden, I heard a strange, unsettling noise inside one of the other rooms. I thought it was my daughter, Tracy, and her boyfriend, Gio Coppola, who were supposed to be there, or my niece, Penny Lee, who was living downstairs in an outside apartment.

"Tray," I called.

Nothing.

"P-Lee," I said, trying my niece.

No answer.

I walked out of my bedroom and looked in the living room. It was long and narrow, with sliding glass doors that provided a 180-degree view of Los Angeles, spanning the high-rise buildings downtown to the Pacific Ocean. At night, though, it was a black carpet of shimmering lights. As I stared across the room, I saw someone run into the den and try a terrace door, which didn't open. I don't startle easily. I've directed seven movies and know a thing or two about dealing with unexpected crises. In an emergency, I'm as calm as a heart surgeon.

Moving methodically, I found the clicker for my alarm system on top of the bookcase, and just as I did, a guy emerged from the den. He had a stocking over his head and a knife in his hand. From his stance, I sensed he was nervous.

"Who'd you let out?" he asked, thinking I'd opened the front gate.

I took a breath.

"My assistant," I said, lying.

Another guy then appeared, this one dressed like a ninja and holding a large sword. That was a nice touch, I thought. I assumed they must have watched Tracy, Gio, and my niece leave and then come up the hill, thinking the house was empty. They told me that we had to go to the bedroom, but we were interrupted by the phone. The first ring caused all of us to freeze and stare at the blinking light. It was the third line, I noticed — the alarm company.

I guessed the clicker had worked.

I picked up the phone and immediately hung it up again. They glanced at me, then at each other, then back at me.

"Otherwise it'll keep ringing," I said.

I knew they wanted to steal something and, unfortunately for them, I didn't have much in the house to steal. I had only lived there a little more than a year after renting a couple of different homes over the years. I had some old couches downstairs, and a piano in the living room. None of it was expensive, valuable, or movable. I noticed them checking me out for jewelry. I had on a necklace and a ring that had been my grandmother's.

The bad robber — the one with the stocking over his head and the knife in his hand — told me to hand over my jewelry. "I can't," I said. "I'm doing a movie. I wore them on camera. I have to match in the shots."

They exchanged looks, and I suppose, this being Hollywood, they understood. They grabbed some cameras on a shelf instead.

By now, my facial mask had hardened, making it difficult to talk. As the bad robber went to look around the house again, he instructed his ninja partner, aka the good robber, to watch me. He said something along the lines of, "If she moves, kill her." He had watched too many movies. Still, I wondered how that would work. Would he impale me with his ninja sword? Cut off my head? Would his blade go through my facemask?

When the bad robber was gone, I turned to his partner and said, "I'm going to wash this mask off my face." I didn't ask. I told him. Then, without waiting for an answer, I went into the bathroom, scrubbed my face, and returned. My robber was surprised when he saw my face.

"Oh, my God," he said. "If we'd known it was you, we never would've come up."

"Well, you can leave anytime," I said.

He didn't move. Neither did I. We stared at each other, unsure what to say next. It was like being in a bad improv class.

"Is this going to be your career?" I asked.

"No, I'm going to college," he said.

"All right," I said. "So this is just a part-time job?"

Then the bad robber returned. He was frustrated by how little I had in the way of loot. He looked at me as if that was my fault. I started to explain that had I known I was going to be robbed . . . But I did have traveler's checks, which I got out. In the meantime, the phone had continued to ring, and this time I picked it up. It was my friend Susan Forristal from New York checking in. I told her that I couldn't talk. Later, she told me that because I had hung up so quickly she thought I was with someone having sex.

Not quite. And when the phone rang again, the bad robber, now annoyed, took the ninja's sword and destroyed it, reminding me of my old friend John Belushi's Samurai Warrior character. Of course, this being my life, as soon as the phone was in pieces, another extension began to ring.

"What can I do?" I said, shrugging.

"Just sign the traveler's checks," he said.

"You know, I think I have to be there in person when you cash these," I said.

"Just sign," he said.

"I'm sorry I don't have more for you," I said. "I have a Roy Rogers plate in the kitchen. I think it might be a collector's item."

The phone rang again, and I answered it. This time it was the police, a Lieutenant So-and-so.

"Are you okay?" he asked.

"So far," I said.

"Do you know these people?"

"No."

He asked a number of additional questions. Since we had already established the basics, they struck me as superfluous. Actually, they struck me as stupid and pointless. I was being robbed. The robbery was in progress. The robbers were in my home. I did not know them. They were *robbers*. What more mattered? Annoyed and frustrated, I turned to the bad robber and held out the receiver.

"It's for you," I said.

I just couldn't deal with the cop anymore.

"It's okay, we know her," I heard the robber say. "She owes us money."

Then he handed the phone back to me. He looked just as irritated with the cop as I was. Neither of us wanted to talk to him.

"Hello?" I said.

"Do you know him?" the cop asked.

"No."

"Do you owe him money?"

"No."

"Are there weapons?"

"Yes."

All of a sudden we heard a helicopter hovering overhead, and the house filled with bright light from its spotlight. I have a lot of glass doors and windows, and all I could think was that the police were going to shoot through the glass and I was going to have to pay for it — in more ways than one. I told the cop on the phone that I had to go. Then I turned to the robbers. It was time to talk common sense, not dollars and cents.

"Listen, you see the helicopter up there," I said. "Now the three of us are in the same situation. They're going to come through here and probably shoot you — and maybe me, too. I don't know. But there is a way out of here, out the back and down the hill."

So they took off one way and I went upstairs. There were cops everywhere. I told them the robbers had scrambled down the hill, adding that they didn't have guns. I didn't want them shooting anyone — especially the ninja going to college. He seemed like a nice kid. I didn't have to wait long for a resolution. Within a few minutes, cops down the hill radioed that they had caught the bad robber. He was hiding in the neighbor's bushes down the street.

They wanted me to identify him. But they wouldn't bring him back to my place because he wasn't on my property. Instead, I had to go outside in my pajamas, in front of all the press that had gathered, get in a cop car, and let them drive me to the bottom of the street where they were holding him. His mask was off, but I nodded in acknowledgment; that was the same guy.

Like a bad ninja, he scowled at me.

"I should've killed you when I had a chance," he said.

"That's pleasant," I said.

The next morning the press knew of the story and media outlets around the world reported "Laverne Foils Ninjas." Around 6 a.m., my phone started to ring. Randy Newman called. "Are you okay?" Paul Schrader called from Guam. "You defended yourself against ninjas?" Jack Nicholson called. "You okay, Pendal? You want to stay here? Only you would wash your face in front of robbers." Others checked in, too. It was nice.

Later that morning I went to work. That's just the way I am. One night I'm at a basketball game, the next I'm being held up by armed ninjas. Shit happens. So even though my life had been in danger, time didn't stop for me. I didn't reevaluate my priorities. They were already in a pretty decent place. I stayed calm and did what I had to do.

As you're going to discover on the following pages, this is the real me. I don't rattle easily. I'm wonderfully, oddly, almost irrationally calm and together in a crisis. It's when everything is calm that I get a little nutty. I've been this way since I was a kid growing up in the Bronx. I've come pretty far since those days, yet in some ways — no, make that in many ways — I'm still the same girl stuck in an aging body. I may not suck my thumb, wear braces, run after boys, or hang out on the Parkway rail anymore, but I rely on the lessons that I learned back then. They've gotten me this far. There must be something to 'em.

My Mother Was Nuts

CHAPTER 1
Five More Minutes

Penny in her dance costume at the Marjorie Marshall Dance School

Hal Altman

N O MATTER WHAT it is that happens to us as adults — and as we all know, shit *does* happen — we can usually trace the reasons back to the things that happened in our childhood. Here's the short version of everything you're about to learn: My mother was nuts. My father was boring. My older brother was funny. My older sister was girly. And I just wanted to play.

I still do. I attend basketball, football, and baseball games. I waste a stupid amount of time playing Angry Birds on my iPad. I watch movies. I talk on the phone. I'm just like I was as a kid. I like to play. My whole childhood was spent pleading with my mother to play outside for five more minutes.

"No, Penny, come in."

"Five more minutes. Please?"

"It's dark."

"No, it's not."

"Yes, it is."

"But I can still see the ball."

"How can you see it in the dark?"

"Just five more minutes."

That was me.

All the kids from my apartment building played together on the sidewalk and in nearby vacant lots. Popular games were stick ball, Skelly, Three Box Baseball, Hot Beans and Fried Potatoes, and I Declare War. It was fun. It was social. Boys and girls mixed. Age didn't matter. If you could round up enough people for a game, everyone was happy, especially me.

I am not much different now. I have never wanted to grow up and stop playing. In many ways, I haven't. In my work and in my personal life, I still try to maintain a connection to the sense of play that I remember from my childhood. Those experiences taught me the lessons that came in handy later in my life: Try hard, play by the rules, help your friends, don't get too crazy, and have fun.

Through all the changes and the challenges of adulthood, I have never strayed too far from those golden rules or from that little girl with the ponytail and the overbite who wanted to keep playing for five more minutes.

Why would I want to be inside at home?

My mother was there. Her name was Marjorie, and she was known across the Bronx as the owner, teacher, and chief choreographer of the Marjorie Marshall Dance School. She had 360 students, and she was beloved by 359 of them. The one that didn't love her unconditionally was the one who she compared unfavorably to all the other girls, the one who wanted to be outside playing, and the one who regularly heard, "Why can't you be more like Lois Rosenberg?"

Lois Rosenberg took dance lessons from my mother. She was blond and beautiful, polite and smart, and she loved dance school. She paid attention and tried hard. She was everything I was not. I was extremely skinny. I had a face like a monkey and an overbite that defied orthodontics three times. My study habits were poor, and I thought telling the truth to one's parents was overrated. It was not for nothing that my mother referred to me as "the bad seed."

In retrospect, my mother and I were more alike than we acknowledged. Blond and sassy, she was from the Bronx, the only child of Margie and Willie Ward, a homemaker and an accountant. She played the piano and taught herself to dance, and then she began teaching the neighborhood kids how to dance. If she got A's on her report cards, her father took her to the latest Broadway musical, and she adapted what she saw onstage for her own students. Though her technique wasn't perfect, she knew how to entertain, and with kids as her stars, her recitals were crowd-pleasers.

She was in college when she met my father, Anthony "Tony" Masciarelli, a handsome, athletic young man majoring in advertising at New York University. He was a clever writer and cartoonist. He wanted to be a big wheel on Madison Avenue. To better his chances, he changed his last name from Masciarelli to Marshall and forevermore denied that he was both Italian and Catholic.

My mother didn't give a shit about religion or ethnicity, not then when they first got together, or anytime afterward. If he wanted to change his name, fine, she didn't care. In him she saw someone who possessed the skills and smarts to be a good provider. She was also interested in his ability to draw and write. She wanted him to make programs for her recitals.

My father was no less guilty when it came to ulterior motives. He thought my mother came from a wealthy family that would help him into a comfortable life of commuter trains and country clubs.

As it turned out, both of their assumptions were wrong.

Later in their lives, my mother and father both kept a glass of water next to their beds and at night they put their dentures in them. Other than children, it may have been the only thing they had in common during their marriage. They married in 1932. My mother said that he fell asleep on their honeymoon, and that was probably the most romantic thing I ever heard her say about him.

After she died, I found some notes that she had typed to herself about the early years of her marriage. They revealed a time more difficult than I ever realized. The first one, written in 1932 following their three-day honeymoon, said, "Tony was rotten to me."

In subsequent notes she complained about money problems, fights, and general neglect. She said that he stayed late at work and went out with friends afterward. She grumbled that he didn't give her a birthday present or an anniversary present. She struggled with buyer's remorse. "New Year's Eve stayed home & in bed at 11:00," she wrote. "Tony out several nights a week alone. Well, he married me against his will didn't he? I practically forced him????"

What?

That was news to me.

They shared a small house in Pelham, just north of the Bronx, with my mother's parents, who helped with the payments. My father worked as an art director, and my mother taught dance in New Rochelle at the Arcaro Dance School. The Arcaro sisters — there were five of them — owned the school. All of them, including those who were married, lived together in the same house near the school. Though their house was full of married couples, they provided my mother with an outlet from the unhappiness of her own marriage.

My father wanted my mother to stop working, but she had zero interest in playing the pretty little girl on his arm. Apparently he tried to change. "Tony got out of bed," she wrote, "went in living room and said he was a new man coming back to begin a happy life all over again." It didn't last. In 1934 she wrote, "This year's the worst so far. He gets younger every yr. Now has the mentality of a 10 yr old."

She was frustrated and took it out on herself. "I feel miserable that such a once-likable fellow should turn into such an awful flop," she wrote. "I thought he was so fine and that he'd be such a loving thoughtful husband who would try so hard to make me happy. If he'd only try, I wouldn't mind, but he just doesn't give a damn. I'm giving him one more chance to prove that he is made of something and that he can be decent and thoughtful. I do hope he'll come through just to prove to myself that I'm not such a bad judge of human beings as to pick an utterly worthless person as a mate."

Life did improve. In November 1934, my mother gave birth to my brother, Garry. In January 1938, she had my sister, Ronny. She was very happy about becoming a mother. After my grandfather battled kidney problems and quit his job, they had to cut costs and moved into a two-bedroom apartment in the Bronx. But that seemed to work out.

Their new address was 3235 Grand Concourse, a six-story building in the heart of New York City's northernmost borough. It was an excellent location. Jerome Avenue was on one side, Van Cortlandt Avenue on the other, and Mosholu Parkway was a couple of blocks away. Their apartment was on the first floor because my mother was deathly afraid of fires and wanted to be able to get out quickly in the event of an emergency.

My father started his own advertising business, The Marshall Organization, and my mother taught tap, ballet, jazz and acrobatics to neighborhood kids in a large room in the building's cellar. She referred to it as the *ballroom,* and it may have actually been a ballroom back when the building was classier and the neighborhood as a whole was much fancier. I always called it "the cellar."

As my father built his business and my siblings grew out of babyhood, my parents seemed to work out their differences, or perhaps they just surrendered to them and enjoyed a manageable peace. He worked long hours, often staying out late with his colleagues, and she built her dance school, putting on shows at charity events, in churches, temples, and anyplace else that needed a show. They entered Garry in a "Cutest Baby" contest sponsored by the New York *Daily News,* and they doted on Ronny, their adorable baby girl.

But the calm ended in early 1943 when my mother found out she was pregnant again. She had wanted Garry and Ronny, but two children were enough for her. I was not planned. One night early in her pregnancy, as she was eating dinner, she started to bleed and thought she was going to lose the baby. Actually, she hoped that would happen. Later, in my teens, she said, "You were a miscarriage, but you were stubborn and held on."

Such a loving thing to say.

CHAPTER 2

What Did'Ya Expect —
Hedy Lamarr?

Penny's birth announcement, drawn by her father, Anthony Marshall

Marshall personal collection

I was born in St. Vincent's Hospital, on Friday, October 15, 1943, at 9:40 a.m., weighing 7.5 pounds and measuring 21 inches. It was the one day in my life that I was a morning person. I had green eyes like God knows who (my father's were brown, my mother's were blue — later they told me it was the postman) and a full head of hair — "much more than her daddy," my mother wrote in my pink baby book. Upon my arrival I had four fingers jammed in my mouth and I sucked them until I found my thumb, which I sucked until I began smoking cigarettes in junior high.

At home, my grandmother, who we all called Nanny, hung a pink flag out the window, informing the neighborhood that my mother had given birth to a girl. A formal announcement followed. My father drew a *New Yorker*-style cartoon of a man sitting on a couch in the hospital waiting room looking shocked as a nurse peeks around the door at a newborn baby. The baby is saying, "What did'ya expect — Hedy Lamarr?"

So that was also nice.

Everyone called me Penny. It was supposed to appease my brother and sister, who had saved their pennies all summer to get a pony and were disappointed when my mother brought home a baby sister instead.

But my full name is Carole Penny Marshall. Yes, Carole — after my mother's favorite actress, Carole Lombard — is my actual first name. It came as news to me, too. At the end of my second day of kindergarten, my teacher, Mrs. Goodblatt, sent me home with a note expressing concern. She thought I might be retarded (her word, not mine) because I didn't respond to my name. My mother took me to school the next day and set her straight.

"Call her Penny," she said. "She doesn't know that she has a first name."

From then on, I started the first day of each school year with a note from my mother. "Do not call her Carole. She will not respond."

Why did my mother even bother with Carole?

I don't know.

I really don't. If you notice, our names all have double letters and end in a *Y*. Pronouncing them, as my mother once explained, made you smile. *Gar-REE. Ron-KNEE. Pen-KNEE.* They were happy names, she said. Other names, such as Susan, Paula, and Katherine, were flat. To her, they were sad names. "And Penny," my mother wrote in my baby book, "is always ready for a hardy laugh."

From what I was told, my brother and sister were both good-natured children who endeared themselves to the family with cute antics like running up to the roof of the building to look for incoming Japanese war planes and promising to yell if they saw any. Those were the days when there were air raid drills. Then I came along like a low-flying plane no one saw. My mother said they loved me best when I finished my bottle. "That's when Penny smiles."

According to my baby book, my personality emerged early. At five months I got sick and lost weight. After a rash appeared on my ass — or my *heinie,* as my mother called it — she took me to the doctor. But he refused to give me an injection. Why? "Because he didn't want to annoy her," my mother wrote.

I had a soft side, though. I spoke early, made funny faces, and, as my mother noted, "When you tell Penny to love something, she puts her little head against your face or neck." The thing I loved most of all was my doll, Nancy. My grandmother made her from a pattern that came in the mail and gave her to me after my first birthday. Nearly two feet tall, Nancy's black button eyes dangled by threads, her hair was matted, and she was full of lumps from being stuffed with Garry's and Ronny's old clothes.

She was proof that my grandmother's days as a brilliant seamstress — she'd once made adorable clothes for my brother and sister and costumes for my mother's students — were behind her, the result of advancing glaucoma, which she refused to treat because she didn't trust doctors. Her eyes were a milky white and she bumped into furniture and walls. Basically, she was blind.

She blamed me, too. She told anyone who asked that she'd lost her eyesight after tripping over my bicycle. Her inability to see made her wary of the world at large. She insisted on having eighty-two locks on the front door. It took her four days to get it open. I wanted to kill myself as I waited in the hallway for her to unlock them one by one. It was not fun when I had to go to the bathroom.

Once inside our apartment, there was a closet on the left and one on the right. My mother's ermine coat hung in the one on the right, in the back (it was deep enough for double rods), and I liked to hide in there, sucking my thumb as I rubbed my face against the soft fur. My mother's desk was a few steps into the foyer. Her typewriter was front and center, and she kept quarters for the washer and dryer in the middle drawer, even though she repeatedly swore that the laundry room wasn't safe because rapists hid there.

We had a dining room table with fold-down sides that was never used because we never had company. We also had a credenza where we displayed the good dishes and serving pieces. Our candy dish also sat on the credenza. *That* we used. It was a green bowl that was usually filled with buttons and paper clips, not candy. It was always fun to watch the delivery boys wait at the door as my blind grandmother carefully unpinned the dollar bills my mother had attached to her dress and then offered them a piece of candy from the bowl.

"How about a treat?" she said.

They looked at the paper clips and buttons.

"No, thank you."

My mother's upright piano was in the living room. Ronny and I both took lessons. After years of instruction, we each knew one piece. My brother played the drums and was in bands through college. He inherited my mother's musical talent. Our TV was also in the living room. In the late 1940s, after the neighbors down the hall from us, the Altmans, became the first in the building to have a TV, my father brought one home. Our favorite shows ranged from my father's dramas to my brother's comedies. I liked to watch *The Lone Ranger* and Charlie Chan on Saturday mornings.

But variety shows were the ones we really looked forward to. We wanted to see the dancers. My mother had to see what they were doing, what they were wearing, what she could steal. We gave my blind grandmother TV duty. Her job was to monitor the shows and yell to us anytime she saw dancing. Of course, she couldn't see. That was the flaw in our plan.

When she called us — "Hurry, they're tapping" — we would fly into the room from all corners of the apartment and see not a dancer but someone typing, usually a secretary on a show. Nanny thought they were tap dancing. If she was upset about the mistake, I would hear her grumble about it all night. She'd remind me that she had gone blind after tripping over my bicycle.

That wasn't the only lie I dealt with. Ronny wet her bed until she was twelve but blamed me. How could it have been me? My grandmother, Ronny, and I all slept in what would have been our dining room if it hadn't been converted into a bedroom for us, and I shared a bed with my grandmother.

The other bedrooms were farther down the hallway. Before you got to them, though, you had to pass the linen closet. Why was the linen closet important? That's where my mother kept her "suicide jar" — a collection of pills. If any of us got a prescription for whatever reason, a few pills went into her jar. They were her safety, her Plan B. She swore she would swallow every damn one of them before she would let herself become a burden.

"I'll just kill myself," she'd say.

Garry and my grandfather shared one of the two bedrooms at the end of the hallway. They listened to Yankee games on the radio (Garry cried when they lost), and if a game wasn't on, my grandfather would stare out the window and avoid my grandmother. Theirs was another marriage not made in heaven. One day he moved into the apartment across the hall. Two spinster sisters lived there. I guess he'd just had enough. We still took him food every day.

My parents were in the other bedroom. They had separate beds, of course, separate dressers — separate everything. My father kept all of our school drawings and family photographs neatly organized and filed in a locked cabinet near his bed. I guess he was sentimental. My mother wasn't. "Why do you need all that junk?" she used to say.

She could barely hide her disgust for anything to do with him. As a little girl, I liked to comb my father's hair after he came home from work. It was my way of playing barbershop. It seemed to make my mother sick.

"How can you touch him?" she would say. "Look at the back of his chair. It's all greasy."

I would feel bad. And yet these were the good times. It would get worse before it got intolerable. They should have gotten divorced. But no, my mother believed that children from broken homes turned into juvenile delinquents. In other words, my parents stayed together so we wouldn't end up in jail. Of course, with eighty-two locks on the door, we already were incarcerated.

CHAPTER 3

The Grand Concourse

Penny's childhood apartment building on
the Grand Concourse in the Bronx

Marshall personal collection

I'M GOING TO CALL the super!"

I heard that all the time. The threat came from my grandmother, who was our building's witch lady (every place had
one), and it was directed at my girlfriends and me. My friends Rozzie, Rina, Wendy, Phyllis, and Natalie were all from the building. We
played on the sidewalk or gathered in the courtyard on the Van Cortlandt side of our building and played King, Queen, Jack; Chinese
handball; jump rope; and potsie, which is what we called hopscotch.

However, the courtyard was beneath the windows in our living
room and kitchen, where my grandmother sat and listened to her
"stories" on the radio. She was hooked on the daily serials. As soon as
she heard our voices rising up from the sidewalk — in other words, as
soon as she heard us having fun — she opened the window and yelled
at us. "Stop making noise. You kids better go away or else I'm going
to call the super."

I ignored her. Most of my friends also lived with at least one grandparent, so they understood. She was a pain in the ass, as were most of
the old people in the neighborhood. They were all spies. They pulled
their bridge chairs out in front of their buildings and watched what

everyone did, or they stared out the window. I couldn't do anything without my mother finding out. *Penny's on the fire escape. Penny's chasing the boys. Penny's walking up on the roof. Penny's playing in the gutter.*

For excitement, I watched for the knife sharpener and the I Cash Clothes guy (he bought old clothes from people). There was a guy with a horse and cart who came around and charged a nickel for rides along Jerome Avenue, which was still cobblestone (so going over the bumps tickled). The ice cream man was also popular. As soon as we heard the melody from his truck, all the kids playing outside would stop and shout up at the building. "Mommy! Mommy! The ice cream man!" Their mothers wrapped coins in napkins and dropped them out the window. My mother was one of the few who worked, so she was never home to drop down money. But not to be denied, I would run inside and steal quarters from her desk.

I would also climb on top of the garage next to our building, retrieve the balls that had landed there during stickball games, and try to sell them back to the older boys playing in the street — that is, if the cops hadn't already come and broken their stick and tossed it down the sewer, as was the practice that usually ended those games.

If the weather was bad, we played inside. We skated across the marble lobby area, slid down banisters, bounced down the stairs on our butts, or pressed all the buttons in the elevators. Two boys once got in trouble for having a peeing contest in front of the mailboxes. Another time I heard that a man was exposing himself on the staircase. I ran as fast as I could to where he had been spotted but arrived too late to see anything. It was still exciting.

Snow days were the best. I would go up to the sixth floor and hang out the windows of my friend's apartment and watch the cars skid on the Grand Concourse. For me, that was an activity.

I would have liked to hang out more with my brother and sister, but the truth was, I barely knew them. Nearly nine years older than me, Garry was always sick or injured. The list of his known allergies ran fourteen pages. He once said that he began to write because it was something he could do in bed while he was itching or throwing up. But I was still a little kid when he started at DeWitt Clinton High School, where he immersed himself in a variety of interests ranging from playing the drums to writing about sports for the school paper.

Ronny was six years ahead of me. Once she hit her teens, our age difference seemed even bigger. She lied about her address so she could get into the co-ed Evander Childs High School. She became boy crazy, and then I became an afterthought to her. If she did pay attention to me, it was because she needed an excuse to get out of the apartment. She would take me to the swings at the Oval, the park where her friends hung out. Then she would flirt with the boys and forget about me.

She also changed my life by teaching me how to cross the street on my own. The Grand Concourse was too big and too busy for a kid to cross on her own. Once I started going to PS 80, though, I had to get myself to and from school. My mother wasn't going to wake up early to take me. She had Ronny take me to the corner and show me how to ask an adult for help. You went up to someone who looked normal and shouted, "Hey mister! Cross me?"

That's what all the kids said. "Cross me? Cross me?" We were like little chirping birds.

Crossing the Grand Concourse was literally a rite of passage, a key to independence and exploring the rest of the neighborhood. St. Phillip Neri Church was down the block, Ciro's Bowling Alley was across the street, and nearby was Jerry's Pizza, which had a fire every week. On Jerome Avenue, there was a shop for everything, including meat, pickles, hosiery, hardware, candy, nuts, vegetables, bagels, shoes, and curtains. We got chicken soup at Schweller's Deli, and Scheff's was our bakery. You want to know heaven? Walking home while eating the warm heels from a loaf of freshly baked seedless rye, sliced.

The Woodlawn-Jerome el rumbled past our building. Up on a

nearby hill was a shrine where Crazy Joseph from Villa Avenue saw the Virgin Mary one day when we all were playing. I'll never forget that day. Jo-Jo suddenly dropped to his knees and started to pray. He'd seen the Virgin Mary, he explained. Most of us didn't even know who the Virgin Mary was. But soon, people came by the busload to see the spot. A shrine was made, and we sold holy dirt for a dollar.

I never knew boundaries, never paid attention to ethnicities or skin color. I lived on the border between the Jewish neighborhood (the Parkway) and the Italian-Catholic neighborhood (Villa Avenue). I was in the smart classes with the Jewish kids, but I went to school on the High Holy Days and sat in class with the Italian kids, cleaning the board and the erasers. People didn't know what we were in terms of religion or ethnicity, and neither did we.

To this day people think we're Jewish, but Garry was christened Episcopalian, Ronny was Lutheran, and I was confirmed in a Congregationalist church. Why such diversity? My mother sent us anyplace that had a hall where she could put on a recital. If she hadn't needed performance space, we wouldn't have bothered.

It got even more confusing later on when we went to a kosher Jewish summer camp. We all had to go to services. We read prayers, blessed the bread before each meal, and lit candles and blessed the wine on Friday nights. Ronny and I could *baruch* like nobody's business.

Identity was never an issue for me. I embraced being from the Bronx. To me, it was the center of the universe, at least the only universe that mattered. I grew up never knowing north, south, east, or west. I only learned uptown, downtown, and "We're going to Alexander's."

Alexander's was a department store, and for us, it may as well have been the capital of the Bronx. Everybody went to Alexander's. My mother only bought things that were on sale, though. She bought Christmas presents at the end of spring and summer and hid them in the closet. My blind grandmother, who only liked dark-colored clothes, ended up in chartreuse and leopard prints. She had no idea. It was hilarious to watch her try on the clothes.

"What color is this, babe?" she'd ask, standing in an outfit that was a shocking pink.

"It's brown," my mother lied.

The next outfit was chartreuse.

"What color is this, babe?"

"It's black."

Everything was either black or brown. I never asked my mother why she lied to my grandmother. I didn't have to; I understood. Sometimes you ignored the facts to make life easier.

CHAPTER 4

Dinnertime

A 1947 portrait of Penny, her sister Ronny, and brother Garry

Hal Altman

I DON'T EAT MUCH. I'm not what you would call a foodie, and I have my mother to thank for that. She was more than satisfied with a bialy and butter or an onion sandwich. She ate standing up in the kitchen rather than sitting down with the rest of us, who she had only the slightest interest in feeding.

She prepared dinner out of a sense of duty and was vocal about her feeling, or lack of feeling, for the culinary obligations tradition had bestowed on women of her generation. The last thing she wanted to do was spend her day standing over a hot stove. To put it bluntly, she hated to cook.

"Only idiots do that," she said. "They don't have any creativity. They just read recipes and do what they're told."

My father rarely came straight home after work anyway. He preferred drinks with his cronies to dinner with us, though my mother offered her own explanation for his absence. "He has another family in Philadelphia that he likes better," she said, her voice thick with sarcasm.

But I didn't know from sarcasm then. I learned later.

His side of the family was a mystery. My father once told us that our family came to America on the *Mayflower,* which made me feel special in school every Thanksgiving when the teacher showed us pictures of Pilgrims. *Those were my relatives,* I thought. In truth, his parents, Joseph and Ann, lived someplace in the Bronx, but I only went there for dinner a couple of times, and my only memory of those dinners was spaghetti noodles hanging over the back of my grandmother's kitchen chairs.

My brother and sister went there more often than I did. Garry said it was while eating spaghetti there and listening to opera that he figured out we were actually Italian, not Pilgrims, and our real name was Masciarelli. By the time I was old enough to figure things out on my own, my father had disowned his family and none of us cared anyway. If he really did have another family in Philadelphia, my mother seemed grateful for the break.

Sunday was family night, the only night we could count on my father being home for dinner, and then he wanted spaghetti and meat sauce, with hot peppers on the side, a salad with oil and vinegar dressing, and red wine. The man who denied being Italian wanted only Italian food.

I had no problem with spaghetti. We had it all the time. If any of us wanted spaghetti other than Sunday, my mother made what we called her "orange spaghetti." She cooked up the noodles and emptied a can of Campbell's tomato soup on top with chunks of mozzarella cheese. It was delicious, and it was even better the next day, when she heated it up in a frying pan. I pity generations who have only known to reheat food in microwaves. I asked for it so often my mother would say, "You're going to turn into a piece of spaghetti."

When I was very little, I would run behind each person's chair, hang from the back, curl my feet off the ground, and scream, "Hanger! Hanger! Hanger!" I don't know why. No one questioned it. I just did it. Once I was too old to run around during dinner, I realized that I had the worst seat at the table. Why? It was across from my brother, whose eating habits were disgusting. For some reason, he was opposed to chewing and mushed all of his food together — and talked throughout the meal, spraying half of what he took in.

Unlike Garry, I didn't want any of my food to touch. The two of us would have driven my mother crazy if she'd paid any attention.

Only Ronny was the good eater. She ate everything and didn't care if it touched or didn't. She wasn't fat, but she had a round face. "Are you storing food in there for the winter?" asked my mother, who also referred to Ronny's thighs — again, she wasn't fat — as "Billy Watson's Beef Trust." Billy Watson's Beef Trust was a turn-of-the-century dance troupe of large women. Dancers had to be more than two hundred pounds to join.

She used to tell me that my buckteeth could open a Coke bottle. She was like that.

My Nanny had no idea what was on her plate. Nor did she care. She finished her meal every night no matter what was served, then pushed her plate to the side and declared, "I eat what I like, and I like what I eat."

Holidays were more of the same. For Thanksgiving, my mother cooked the obligatory turkey, and each year, after telling us how she planned to brown it, the bird slipped out of her hands and dropped to the floor. "That's what makes it so good," she said as she wiped it off with a dishtowel and put it in the oven. "No one will know."

On Christmas Eve, my father came home slightly tipsy, lugging a tree into the apartment. My parents decorated it and put out the presents that my mother had bought on sale at Alexander's throughout the year. One year Garry asked my mother what she wanted for Christmas. She looked toward my father. "I don't want you to get *him* anything he wants," she said. When I asked her the same question, she was ready with another request. "I want the kitchen boarded up," she said.

I had to laugh or kill myself.

CHAPTER 5

Strictly Ballroom

Penny (far right) and friends in costume at the
Marjorie Marshall Dance School

Hal Altman

MY MOTHER'S BALLROOM was located in the cellar between the incinerator and the storage room for bikes and sleds. There were pipes on the ceiling, and the bulbs that lit the room were plain. Every year we painted the walls turquoise. It was nothing fancy, but for those who took lessons at the Marjorie Marshall Dance School, it was a special place.

You heard the music before you arrived. Then, once inside, you saw my mother at the upright piano, dressed in black slacks and a pale blouse, with a Yoo-hoo and her cigarettes sitting on top of the piano.

Class began with a group sing around her piano and then moved on to dancing: Ballet and acrobatics were on one side of the ballroom, and jazz and tap were on the side with the piano. A thin curtain on a rope divided the two sides. My mother's partner, Mildred Roth, who lived on 208th Street, collected money and took over costume-making chores from my grandmother.

Mildred's daughter, Paula, was my age and she was good in school. I didn't like her so much. She was always around, being forced on me. That annoyed me, and I took it out on her. I was much nicer to my friends from the building, Rozzie, Wendy, Phyllis, Natalie, and Rina.

My mother's school had girls from all across the Bronx. Boys not so much. If a delivery boy came to the door and my mother was home, her first question was, "Do you dance?" She had no use for anyone who didn't go to class, such as Rina's younger sister, Marsha. "Is that idiot here again?" she said one day after seeing that we were playing together after school. "Doesn't she have a home?"

"I don't think your mother likes me," Marsha said.

"No, she likes you," I said. "She just says things like that."

I convinced Marsha to sign up for dancing school. It made my mother happier.

She would have been ecstatic if I had become a dancer like her. She tried her best to mold me into one. At eleven months, I learned to do a backbend, an arabesque, and a somersault. She said I clapped enthusiastically when she did a cartwheel in front of me. At four, I debuted in my first recital. She praised my sense of rhythm and memory. By eight years old, though, I hated every minute of the hour-long classes. I knew the other girls adored my mother and wanted to please her. Not me. I wanted to give her a heart attack.

Why?

Because she was *my* mother.

For me, dance didn't end after class. At night, following dinner, I would sit at the kitchen table with Ronny, or my fake aunt Tina (a former student of my mother's who had children of her own; like all of my mother's friends, she was an "aunt"), or whoever else was around, talking about students, comparing one girl to another, and discussing upcoming shows, all the while pasting tiny colored stars on paper that my mother gave to the little kids after their lessons as a reward for working hard. It was nonstop.

But she meant well. This was her life's work, and she approached it with an obsessive, missionlike zeal. She believed every child should know what it feels like to entertain. It didn't matter if they were short or tall, talented or just a kid whose mother dropped her off to get her out of her hair for an hour. She felt it was important to have the experience of hearing applause and making people happy. She also believed everyone, regardless of their build, deserved a turn in front — "even the fat girls," she said.

In 1952, my mother met June Taylor, the choreographer best known for appearing each week with her June Taylor Dancers on *The Jackie Gleason Show*. My mother pitched her on having us — her "Junior Rockettes" — perform on Gleason's show. Approaching June this way was typical of my mother's ambition and fearlessness. June said she would consider it but cautioned that Mr. Gleason had to approve everything on the show, and he wasn't known as a big fan of children.

However, my mother soon received a call inviting her to bring us in for a tryout. She was thrilled. Even I got excited about the possibility of being on *The Jackie Gleason Show*. We were always rehearsing, but we practiced extra hard for a couple weeks. At the audition, my mother lined us up in front of June and several others, sat at the piano, and started to play, expecting us to begin as we'd practiced a hundred times. But none of us moved. We stood in place, frozen, staring at ourselves in the mirrors on the wall.

My mother realized immediately what had happened. Our ballroom didn't have mirrors. We had never seen ourselves dance before. She jumped up from the piano and instructed us to turn away from the mirrors and start over. That worked. We performed flawlessly.

Afterward, June spoke with my mother. Then, I guess, she spoke with Mr. Gleason, because a few weeks later we learned that we had the job.

We were on the last episode of the season. June put together a number where her high-kicking dancers stepped up a riser and disappeared behind large, hollow columns. After waiting a beat, we danced out from behind and down the stairs, looking exactly like them except we were children. The sight gag was simple but effective. Rehearsals ran through the week. We learned the moves easily, and we were given costumes that matched those worn by the professionals.

Hours before the live broadcast, though, we were informed that our white tap shoes were the wrong color. Apparently you weren't supposed to wear white on TV. My mother saved the day again. She had us paint them with pancake makeup until they were the same color as our costumes, rose. I had one more problem: I was sick with the flu. Slumped in a dressing room chair, I watched my mother apply makeup to the other girls as the fever radiated from my skin and caused me to shiver uncontrollably.

When it was my turn to get made up, my mother stooped in front of me and looked directly into my droopy eyes. Then she glanced at my backup, another girl who was standing a few feet away, talking to some of the other girls, the other Junior Rockettes.

"Do you want her to be in the show instead?" she asked.

This appearance on *The Jackie Gleason Show* meant more to my mother than it did to me. For her, the show always came first. So I stood up on my shaky legs and shook my head.

"Okay, I'll dance," I said.

I looked bored throughout the performance. In reality, I was concentrating on not throwing up on live TV. But everything worked, and the number was a hit. After the show, June and her sister, Marilyn, who became Jackie Gleason's third wife in 1975, complimented each of us. I liked Marilyn. Later, I sent her a bottle of perfume and she sent me a picture, thanking me.

Before leaving, one of the show's producers approached my mother and Mildred and suggested we buy our costumes for fifty dollars each. Aghast, Mildred turned to my mother and said, "I can make those for a buck eighty." So we left them. But when June asked us back the next year, there was a catch: We had to wear the same costumes. As a result, only the girls who could fit into them were able to be in the show again. I didn't have a problem — I was still built like a beanpole.

As would be the case many times throughout my life, I managed to shine despite my general apathy. After our second appearance, June said that I had the potential to become one of her dancers someday if

I took a few years of ballet lessons. I thanked her as my mother patted my back, but both of us knew I wasn't going to end up a June Taylor Dancer. I hated ballet.

A short time later, in fact, I tried to quit dance altogether. My mother responded the same way she always did to such outbursts. "Fine," she said. "On Saturdays you'll go shopping and do the laundry and clean the house like everyone else."

Well, I checked with the other kids and nobody had those kinds of household chores. She was just making shit up.

My mother had us entertain at any place that would feed us, and she made sure we were prepped to say the right thing, depending on where we were booked. If we were at a church, we might be Episcopalian or Catholic. If we were at a temple, we might be Jewish. We appeared on TV — *Star Time,* the talent show starring Connie Francis, and *The Horn and Hardart Children's Hour* — and at prisons and shipyards, charity events, telethons, and Alexander's annual gala. Local newspapers wrote stories about us: "Youngsters Aid Polio Fund," "Strutters Aid Blind Children," "Junior Rockettes to Dance on Arthritis Telethon."

Whatever my mother lacked as a homemaker she made up for as a producer/choreographer/road and stage manager. She taught us to pack our suitcases with costumes for the last number at the bottom and the first one on top. She rehearsed us on subway platforms. People stared. She didn't care. Backstage, she put rouge on our faces with a bunny tail brush and added lipstick. Other parents helped with costumes. Sometimes Mildred's husband, Adolph, pulled the curtain. One time a girl couldn't find her white blouse between numbers and my fake aunt Tina quickly unbuttoned her own white blouse, gave it to the girl, and stood backstage in her bra.

My mother had her littlest students sing songs during costume changes and she wrote them original recitations to perform in front of the curtain.

Every Monday Mommy goes
to Alexander's store.
She buys me skirts and tops
and shoes and socks galore.

She brings them home,
we try them on,
she takes them back that night.
She doesn't like the look —
or some don't fit just right.

Last night I read of a baby sale.
It gave me such a scare.
I'm glad I was born in a hospital
because you can't return things there.

Each venue was an adventure. At Delmonico's, our feet slid out from under us on the slippery floor. We all landed on our butts. In the Village, my mother ushered us through a club full of women, whispering to us, "Keep close. Keep close." Later, I realized we were dancing for a party of lesbians. But I don't think my mother cared who was in the audience as long as we got to perform. We danced at an insane asylum; at an Army hospital where the soldiers were lying in bed and holding mirrors so they could see us; and at the Brooklyn Navy Yard for a group of Greek sailors, who clapped like crazy watching a bunch of teenage and pre-teen girls kicking their legs up.

We went to Fort Dix, Fort Jay, and Fort Hamilton on the Brooklyn shore where the water splashed over the wall and got us wet as we tapped. I think we invented a new step: tap-splash, tap-splash, tap-slip-fall, get up again. At a place in upstate New York, they put us on a gravel driveway. Then they told my mother that there wasn't going to be a piano. Rather than complain, she pulled a kazoo out of her purse. She played the kazoo as we kicked gravel around.

We were on *Ted Mack's Original Amateur Hour* three times. To better our chances during the first appearance, I helped lock our competition, a group of Irish folk dancers, in their dressing room. They nearly missed their cue. But my mother played by the rules. Before each show, she put up signs in our elevator, telling people to call in and vote for us. It must have worked. We won each time and went to the finals at Madison Square Garden, where we opened for Pat Boone but ultimately lost to child star Jojo Vitale singing "That's Amore."

Even though I danced like this through high school, I never thought of myself as an entertainer. I suppose I was. I do know that I got way more out my mother's insufferable dance classes than I ever realized at the time. Years later I fell back on my ability to dance. I tapped on *Laverne & Shirley*. I did the lindy with Barry Manilow on his first TV special. I break-danced on TV before most of America had even seen break dancing. Those classes I hated so much had given me a Plan B and a lifetime of confidence. But like most people, I needed to live most of my life before I could look back and understand how lucky I was to have been tortured.

CHAPTER 6

Dear Mom & Dad

A portrait of Penny's parents, taken in the 1930s

Godfrey Durr

I WENT TO CAMP EVERY summer starting at age nine, and every one of those days I was there I wrote a letter home. You had to in order to get into the mess hall for dinner. My letters were all variations on the same theme:

Dear Mom & Dad,
    Hi, how are you? How are Nanny and Grandpa?
    Send candy.

                                                    Love,
                                                    Penny

Aside from wanting to satisfy the daily requirement to get into the dining hall, I might have asked for food so I could build up a reserve and not have to come home. I would have gladly stayed at camp year-round if it had been possible. Going was a family tradition. Both of my parents had spent their childhood summers at camp. My mother had been the dance counselor at Camp Geneva in Lake Como, Pennsylvania, and she kept going even after she was married.

Before any of us went away, though, we spent summers taking family trips to Avon-by-the-Sea on the Jersey Shore. I enjoyed going there, too. It meant no dance school. My mother closed the ballroom for two months and we loaded up the family car and headed south on the highway. Within an hour or two, Garry, Ronny, and I began to throw up. Once one of us vomited, it set off a chain reaction. We all threw up. It was a sure sign summer had arrived.

In Avon, we rented rooms in a large two-story home a short walk from the beach. After we unpacked, my father drove back home and went to work. I guess that was his idea of a vacation — life without the rest of us. However, he returned on the weekends. As a little kid, I enjoyed his company. He took me to the arcade in Asbury Park and horseback riding in Belmar. Without him around, though, my mother exhaled. She put on her satin bathing suit, covered her hair with a scarf, and spent the day in the sun, visiting with friends.

I could tell she had started to relax when she began talking about the young men she had liked in college before settling on my father. It took a week or two of her watching other couples on the beach ("Look at that niceness.") before she started in on how she should have married Godfrey Durr, Matt Chambers, or Tom Farrell instead of my father. It was hard to tell if she meant it as a joke.

I went topless until I went to camp. In every picture I have from Avon, I am only wearing bathing suit bottoms. Sometimes I wore suspenders — but no top. Why didn't my mother get me a top, too? I don't know. No one ever said anything, though, and I never felt like a centerfold-in-training as I ran around the beach, digging holes and poking my nose into other people's business.

One of my favorite days in Avon was when the lifeguards pulled someone out of the water and I found myself standing right next to them. People formed a circle around us as they watched, and I loved having a ringside seat for the drama. The next summer a friend of my sister's cut her foot on a piece of glass, and a lifeguard carried her away. That was also an exciting day for me. So were the days when the jellyfish invaded the beach and swimmers limped out of the water in tears to the lifeguard station.

The lifeguards made a big impression on me. At home, I hugged any man I saw wearing a uniform. "Don't ask," my mother explained to friends and neighbors who wondered why. "She just does that."

Then one summer Garry went to a Boy Scout camp instead of going with us to Avon. We knew he would get sick or injured, and he did. He got poison ivy. But he survived. He sent letters every day. He was doing fine. In addition to clean underwear, he had taken four hundred gallons of calamine lotion. The next year my sister went to camp. Now both of them were sending letters. I was deeply envious. They were having a good time while I was left with my mother and Nanny, whose old lady friends would ask me to play canasta with them.

"We need a fourth. Can Penny stay home from the beach and play cards?"

I was good, too. I was only eight, but I could meld like a seventy-year-old.

The next year it was my turn to go away. I went to Camp Odetah in rural Connecticut. On the first day I was placed in the extra milk line, given two chocolate milks every meal, and told to play. I never wanted to go back home.

> Dear Mom & Dad,
>   Having a great time. How's everyone? Send me a salami.
>
>   Love,
>   Penny

After one summer there, I switched to Camp Geneva, the same camp my mother had gone to as a teenager. My sister was there, too, and my brother was on the boys' side, Camp Onibar. My mother wrote one letter each week and sent a copy to all three of us. Ronny always complained that she got the third carbon every time. "Here, take mine," I said. I didn't care whether I heard from her all summer. Family? What family? This was my escape.

Geneva was a kosher camp for rich Jewish kids. We, of course, were neither. We got in because my mother's best friend, my fake aunt Blanche (she and my uncle Leo were my godparents) was a Rabino, and they owned the camp.

I arrived with strep throat and spent the first week of camp in the infirmary, where I found out that I was allergic to penicillin. That was fun. Once recovered, I threw myself into the activities. Geneva was a paradise of green fields carved out of a thick Pocono forest, with social hall, bunks, tennis courts, a lake, a baseball diamond, golf, and an archery range on the edge of an apple orchard. It also emphasized singing and dancing.

After a morning reveille, we lined up around the flagpole and put our hands over our hearts as the stars and stripes were raised. After breakfast, we sang songs — a primary activity — cleaned our bunks, and then received our first activity for the day: basketball, softball, swimming, volleyball, archery, baton twirling, or golf, which I never liked. What was the point? You hit the ball and walked. I was bored in five minutes. I liked sports where you ran.

I was assigned to bunk 7, where I became instant friends with Dede Levy from Long Island, Sherry Arbur, Barbara Peltzman (or Peltzy) from Forest Hills, Nancy Cohen, and Jill Rubenson and Andy Stein, both of whom were superb athletes. We spent the next four summers together, trading stories and teaching one another about music, boys, and our changing bodies. This was a time when no girl's parents talked to her about that kind of thing, so, for instance, if one of us started our period, it became a group activity. *Who's got a tampon? Who knows how to work a tampon? Who's got a mirror? Ouch, this hurts.*

We shared everything. Our different backgrounds melted away. We were bunkmates and friends for the rest of our lives.

I recited the Sabbath prayers on Friday nights like everyone else, and learned the history of the Onibar Indians who had first settled the area. Eventually we figured out that Onibar was Rabino spelled backward. Many years later, my brother wrote for Jack Paar and he did a bit called "Letters from Camp," which included the joke: Dear Mom and Dad, we found out Camp Nehoc is not an Indian name. It's Cohen spelled backward.

> Dear Mom & Dad,
>   How's Nanny? How's Grandpa? I hope everyone is good.
> I love camp. Send chocolate.
>
> > Love,
> > Penny

Each session included an athletic competition known as the Color War. It lasted a week, and all the campers, girls and boys, divided into teams. On the boys' side, you were either blue or buff, and on the girls' side, you were green or buff. During Color War, you had to sing to your color. We sang to buff. "Buff is the team with the gleam of victory in its eye . . . B-U-F-F is the team! Rah-rah-rah . . ." It was hard to get excited about singing to buff.

There were also weekly shows featuring original songs and dances. Every bunk did one, as did the older staff, the counselors, and the waiters and waitresses. These performances were taken seriously, and the bar was extremely high. Mark "Moose" Charlap, who wrote the music for the Broadway production of *Peter Pan*, had been the musical director for several years, and he was succeeded by seventeen-year-old Juilliard student Marvin Hamlisch. He wrote new songs every week.

At thirteen, I took a year off to attend Camp Edgemont, a horseback riding camp in Deposit, New York. My mother was upset. "It's not kosher!" she said. What did it matter? We weren't even Jewish. I spent the next two summers back at Geneva, working as a waitress. It was a coveted job; you received tips and didn't have to pay for the summer session.

Even better, I was assigned the staff table. That's where I got to know Marvin Hamlisch. He sat at my table. I knew all of his food allergies.

Midway through that summer, the waitresses' bunk burned down.

My mother thought it was my fault. By this time I was smoking cigarettes, and she assumed that I'd left one burning. It shows how highly
she thought of me.

Eventually, though, one of the other waitresses confessed to setting the fire. She turned out to be a pyromaniac.

We all were just grateful that drama didn't get in the way of the
even more exciting end-of-summer musical. My friend Caren from
back home was the dance counselor. She worked all summer on the
choreography, much of which she credited to my mother, whom she
adored. She took lessons in the ballroom for years. As testimony to
the regard she had for my mother, she used Marvin as her rehearsal
pianist but insisted on having my mother play the piano for the actual show. In fact, her parents drove my mother to camp.

It's mind-boggling to think that she trusted my mother's playing
more than she did Marvin's. What can I say? I think it was because
my mother knew how to jump around in the music if someone made
a mistake. Most Julliard students can probably play that way, too. But
they don't.

At the end of camp, my parents picked me up and we caught up
during the long drive back to the Bronx. Everything was the same,
my mother said, nothing was new, that is until I asked how my grandfather was doing.

"Oh, he died," my mother said.

"Excuse me?" I said, shocked.

"He died," she said.

"When?" I asked.

"Around the beginning of the summer," she said.

"But in my letters I asked how he was doing, and you said he was
fine. Why didn't you tell me?"

"We didn't want to ruin your summer."

CHAPTER 7
The Marshall Plan

Penny at Camp Geneva in 1954

Marshall personal collection

I N 1952, MY BROTHER started at Northwestern University. Garry was eager to get out in the world and away from my parents. However, he was concerned about leaving Ronny and me behind. Before departing for Chicago, he asked us to meet in his bedroom. When we were all together, he shut his door and stood in front of us looking as if he had the weight of the world on his shoulders. What was on his mind was a topic that would occupy the three of us for the rest of our lives: family.

"As you may have realized," he said, "Mom doesn't understand much about life beyond her ballroom, and who knows where Dad is most of the time. Nanny's walking into walls, and Grandpa is living across the hall."

Ronny and I nodded.

"Basically, we got no shot with these people," Garry continued.

He paused to let his thoughts sink in, and after a moment of silence he leaned forward.

"If something goes wrong, they aren't going to be there for us," he said. "That's just the way it is. So as we go forward in our lives, we have to stick together. We're the only ones who are going to understand each other."

After Garry finished, we all stood up and hugged. At nine years old, I didn't understand everything he said. But I knew his assessment was accurate. In fact, two years later, Ronny followed him to Northwestern and I realized Garry's worries had been prophetic. Once my brother and sister were out of the house, my parents quit pretending to like each other. Whatever pretense they had maintained for our benefit disappeared.

She layered her sarcasm on even thicker. Hearing his key in the door at night, she would turn to me and sneer, "Better get up and give *him* a kiss if you want your bank money." Sometimes she dragged Mildred or one of her other friends into their bedroom and pointed to his closet where his clothes hung neatly. "Look at that," she'd say with disdain. "He's such a pansy."

My father thought that my mother was holding him back. His business was thriving, thanks to the commercials he made for the American Medical Association, the biggest and best of his clients. "He's such a phony baloney," my mother said. "He thinks he's such a big shot." He wanted to move to Sutton Place, an affluent neighborhood on Manhattan's East Side. But when he brought home floor plans, my mother said, "And what am I going to do there? What am I going to do in Sutton Place?"

I wondered the same thing.

Did he not know this woman?

At least I had my own room now. It was Garry's old bedroom. After Ronny left for school, my mother painted the walls turquoise, installed new closet doors, added a bookshelf, and bought me a white, Danish-style bed, which I liked. Even better, I didn't have to share a room with my grandmother anymore. I had privacy. I stayed up at night, reading Nancy Drew and Dana Girls mysteries, as well as stories about animals and kids running away from home. I kept a diary. Sometimes I snuck down the hall and secretly watched whatever TV show my mother had on in the living room while she waited up for my father to come home.

My brother once observed that when you watch our home movies, you see me grow progressively more depressed, and it's true. I suppose that's why my father came home one day with a dog, a cocker spaniel that I named Mr. Belvedere. My mother loved him, and my father walked him at night, and he kept me company. After about a year, though, I woke up one day and he was gone.

"Where's the dog?" I asked.

"He went to a place in the country," my mother said.

"He's gone?" I asked.

"He's much happier where he is," she said.

My parents let me replace Mr. Belvedere with two parakeets, Charlie and Pete, and two goldfish, Charlie and Ebenezer. I was into the name Charlie. After a while, the fish stopped swimming and floated on their side. I thought they were resting.

Every few months, I considered running away to Arizona. Don't ask me why Arizona. I don't know. After I started junior high, my parents got me another dog, a beige mutt I named Nickel. He stuck around for a few years before being shipped off to the country, too. By then, though, I had turned into a typical teenager. I was a member of the Elvis Presley Fan Club (I still have my membership card), collected all the latest 45s, and thought constantly about boys.

When my friends referred to the Marshall Plan, they were talking about my interest in getting boys to pay attention to me, not the United States's effort to rebuild postwar Europe. I would hit boys on the Junior High School 80 schoolyard and run, hoping they would catch me. But they couldn't. I was too fast.

One day I snatched Jeffrey Strauss's baseball mitt and sprinted away, taunting him to run faster. He couldn't. My mother told me to slow down. It was the only advice she ever gave me about boys. "You have to let them win," she said. "They don't like it when you're better than them."

That turned out to be true. Then Ronnie Kestenbaum let me carry his mitt. I thought he loved me.

• • •

At thirteen, I had my first real kiss. My friend Tema Aaronson and I were baby-sitting and Stuey Seltzer and Lenny Cohen came over to keep us company. We were so lonely, you know? After talking about homework, we asked if they liked The Five Satins and The Del Vikings, and then pretty soon we were all French kissing. As soon as they left, Tema and I hurried to the bathroom and rinsed out our mouths. Laughing, we called them "the water boys."

I never liked the way I looked. As an adult, I was once asked what my least-favorite feature was. I said everything. I always wanted to be prettier. All the girls in my neighborhood were Italian or Jewish and they had brown or blues eyes. Mine were green. One day I came up with a cockamamy theory that my grandmother's glaucoma eye drops would turn my eyes brown like everyone else's. They didn't. They nearly blinded me.

"What did you do?" my mother asked.

"Nothing," I lied.

"What did you do?" she asked again.

"Nothing," I said. "I just woke up like this."

I had to stay home from school, which wasn't the worst thing in the world. I tried to skip school as often as I could. Every week I would go through the *TV Guide* and circle movies I wanted to see. If enough of them were on the same day, I would hold the thermometer up to the lightbulb and tell my mother that I had a fever. "See, one-oh-two." By three o'clock, I would feel better and run out to see my friends and ask what had happened at school.

All of my friends hung out at the same place: the Parkway. The Parkway was the center of my social life — of my life, period. It was a stretch of fence that started directly across the street from JHS 80 and ran for a good distance along Jerome Avenue. The high school kids gathered around the Mosholu Cafeteria. They didn't want to be around the younger kids. Every group had their own piece of real estate. Even the loose Rocky girls — the cool girls — had a spot.

I went there every day as soon as school let out and met up with

Tema Aaronson, Irma Gottlieb, Carol Cohen, and other friends. There was a reason my friends joked that one day I would have a permanent dent in my ass from sitting on that fence: I was always there. I didn't want to miss a thing. I snuck there at night, too. After dinner, I would volunteer to take the garbage to the incinerator, run to the Parkway, see my friends for ten minutes, and run back home.

"What took so long?" my mother would ask.

"There was a line," I would say.

On Saturdays we'd race home for fifteen minutes to check out *American Bandstand.* We would want to see the latest new dance. Then we would race back and talk about what we'd seen. Our world revolved around weekly dances. The school hosted a dance every Friday afternoon and the Jewish Community Center had one on Saturday nights. Those were important social occasions. They were fraught with drama. Everything revolved around who you'd danced with the previous week, and who you hoped to dance with at the next one.

At the dances, the girls went on one side and the boys stood on the other side, and eventually the music lured those of us more confident about our ability into action. Calvin Klein, the future fashion mogul, was one of the boys who liked to dance. He was good, too. He was a year older than me and later married my friend Jayne Center. When I was in seventh grade, my sister gave me a diary for Christmas and I filled pages with concern and speculation about being asked to the Valentine's Day dance. "I hope either Joel, Ronald, or David asks me!" I wrote. Two weeks later, I was still waiting. "Please make one of those boys ask me to the V. dance," I added hopefully.

By the week of the dance, I was waiting for either Jeffrey "Mousey" Strauss or Joel Permsian to ask me. I liked both of them. Now, fifty-five years later, I don't remember who took me. Thanks to my diary, all I know is that I danced with Jeffrey, Norman, Joel, and Yohan. Gene wouldn't dance with me or anyone else, but I excused him because, as I wrote, "He's sooooo cute."

Like most thirteen-year-olds, I didn't realize that my dramas were actually normal life. But they were utterly normal. Consider this diary entry: "Today in school I was sitting in back of Joel and next to Anita. We were laughing and talking so we have to stay in on Thursday. I tripped Joel and he went flying and landed on his side. I got scared because I thought he got hurt. I also got my period today. By the way, Eddie broke two of his fingers playing basketball."

Two years later, my friends and I moved on to high school, believing we were wiser, smarter, and more experienced. Were we? I dug out my ninth-grade autograph book, looking for pearls that would show that some of us at least knew what the hell was going on. I found this note from my friend Kenny, who clearly had figured out what mattered and passed it on to me:

> *Penny,*
> *When you are kissing*
> *don't be hasty.*
> *Take your time*
> *and make it tasty!*

CHAPTER 8
Mucho Grath-e-ath

Penny at the 1960 Westbury High School prom with her date,
Frank Ryder

Marshall personal collection

I CAME HOME FROM school one day when I was fifteen and my mother surprised me with the news that she and my father were getting a divorce. She said it matter-of-factly, as if it was on her list of things to tell me before dance class, and in fact, it was. She didn't give me a chance to ask any questions.

"Decide who you want to live with," she said. "Him or me."

"Do I have to decide now?" I asked.

"Yes," she said. "And take out the garbage on your way out."

I went outside and stood next to the incinerator, wondering if my life had just gone up in flames. What had happened? Why were they splitting now? But more important, which one of them did I want to live with?

I weighed the pros and cons of each. My mother was funnier — and that counted for a lot. But she would insist that I continue dance school, which I hated. My father was boring and humorless but more lenient. He wouldn't care where I went. However, he would probably move to Manhattan and I didn't want to leave my friends in the Bronx.

I was still trying to decide when my father came home from work. I told him that I had to talk to him and pulled him into the kitchen. Then I started asking him questions, like where he planned to live.

"What are you talking about?" he said.

I filled him in.

"We aren't getting divorced," he said.

"But Mom said —"

"Don't listen to her," he interrupted. "She's crazy."

Inside, they had a scene where the truth came out. It turned out that my father was about to make a commercial for the A.M.A., and my mother had suggested that her dance students could dress as pills and tap around a large prescription bottle. When he said no, it wasn't appropriate, she stewed until I came home from school and then hit me with the divorce story.

Who was she punishing?

My mother was right about one thing. Broken homes did lead straight to juvenile delinquency.

A few weeks after that shocker, I was still reeling. This was just more proof of how I bore the brunt of my parents' hatred for each other after my brother and sister left home. Despite the pledge Garry, Ronny, and I made to take care of one another, I felt abandoned. One day, as I left school with my friend Marsha, I suggested going to Alexander's.

"To do what?" she asked.

"Let's shoplift," I said.

My friends Sharon and Gail had recently bragged about taking some clothes and makeup. It sounded exciting, like fun.

Marsha followed me into the department store, where I stole some shit I didn't need and then headed for the door, thinking I had been pretty slick. But the cops were waiting for us outside. They knew we were two foolish high school girls rather than hard-core criminals warming up in Alexander's before hitting the Bank of New York. In fact, I thought I detected a look of pity from the one cop who asked why I had shoplifted.

I probably could have explained that my mother put on the store's annual show and gotten away cleanly after receiving a lecture from the store's manager and offering an apology. Instead I was a smartass and told the cops that we were "pixilated." It was a word I remembered from the scene in the movie *Mr. Deeds Goes to Town* where an old woman testifies to Mr. Deeds's sanity — or temporary lack thereof — by describing him as *pixilated,* or possessed by pixies.

Not amused, the cops took us away. Both Marsha and I ended up going to night court, where we got probation. Other than my parents being upset, it wasn't too bad. In the Bronx, night court was a big date night. I'm not kidding. You watched people get put away. It was entertainment. My brother later wrote a joke that you even wore a tie and jacket on Fridays. It was felony night, and you didn't want to be underdressed.

I attended Walton High School, an all-girls school. It was only one bus ride from home. My sister had lied about her address and gone to Evander Childs because it was co-ed. But that was two bus rides. I couldn't handle that in the morning. Nor did I care. My social life was at the Parkway.

As a sophomore, I took calculus, chemistry, and physics with the smart kids. I was good at studying things like the periodic table of elements, charts, and graphs. But essays gave me trouble. I remember a question on the history Regents, an end-of-the-year test that all New York high school students had to pass in order to go to college. It asked why the Roman Empire fell. I wrote, "Carelessness."

After my grades slipped from A's to B's and C's during my junior year, the guidance counselor called my parents in for a conference. He was worried about my chances of getting into college.

"How can we make her do better?" my father asked.

"Send her to school in Turkey so she doesn't know the language and can't make friends," he said.

I was probably too social for my own good. But I wasn't about to trade the Parkway for the library. After graduating from Northwestern, my sister had gone to secretarial school so she could get a job. If that was the case, why did I need to give a shit about grades? If my choice was boys or books, I picked boys. I had loved them ever since my friend Phyllis Altman's brother, Robert, and I had played doctor as little children.

My mother called all of my boyfriends bums. But they were upstanding guys. I dated Bobby from the neighborhood, and then Matt, who went to Cardinal Hayes, and also Harold, who wasn't allowed to date non-Jews, so he had to pick up Tema and all the other Jewish girls his mother knew before getting me. I also went with Gus, the son of a super in a building near mine. I still have the love note he wrote me: "To the most perfect girl I have ever met. And the only one who has ever brought me happiness and joy."

Poor Gus.

I don't know which one of us aimed lower.

There were other boys, including Lefty, who was close to being a hoodlum and could spit farther than any human being on the planet. My mother saw him in our apartment and pulled me into another room. "Don't tell me you can take care of yourself," she said. "I know the bums you're hanging out with."

"They aren't bums," I said.

"You're necking, aren't you?" she said.

I didn't know what necking meant. What did two necks do? We called it making out.

"I can take care of myself," I said.

My junior year ended with Frank Ryder, a handsome boy I knew from camp, taking me to his prom at Westbury High on Long Island. My mother thought I looked very nice. If dancing was involved, she approved.

As a senior, I took typing and shorthand with the expectation of someday becoming a secretary. I also took Spanish, though Walton was the only school in the country to teach Castilian. So I learned to pronounce everything with a lisp — *mucho grath-e-ath* — which wasn't hard for me because I had an overbite.

It added to my well-roundedness. According to *The Periwinkle*, Walton's yearbook, I had over the past three years distinguished myself as WSSC Volunteer Aide, Homeroom Vice President, and Aide to Miss Chambers. Translation: I was the rag monitor and wiped the tables in the cafeteria after lunch.

Although it may have seemed as though I wasn't trying very hard to reach the end of the school year before I flunked out, I never doubted that I would go to college. Like most seniors, I had to decide where. Like a smaller subset, though, I also had to figure out where I could get in with a C average.

My first choice was Ohio State because a guy I liked from camp went there. But I didn't have the grades to get in. Another guy I liked was at Brooklyn College. But my father said that he'd rather sell pencils on the corner than send me to a city school. One day he brought home a brochure from William & Mary, the liberal arts college in Williamsburg, Virginia. "Are you going to be a Magnolia Queen?" my mother asked. "I don't think so."

We also discussed Fairleigh Dickinson, the private school in New Jersey. But I couldn't figure out how you could cheer for Fairleigh Dickinson at a game. Go Fairleigh? Go Dickinson? What were you supposed to say? Finally, my father brought home a pamphlet from the University of New Mexico. As I read the description, I realized this school was different from the others. They accepted anyone from out of state, which upped my chances of getting in.

As promised, I received an acceptance letter. I was thrilled, but what surprised me even more was my mother's reaction. She wasn't the slightest bit emotional about her last child leaving home. Then I realized that she was under the impression that all the "New" states were bunched together — New York, New Jersey, New Hampshire, and New Mexico — so she thought I'd be close to home.

I didn't bother to correct her.

CHAPTER 9
The Facts of Life

Penny's 1961 Walton High School graduation photo

Marshall personal collection

M Y FATHER TOOK ME to Albuquerque. Our plane stopped in eight million cities along the way. I think we flew the milk route. Once there, I found the campus was relatively empty since I had arrived a couple weeks before classes in order to go through rush. My sister, a Chi Omega at Northwestern, advised me that joining a sorority was the best way to meet people. I was a legacy, she added — whatever that meant.

Hundreds of girls went through rush, and we followed one another from house to house, where the sorority girls sang us songs, threw parties, and asked questions. I thought the conversations were inane.

"Where are you from?"

"The Bronx."

"Do you live on campus?"

No, I commute. "Yes, I live on campus." *What are you, an idiot?*

One of the rules during rush was that pledges couldn't speak to any boys. I had no problem withholding conversation from the boys rushing fraternities, but there were football players on campus, too, and I wanted to hang out with them. They were practicing before the season started. They were enormous. I had never seen a guy my age over 5'6" or 5'8". I said if I can't talk to them, the hell with rush, and I quit.

Coming from New York, I thought that I would be the fast, big-city girl among the freshmen in my dorm. Then I walked into my room and found my new roommate sitting on her bed, smoking a Hav-A-Tampa cigar. She looked at my cigarettes as if to say she had outgrown those in fifth grade. She wasn't an isolated case. I met girls from Texas, Oklahoma, Kansas, and Arkansas who'd slept with their cousins at fourteen. By comparison, I'd done nothing.

At registration, I signed up for math, accounting, psychology, and anthropology classes. After receiving some bad grades in math and accounting, though, I changed my major to phys ed. Then, because I didn't want to take anatomy or kinesiology, I changed my major again, this time to recreation. I know. I hadn't heard of it either. But my advisor said people would have a lot of free time in the future.

I adjusted to college life easily. In letters home, I assured my mother that I was happy and busy. "I've been going out with mostly boys not in fraternities and the football players," I wrote. "They're real cool guys." I stayed on campus for Thanksgiving and continued sending letters home. "I happen to have a lot of friends and am very well known in the school in regard to being from New York, my accent, which I haven't lost, and also the way I dance — the Twist, not tap."

In March 1962, I spent spring break in Los Angeles with my friend Sharon Martin, her boyfriend (and later husband) Clint Helton, and his younger brother, Del, who I liked. We visited Disneyland, went to the beach in Santa Monica, and spent time with my brother, who was writing for Joey Bishop and *The Lucy Show* and seemed to be doing well.

We stayed one night at his apartment in Hollywood, but the next day, after he had gone to work, the manager said we were making too much noise and asked us to leave. Mad, I threw a chair and a chaise in the swimming pool. Later, the manager yelled at Garry, who apologized and said, "Yeah, my sister Penny is good at that kind of thing."

Later that semester, I dated a freshman football player from Texas who called me "ma'am" and scared me with his politeness. I couldn't understand his drawl, and he couldn't understand my Bronx accent. We got along perfectly. But getting along with people was one of my talents. As a New Yorker, I was an outsider, and I was ignorant of a lot of the biases that the Southern boys possessed. At the dances, I usually partnered with black guys from the football team. They were the best dancers. It never dawned on me that some of their teammates might have had a problem with a white girl and a black guy dancing together.

But some did. One day I went into the student union and sat down on the team's bench — it was called the "animal bench" — next to a couple of the black guys from the team. They were friends of mine. Ordinarily they would have shot the shit with me, but someone must have said something after the dance and so this time they said it wasn't a good idea for me to sit with them anymore.

What?

I didn't understand why. As I said, I was naïve.

"It's not cool with the Texas boys," one of them explained.

I dismissed their warning with a shake of my head. Screw that. Growing up, I had always been able to cross boundaries. I had gone into whatever neighborhood I wanted and played with whomever I wanted, and I wasn't going to stop now. "I'm going to sit with you if I want to sit with you," I said. "I don't give a shit what the Texas boys think."

And I didn't.

My admirers included the football team's captain, Chuck Cummings. We dated for several months. He had starred in the team's biggest victory of the year, the 1961 Aviation Bowl Championship, in Dayton,

Ohio, and one night we were reliving some of those magic moments and creating a few of our own in the front seat of his car. Now, this is where life gets embarrassing. I thought that I'd already had sex, which shows how ignorant I was. If you think you've had sex but aren't sure, you probably haven't done it.

As it turned out, I hadn't — until that night when I was making out with Chuck, and even then I wasn't sure what was happening other than that this guy who weighed two hundred plus pounds was on top of me and I couldn't push him off. Unsure what he was trying to do, I quit struggling and said, "Hey, if whatever you're trying to do means that much to you, go ahead."

It was after curfew when I walked back into my dorm and the tight-ass monitor immediately slapped me with twenty-eight "late" minutes. That pissed me off. Once upstairs, I changed clothes and discovered there was blood in my underwear. The next morning I called Chuck and yelled at him for making me start my period. He was quiet for a moment. He took a deep breath before explaining that he didn't think I had started my period.

"No? I'm bleeding," I said, annoyed.

"Penny, let me talk to you about what happened," he said.

Like the good guy that he was, he came over and took me for a walk, and with more compassion and gentleness than you'd ever expect from a star football player, he explained the facts of life to me. This was the talk that I never got while growing up. I guess it says something about me that I didn't just have sex with the captain of the football team. I learned about it from him, too.

Tragically, Chuck died in a car accident the next year. In his honor, the university created the annual Chuck Cummings Memorial Award for the most inspirational player. They still give it out. I also think it's kind of cool that there's a memorial to the first guy I did it with.

I know that I've never forgotten him.

CHAPTER 10

Mrs. Henry

Penny and Mickey Henry cutting the cake at their 1963 wedding
in New Mexico

Anthony Marshall

*T*OWARD THE END of my sophomore year, I met Mickey Henry and I quit thinking about all the other boys I had been dating or wanted to date. A freshman, Mickey was in school on a football scholarship. An All-State end from Highland High, he was large and strong — exactly the type I liked — with short, dark hair and a puckish grin like a young Burt Reynolds. I came up to his shoulder and practically disappeared when he wrapped his arms around me.

You couldn't find two more different people, though. Mickey and his two sisters had been raised by his grandmother. His mother worked at the local military base. His father had been in an institution since Mickey was a baby. If not for football, he wouldn't have traveled outside of Albuquerque. He was shocked by the stories I told about my family and growing up in New York. If I didn't amuse him, I confused him. Like when I tried to explain why my brother, sister, and I had all been confirmed different religions but were atheists.

Then summer came. I was a counselor for the second year in a row at Diana-Dalmaqua, a camp in the Catskills run by the parents of my mother's dancing school favorite, Lois Rosenberg. Mickey worked construction in Albuquerque. We kept in touch with letters and lengthy long-distance phone conversations.

When we returned to campus late that summer for what was my junior and his sophomore year, we picked up where we left off. We even discussed marriage in that dreamy, what-if way kids do when they're in love for the first time. But I wasn't in a rush, and Mickey said we needed to wait until after graduation when he would have a job and could start building a stable and solid future. I admired his self-control and common sense.

Then, one weekend early in the season, Mickey didn't make the travel team and he sunk into a deep depression. I'm sure it was the first time in his sporting life that he had been left behind, and he didn't know how to handle the setback. We went out the next night and in the process of consoling him, we ended up getting romantic in his car. I'd been in a front seat before, except this time I knew what I was doing.

Or so I thought — until I missed my period. I made an appointment with the campus doctor, who gave me a cursory exam and said I was stressed. I knew stress didn't affect me that way, though. Without going into detail, I asked the doctor to give me a blood test. Even though the chance of me being pregnant from that one time was one in a million, I knew a baby was growing in me. And a few days later, the test results confirmed it.

For the first twenty-four hours, I was numb. All I could think about or hear in my head was my mother. She epitomized all my fears, frustrations, and sense of failure. I knew I was going to have to tell her, and before her, I had to tell Mickey. But before telling either of them, I wanted to think through my options, because maybe, just maybe, I might come up with a solution.

The most obvious option was to get an abortion in Juarez. I knew some girls who'd gone there. But I ruled it out immediately. Another option was to ride horses and push myself physically in an effort to cause a miscarriage. I'd also heard stories about girls who'd gone that route, but I didn't know if they were true, and I thought, with my luck, I'd botch the job and make a tough situation worse.

Still another option was to move to Amarillo and have the baby on my own. I don't know why Amarillo. I'd never been there. It started with an "A." It sounded far away. I had made my bed, and I would sleep in it — but out of town. I liked that scenario. I would be running away from Mickey and my mother, the two people I didn't want to face.

Yet they were also the two people that I needed to tell. I don't know why, but something about me would rather face the fire than torture myself, so I worked up my courage and broke the news to Mickey.

His reaction was much better than when he didn't make the travel team. He listened to me run through the possible scenarios, and after I finished, he brought up another option — marriage.

"It's mine, too," he said. "We'll get married."

I had purposely avoided the M-word. Despite whatever Mickey and I had said in the past, I knew deep down that I wasn't ready to get married, and I probably didn't want to spend the rest of my life with him. But Mickey wrapped his strong arms around me and assured me that we were doing the right thing and would get through this together.

I called home, and my mother answered.

"I have news," I said. "I'm getting married."

"You're pregnant," she said.

It wasn't even a question.

"No, I'm not," I said reflexively.

"Yes, you are. And I'll tell you right now that I'm not coming for the wedding. You'll need me more when the baby is born."

I suppose the conversation could have been worse.

My father was upset. He blamed Mickey and said he wanted to fly out and "kick that Indian's teeth in." Mickey was half Irish and half Mexican, hence the slur. My father was 6'1", but Mickey was 6'4" — and younger. I didn't think any teeth would be kicked in. Daily phone calls helped everyone cool off. It was like we all went through the five stages of grief: denial, anger, bargaining, depression, and acceptance.

Mickey and I set November 23 as our wedding date. We picked up a marriage license at city hall. They also gave us a marriage "starter kit" — a cardboard box containing Tide, a bar of soap, and a tube of toothpaste. My father flew into town on November 22, the same day President Kennedy was assassinated. The news set a tone for the weekend.

On Saturday, after playing in a game against Brigham Young, Mickey changed into a suit and drove to his mother's house, where the two of us were married in a simple and somber ceremony in the backyard. I wore a beige winter suit with a thick fur collar. My father had brought it from New York. I looked like an animal was swallowing me. I never wore it again.

Afterward, Mickey's mother served cake and Kool-Aid. Then Mickey and I went to a motel, where we spent the rest of our honeymoon weekend watching President Kennedy's funeral on TV.

Once married, we left our dorms and moved into an apartment near school. There was an avocado tree in the backyard, and I discovered that I liked them. So there was that. There was also an effort to make the best of the situation. My parents sent Mickey's mother a letter expressing their appreciation for her watching out for me. They included a loaf of New York rye bread.

Mickey responded with a multipage thank-you, asking my parents to forgive me for not telling them sooner ("She was so upset that she had let you down.") and assuring them that we were going to make it. "I want you to know that I do love Penny very much and will do my best to make her happy and provide for her every need," he wrote. "Please don't think I'm helpless or irresponsible. I realize the overwhelming responsibility and pressure that I now have."

Before Christmas, I found out that Mickey's family members were Jehovah's Witnesses. His sisters pushed me to go with them to the Kingdom Hall. I tried it once. The big joke there was "How do you tell Adam and Eve apart in Heaven?" The answer: "They don't have bellybuttons." I didn't get it — and I didn't go back.

As a Jehovah's Witness, though, Mickey didn't celebrate the holidays, so I took him to New York and we had Christmas with my family. It was his first time in the city. He was nervous but excited. My father showed him the Empire State Building, the Statue of Liberty, and the other sights. They went by themselves. I didn't do tourist attractions. I had seen them all in school.

But I did take Mickey to his first Broadway show. As we waited for the subway to take us downtown, I got nauseated. My morning sickness struck at night. Mickey turned away from me as I bent over the garbage can to throw up. I thought I detected some small-town embarrassment. "What?" I said. "This is New York. I'm not the first person to throw up in the subway."

Back home, our lives changed. I realized why it takes nine months to have a baby. You need the time to adjust and prepare. Money became an issue. To cut expenses, we moved into Mickey's mother's house. It was shades of my own parents as I found myself living with his mother and grandmother. Mickey also sold his station wagon and got a job at night after school. Wanting to contribute, too, I dropped out of school midway through the year and signed up for office temp work as a Kelly Girl.

Before accepting any jobs, I had to learn to drive. Mickey taught me on his mother's car, an automatic sedan. Then he bought an old stick shift. I don't know what was he thinking. I spent months riding around in first gear.

That spring, as my stomach grew beyond a bump, Mickey's mother moved into an apartment in a new development. She had her own money problems. Mickey and I scraped up enough cash to rent a studio apartment in her development. But that tapped us out. If my parents hadn't bought us a hide-a-bed, we wouldn't have had anything. Some nights I wrestled Mickey for food.

By June, I had gained fifty pounds. At night, I laid on the floor like a beached whale. Tracy was due in early July. I couldn't wait to give birth and feel normal again, if that was possible. I counted the days and braced myself for the big event: my mother's arrival.

CHAPTER 11

Forget the Gas, I Want the Jell-O

Penny and her young daughter, Tracy, in 1965

Marjorie Marshall

*M*Y MOTHER ARRIVED after the Fourth of July. I wasn't due for a few more days. At that point, my sole preparation for the baby had been to choose between the two local hospitals, the Presbyterian one or St. Something. I'd asked which one had a TV in the room. A day later I began to hear gurgling sounds in my belly. I thought it might be time and I turned to my mother, who had come, as she said, because I was going to need help.

"So?" I asked.

"What do you expect me to say?" she said. "I'm not a doctor."

I didn't know anything about labor, and she couldn't remember shit. Neither could Mickey's mother. Between them, they had seven children and neither of them knew a thing. They were mute when my water broke the next afternoon. I grabbed my Dr. Spock book, went into the bathroom, and looked up water breakage. It said, "Call the doctor."

For some reason my doctor said I didn't have to go to the hospital yet. My mother opened the pullout couch, spread some newspaper, and we watched TV until my contractions grew stronger and more frequent. Then even I knew we had better start timing things. Finally, I decided to go in. It seemed early, but I thought it was better to be safe than have my mother deliver the baby.

I also wanted to be in the air-conditioning at the hospital. It was summer and close to a hundred degrees outside. I was dying. We got word to Mickey, who was working construction. At the hospital, they ushered me to the maternity ward and assigned me a bed. I remember there was a curtain between me and some other lady who kept screaming, "I'm doing it myself."

I soon understood why. As I waited, everyone and their uncle stuck their fingers in me to see how much I was dilated. I think the janitor checked, too. It didn't seem to matter. Mickey came and went because my labor went on for twenty hours without any signs of a baby. At some point, the nurse asked whether I wanted gas or a spinal block during delivery. No one thought of natural childbirth then. I leaned toward the gas because I don't like needles. I'd never even had Novocain. But it was still too early for either. They told me to walk around or take a shower.

I mentioned that I was very hungry. I hadn't eaten since the previous day, and this was when I would fight Mickey for food, so just imagine how badly I wanted something to eat. I asked the nurse if they had any food they could bring me.

"You can't have any food with the gas," she said. "If you have the spinal, I can give you Jell-O."

"Okay, forget the gas," I said. "I want the Jell-O."

The final six hours were hard labor. They continued to check how much I was dilated and they preferred to do it during a contraction. But something came over me when the nurse tried, and I said, "Get the hell away from me," and hit her. It was a reflex. Enough was enough. The woman on the other side of the curtain yelled, "You tell 'em, sister!"

Soon after, on the afternoon of July 7, 1964, amid much relief from all those around me (by this time the spinal had kicked in and I didn't give a shit), especially the nurse, I gave birth to a baby girl. Checking in at seven pounds, fourteen ounces and twenty-two inches, she had a full head of dark hair and brown eyes just like her father. She looked like a miniature Beatle.

Mickey had hoped for a boy, but by the time he finished counting her fingers and toes he was in love with his little girl. As for her name, all Mickey knew was that he didn't want Robin or any other birdlike names. As we traded suggestions, I remembered the name of a girl I liked from camp, Tracy Saturn. Tracy was a happy name, as my mother would have said. I liked it. She was Tracy Lee Henry.

I tried breastfeeding Tracy, but my milk didn't come out. They put her on Similac and gave me a shot to dry up the milk in my breasts. In the meantime, I developed a kidney infection. So there I was, with an ice pack on my chest and a heating pad on my sides. It was lovely.

They kept me in the hospital for nearly a week. Back then they didn't kick you out in two seconds like they do now. When we finally took Tracy home, our studio apartment seemed even smaller. I emptied out a dresser drawer and she slept there. It was an instant nursery. Despite my happiness and relief, I was disappointed at not being able to go to camp that summer. If not for getting pregnant, I would've been at Diana-Dalmaqua again.

But I adapted and turned my attention to being a mom. I fed Tracy, bathed her in the kitchen sink, and learned to rest her in an infant's seat on top of the dryer or the idling car when she couldn't go to sleep. I didn't like the morning feedings, which I had to do when Mickey started school again in the fall and traveled with the team. Otherwise he was good about getting up with her.

I lost twenty of the fifty pounds I'd gained right away. It melted off. I'm sure it was all the running around I did. Like most new mothers, I was amazed at how much work was required for this tiny thing that didn't do much. I remember being thrilled when Tracy was finally old enough to prop herself up in her playpen and hold her own bottle just like my mother had me do.

• • •

At the end of summer, we moved to a two-bedroom apartment. It was roomier and cheaper than our studio, and Mickey was closer to school. After seven weeks at home, I went back to work, too. Mickey's grandmother watched Tracy, as she'd done with Mickey and his sisters. We also used their swimming pool. I don't know what we would have done without them.

We had nothing. Our one luxury was a diaper service. It had been a gift, and we had it for three months. I was supposed to rinse the poop in the toilet before putting it in the diaper pail. Sometimes I forgot and the toilet clogged. Hey, I didn't pretend to be the paradigm of motherhood or domesticity. But I never forgot the strong smell of ammonia in the diaper pail. Just lifting the top for two seconds let out a blast that burned my eyes.

In 1965, my New Year's resolution was to find work that didn't require me to get up in the morning. I wanted some kind of life back. My mother suggested that I try teaching dance. Ordinarily I ignored whatever advice she gave me. It was a reflex response. She said something, and I kicked back. But this time I listened. I made a list of dance schools and looked for a job.

My first stop was the Litka School of Music, the city's top dance school. The owners, Muriel and Adolph Litka, liked my experience and hired me on the spot. They knew how to sell. In a press release, they described me as a Junior Rockette, a June Taylor Dancer, and the winner of the *Ted Mack Amateur Hour*. Even I was impressed. "At the Litka School, she will specialize in precision dancing, acrobatic ballet, and tap dancing," they said. "She can also teach some jazz."

As if that wasn't enough, they added, "Her brother, Garry Marshall, is a writer for Danny Thomas's production company, which includes shows starring Dick Van Dyke, Danny Thomas, Lucille Ball, and Gomer Pyle."

I knew Gomer Pyle wasn't real. Likewise, my credits weren't entirely accurate, either. But why correct the Litkas? They were happy, and I was employed. The hours were exactly what I had in mind. The preschoolers came in at eleven o'clock and the older kids arrived in the afternoon. I played the same songs my mother had used and taught the same routines. It was easy. I sat next to the record player, smoked, and said, "Left, right, left, right."

CHAPTER 12

Take Everything

Penny and Mickey at the 1965 New York World's Fair

Marshall personal collection

B Y THE MIDDLE of spring, I had lost the remaining thirty pounds of my pregnancy weight. I felt much better. Later, when Tracy turned one, the three of us went back to New York and spent a week on the beach in Avon-by-the-Sea. We also went to the World's Fair to see my mother's students entertain on one of the stages. When my mother insisted on hiding an entire roasted chicken in the front pouch of my cotton pullover so we could save money and not have to buy dinner there, I thought I might be getting my life back, the crazy life that I knew.

My mother was eager to spend alone time with her one-year-old granddaughter, but with a condition. She didn't want Tracy to talk as much as she did, which was all the time — and in complete sentences. She was very verbal and had a large vocabulary, thanks to all the time she spent with Mickey's grandmother. One of her favorite phrases was "Oops, Nana has gas."

It was cute. But my mother didn't want so much cuteness. She was pretending that Tracy was six months younger so she wouldn't have to tell people in the building that I had been pregnant before getting married.

That Christmas, having had his fill of New York — and my family — Mickey stayed in Albuquerque. He was a Jehovah's Witness, so he didn't celebrate Christmas. However, after coming home, I found a receipt for flowers. I confronted Mickey. He confessed to having sent them to an old girlfriend. I had problems with that. He couldn't buy his child a birthday or Christmas present because it was pagan, but he could send an old girlfriend flowers?

After a number of angry arguments, I stopped being angry. I realized the rest of my life, however that turned out, wasn't going to be with Mickey. I wasn't mad at him. What was to be mad at? We were two different people trying to do the right thing under circumstances that neither of us was prepared for yet. Mickey knew it, too. I think he came to that same realization when he sent flowers to his ex.

As for what to do next, we had no idea. We had a kid, and we were too young to know how to make a clean break quickly. We didn't even know how to talk about it. We needed events to push us into action, as they eventually did.

One day a man from the Albuquerque Civic Light Opera came into the Litka School of Music, asking for me. Explaining that he had read about me, he said he wanted me to choreograph their production of *South Pacific.* I said no. It sounded like more than I could handle. Then he asked if I wanted to be in it.

"Do I have to audition?" I asked.

"No," he said.

"Then okay," I said.

With Mickey's encouragement, I signed on. I was in the chorus of *South Pacific,* as well as *Carnival,* and *High Spirits.* For me, the best part of these productions was discovering other people in town who liked to stay up at night and smoke. Mickey wasn't a night person; now I had company, people who were fun and had interests similar to mine.

Like Phil Crummett, a handsome, energetic actor with a big singing voice, who was involved in theater in town. Older and ambitious, he was putting together a production of *Oklahoma!,* and he hired me to be his assistant. As he auditioned people, he asked for my opinion. Then one day he asked if I wanted to audition for Ado Annie.

"Yeah, sure," I said. "Okay."

I didn't have any confidence yet. And during rehearsals, I discovered that I couldn't sing worth shit, but I could sell. Once the play opened, reviewers agreed. One local paper called the production "superlative" and said, "the two comic leads, Bill Cook and Penny Henry, almost steal the show." Another paper also applauded the show but created a problem for me by saying that Phil was "up and down throughout the show" while my "rendition of a girl that can't say no is head and shoulders above the rest of them."

After that, Phil Crummett hated me.

The next summer, I played Ado Annie again in a production of *Oklahoma!* staged at a theater-in-the-round in Durango. Going away for more than a month motivated Mickey and me to get divorced. Both of us agreed there was no point belaboring the situation any longer. We were living separate lives. We didn't want to end up hating each other.

We didn't have anything to haggle over. "Here are half the pots and pans," I said. "What else do you need?" Mickey didn't want anything. And all I wanted was my name back. I dropped "Henry" as quickly as possible. I was tired of hearing the joke, "Penny Henry, the sky is falling."

The only trouble we had came from our parents. As soon as we decided to make the split legal, his mother and grandmother hid Tracy from me. They were afraid I was going to take her to New York. What made them think I'd move back in with my parents? My mother heard about Tracy and came out to get her back. It seemed like a fight was about to break out.

But after she talked with Mickey's mother, the two of them went to court and asked for custody of the baby. Or so she said. Mickey and I never actually went to court. My mother could have made the whole thing up. I don't know. What I do know is that she and Mickey's mother made us feel so inept that we believed her when she said the judge awarded them joint custody.

Who knows?

It didn't matter.

Mickey's mother and grandmother took care of Tracy most of the time anyway. What was done was done. Mickey came over and we cried together. We didn't know how all this had happened. We were just young and in over our heads. It was time to start over.

CHAPTER 13

A Work in Progress

Penny's first friends in Hollywood: her brother, Garry Marshall,
and his writing partner Jerry Belson

Marshall personal collection

AFTER THE PRODUCTION in Durango, I decided to move to Los Angeles. Where else was I going to go? New York with my parents? I don't think so. Two guys from the play — Bill Cook, who had played opposite me, and his boyfriend, Randy — were going to L.A. I decided to go with them. I sold my Chevy Corvair to my friend Gerry Puhara, who was also in *Oklahoma!*, and I was ready to go.

On the night before we left, Bill, Randy, and I went to the drive-in and saw *The Trip*, director Roger Corman's movie about a TV director who takes LSD and goes on a mind-bending journey. Bill lit up a joint, and I smoked pot for the first time. It didn't even make me hungry.

Except for a flat tire in Arizona, our road trip was uneventful. I collected matchbooks from every place we stopped. They didn't take up much room. All I had was a little bag of clothes. In L.A., I stayed with Betty Vaughn, a girl who had also been in *Oklahoma!* She lived in Canoga Park, a suburb in the northwestern part of the San Fernando Valley — so far away from everything that when I checked in with my brother, he asked, "Where's Canoga Park?"

Garry's career was on the rise. After graduating from Northwestern, he spent two years with the Army in Korea, despite fourteen typewritten pages of allergies (they gave him a special, hypoallergenic uniform and put him on the USO radio shows), and then returned to New York. He tried stand-up comedy and wrote jokes for Phil Foster and other comedians. My mother worried that he was going to get hooked on reefer. My brother, with all his allergies, wasn't going to get hooked on reefer.

His only addiction was work. In 1961, he and his writing partner, Fred Freeman, a friend from college, had moved to L.A. to write for Joey Bishop and *The Tonight Show Starring Johnny Carson*. After they split, Garry met Jerry Belson, the funny, smart, pot-smoking younger brother of an Army buddy from Korea. Although opposites (my brother was upbeat and clean-shaven, Jerry was dark and had long hair and a beard), they were a perfect match—and prolific. They wrote for *The Danny Thomas Show, The Lucy Show,* and *The Dick Van Dyke Show,* the Emmy-winning series created by Carl Reiner, who had once lived across the street from us in the Bronx.

One time Garry took Jerry back to the Bronx to show him where he had grown up. He took him down to the cellar to meet my mother and show him her famous dance school. One of the women there turned to my mother and asked, "Which one is your son?"

"Not the one with the beard," my mother said.

"Oh, thank God," the other woman said.

When I arrived in town, they were involved in TV, movies, and even talent management. Since I had last seen him, Garry had acquired a wife, Barbara, a former nurse, who had been his neighbor in his old apartment building. His life was perfect. He was writing, and he had live-in health care.

He offered to help me. He asked what I wanted to do. I didn't know.

"What are you good at?" he asked.

"Nothing," I said.

"When was the last time you were happy?" he asked.

"When I was sitting on the Parkway fence watching the boys play softball," I said.

While telling him about my performances as Ado Annie and the other shows I'd done with the Civic Light Opera, Garry saw a glimmer of light in my eyes. As he knew, for me, that was equivalent to doing cartwheels. He suggested that I try acting in TV and movies. I would need lessons, he explained, but he would give me names of teachers. It sounded good to me. But not everyone agreed. My mother called in a panic. She told me to change my name.

I didn't want to change my name. I had just changed it back to Marshall.

I told Garry.

"Mommy said I should change my name," I said.

"Why?" he asked. "What was her reason?"

"She doesn't want me to embarrass the family," I said.

"Don't listen to her," he said. "She's nuts."

Garry had me move into his office, a two-bedroom apartment in Hollywood where he and Jerry wrote every day. He and Fred Roos, a friend from Korea, also ran Compass Management from there. Compass represented a bunch of young actors, including Harrison Ford, Teri Garr, Candy Clark, and Cindy Williams. The girls were known as "the Compass cuties."

Although living there was convenient, it wasn't ideal. They started work in the morning and I slept late. Garry moved me into an apartment just off Sunset Boulevard that belonged to a friend who was out of town for a couple months. He also provided the names of people I should meet. He said one guy was good for lunch, another would talk to me about acting, this one would tell me about unemployment, another was a good contact but don't go to his office by myself, and so on.

I took Harvey Lembeck's improvisational workshop. I also signed up for classes with acting coach Justin Smith (who I called "Just in

Time" so I could remember his name). And I tried a workshop run by The Committee, an improv group based in a theater on Sunset whose members included Alan Myerson, Leigh French, Del Close, Don Sturdy (who later changed his name to Howard Hesseman), Carl Gottlieb, Larry Hankin, Richard Stahl, and Garry Goodrow.

In Justin Smith's class, I discovered a knack for making people laugh just by talking about myself. I introduced myself, as was the protocol, and started describing my family and childhood. People were cracking up. Maybe it was the sound of my voice. Maybe the stories were funny. I didn't know. I was just being me. Garry suggested I try stand-up. There weren't many female comics. He thought his pal Buzz Cohen could write an act.

"Why don't you do that?" he said.

I didn't even consider it. Being on the road alone was not my idea of a life. I wasn't so good on my own.

"No, I don't think so," I said.

I also liked Jeff Corey's acting class. He started on time, and he let you do your scene if you came prepared. One day he questioned the scenes I chose.

"Are you always going to play the victim?" he asked.

I thought about it for a moment.

"Yeah, why not?"

I wasn't going to play the sexy bombshell. I had been insecure about my looks my whole life, and being in Hollywood raised that insecurity to a new level. I thought actresses had to be beautiful. You only had to look at the top TV shows and movies to see that I was right. My brother, ever the realist, warned that I might not work until I was older. Perky girls like Sally Field and Karen Valentine were hot, and as both of us knew, I wasn't perky.

Still, there was reason to smile. My friend Gerry Puhara moved to L.A., arriving in my old Corvair, and we got an apartment together on Hayworth. Both of us got temp jobs, me sorting W-2s and W-4s at Cedars of Lebanon Hospital, and her on *Let's Make a Deal.* Then my brother gave me a job on the movie *How Sweet It Is!*, a comedy about a photographer (James Garner) who takes his wife (Debbie Reynolds) and teenage son to Paris on an assignment, and I was part of a group of girls on a summer vacation tour.

Garry and Jerry had written the script, and their *Dick Van Dyke Show* pal Jerry Paris directed the film. The job began with a working cruise to Acapulco. We went there and back. I lived on Dramamine. But even seasickness was better than typing numbers. I was in a bunch of scenes, but my big one was at the Louvre (it was re-created on a soundstage), where I was in a montage of girls smiling in front of the *Mona Lisa*. When my turn came all you saw was a mouthful of braces. It was a visual joke.

I was probably the only actress who would agree to have real braces put on for the week. Jerry sent me to his dentist in the Pacific Palisades. My teeth hurt like hell. I whined to my brother, who wanted to kill me. But once they said, "Penny, you're on," I was perfect. Then, after we cut, it was back to complaining.

As a reward, they gave me a line to speak. I was supposed to say, "It was made in Japan." Determined to do a good job for my brother, I shouted it as if I was onstage with the Civic Light Opera. The soundman nearly fell off his seat. Garry rushed to my side.

"We aren't in the theater," he said. "We have microphones."

I felt stupid. But I looked around and nearly everyone was laughing or had a smile on their face. Maybe I wasn't terrible.

Penny in costume in 1972 as a member of the Celanese Players, a group
of actors and writers that included Steve Martin and Valerie Curtin

Nurit Wilde

F RED ROOS, MY BROTHER'S partner in Compass Management, put me in an episode of *That Girl*, the popular sitcom starring Marlo Thomas and Ted Bessell. I played an assistant librarian, and I had one line — actually one word. As Marlo walked by, the head librarian said, "There goes a girl with a head on her shoulders." I said, "Who?" And the librarian replied, "*That* girl."

For saying that one word I was paid $140 — more than I made during an entire week of temping in the dental lab where I was being driven crazy by the sound of drilling all day. For $140 a word, I figured I could say "What?" "Where?" "How?" and be both wealthier and saner. So I quit temping and signed up for unemployment.

At that moment, I became a real actress. In Hollywood, unemployment is a lifestyle. You have to work hard to get on it. Then you're free to go on auditions, as well as to sit around and drink coffee, smoke, and flirt with whoever's cute in your acting class. I'm not going to lie, though. It helped that my brother had an important job in the business. He made it clear that he wouldn't risk his career for me, but he would open doors. It would be up to me to get through them.

The formula seemed to work. Dick Clark, who liked my brother, gave me a small part in *The Savage Seven*, a low-budget movie he was producing about a biker who falls for an Indian girl on a reservation, angering her brother and leading to a lot of fighting. It was a good group of people. Richard Rush was the director, future Oscar-winner Lazlo Kovacs was the cinematographer, and the cast included Robert Walker Jr., Joanna Frank, and Larry Bishop, Joey's son.

Despite having only one line of dialogue, I was on location for three weeks in a couple of not-so-beautiful desert towns in California and Nevada. But I had fun. Walter Robles, one of the stuntmen, taught me to ride a motorcycle, and Hell's Angels boss Sonny Barger spent a few days on the set. I regretted having to go home. I'd had the same problem as a kid when camp ended. After making new friends, I didn't get to see them again. It made me lonely. I told my brother I might not want to do any more movies. "You'll make new friends," he said.

Veteran producer Sheldon Leonard, who mentored my brother and Jerry Belson on numerous TV series, cast me in the role of a secretary in the pilot of his new detective show *My Friend Tony*. It was the first of God-knows-how-many secretaries I played. All I had to do here was pick up the phone and say, "Hello, Woodruff-Novello Private Investigators."

But Garry and Sheldon asked the near impossible. They wanted me to say the line without sounding like I was from New York. Accents were not and never would be my forte. I talked the way I talked. But I couldn't say that to Sheldon and my brother. So I practiced different options in my head and ultimately decided to add an extra *R* to the word "investigators."

When I answered the phone it came out as, "Hello, Woodruff-Novello Private *Investergaters*." Yes, I mispronounced the word. But no one noticed. Garry and Sheldon, both of whom spoke with the strongest New York accents of any two people I knew, thought it was perfect.

. . .

That summer, Garry put me in the movie *The Grasshopper*. He and Jerry Belson had adapted the script from a novel about a beautiful girl who runs away from her small British Columbia home to L.A. to be with her boyfriend and ends up letting her looks lead her down a troubled path of bad jobs and worse men. Jerry Paris directed again. I played "the plaster caster"—look that up if you need to—and in my brief scene as a wild rock chick I held up a tape measure.

One day Jerry Paris, who, like my mother, was famous for saying whatever popped into his head and not ever censoring himself, introduced me to the movie's star, Jacqueline Bisset.

"Look at her. Isn't she beautiful?" he said.

"Yes," I said.

"She can't act. But look at that face!"

Jacqueline smiled, showing only a touch of annoyance, as if Jerry's comment was one of those things she had to endure for being so breathtakingly beautiful. I bet she lived for those moments when people complimented her work and praised her talent. Despite my brother, I wasn't shielded from Hollywood's cruelty. My first commercial, for instance, was for Head & Shoulders shampoo. I played one of two roommates primping in the bathroom. I was the girl combing her hair, and Farrah Fawcett was the girl in the shower asking to borrow my shampoo.

"I know it really works against your dandruff," she said. "But what about my gorgeous hair?"

"Your gorgeous hair will love it," I said.

The implications were obvious. Although Farrah was a doll who went out of her way to make sure I didn't feel insulted, it was still hurtful. I went home feeling horrible about myself. If I had been able to think of an alternative career, I might have quit the business. I felt like I was on the verge anyway.

But I did another episode of *That Girl* and then I landed a part on the opening episode of *Then Came Bronson*, a new series starring Michael Parks as a disillusioned journalist who quits his job at a newspaper and jumps on his motorcycle to find the real meaning of life. It was the first job I got on my own, and it kept me in the business.

At the audition, the director, Marvin Chomsky, told me the story of the episode: Jim Bronson visits a former girlfriend at a camp she runs for children with special needs. I got it. She had found her life; he was looking for his. Yes, but Marvin asked what I knew about summer camp. My face lit up with confidence.

"I went to camp for twelve years," I said. "I love camp. I know everything."

"No," he said. "This is about a camp for disturbed children."

I told him about the pyromaniac who had burned down the staff bunk at Geneva.

"My mother thought it was me," I said.

"Why'd she think that?" he asked.

"She thought highly of me," I said.

Excited, I told my brother that the episode was shooting in Jackson Hole, Wyoming. He wanted to know who else was in the episode besides Michael Parks. I told him the biggest names: Jack Klugman, former child actor Mark Lester, and Karen Ericson. Garry told me to introduce myself to Jack and ask if he wanted to be in a new TV series that he and Jerry had in the works.

"What's that?" I asked.

"*The Odd Couple,*" he said. "We're adapting the Neil Simon play. I want him for Oscar."

"All right," I said.

So I went to Jackson Hole, where I'd never been, and it was a very nice place. There was plenty of down-time between scenes. And Jack and I both liked to sit in the sun. One day the two of us were lying out on chaises beside the lake and I remembered my brother's request. I'm fearless when it comes to talking to people. I'll ask anything. So I got Jack's attention and said, "Would you be interested in doing a TV series based on *The Odd Couple?*"

Jack was confused. He had barely noticed me, yet here was this girl pitching him on a TV series.

"Who are you?" he said.

"Penny," I said.

"Why are you asking me this?" he said.

"My brother is Garry Marshall, and he is going to do *The Odd Couple* as a TV series. He wants to know if you'd play Oscar."

I'm not sure what either of us said next. It's not important. What matters is that Jack obviously didn't say no and as a result went on to costar with Tony Randall in one of TV's greatest sitcoms. I also learned it never hurts to ask. You never know until you do.

CHAPTER 15
The Manson Murders

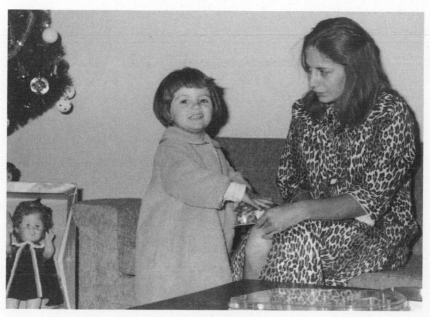

Penny celebrating Christmas with a young Tracy in 1966

Anthony Marshall

*T*HEY SAY IF YOU remember the '60s, you weren't there. (I feel that way about the '80s.) Because I had a child, I was largely unaffected by the decade's changes — that is, until 1969. That was the year my mother told Ronny that I knew Charles Manson. For the record, I didn't. It was also the year she told people that I was going to take LSD and jump off a roof. She was wrong. That was the '80s.

In 1969, I moved several times, changing roommates for reasons that aren't interesting and offering my couch or floor to whatever friends from the Bronx had come out to sample the culture. There were more than a handful of them, like Arlyn Dunetz, who crashed on our floor until she went off with a guy in a van. The next time I heard from her, she'd changed her last name to Phoenix, lived on a commune, and had seven kids, including River, Rain, and Leaf, all of whom she wanted to get into acting — and of course she did.

My mother, my father, and my grandmother were the last three people I expected to see near the Sunset Strip, yet they arrived mid-year, reeling from financial losses and upheavals in the neighborhood. My father had lost his best accounts and much of his income when his friend who was head of the American Medical Association retired and his replacement hired another agency. My mother's dance school had also declined. The hippies didn't send their children to learn tap and ballet the way parents had in previous decades.

My brother said he could help them if they moved to L.A. As unthinkable as it seemed, my mother closed her school and soon arrived with my aging, blind grandmother. She made an entrance, too. At the airport, she jumped on the baggage carousel after missing her luggage and rode it around, yelling at Garry and his wife to get her bags and watch Nanny.

Nanny went into an old folks' home in Hollywood while my mother moved into a place on Laurel Avenue. My father, who stayed in New York to close the apartment and tie up loose ends at work, arrived a few weeks later. He was not given a warm welcome.

"I'd kill myself," my mother told us, "but I can't find my suicide jar."

Garry covered their $155-a-month rent. My mother handled the rest of their finances, keeping track of every penny and putting my father on a strict allowance. One month she refused to give him $100 for his car insurance because he still owed her $50 for repairs from the month before. "If I give him money," she told me, "I'll never get it back." She talked about applying for work at one of the local department stores. Garry also tried to set her up at a talent agency, but she proved too difficult. She thought everyone was a moron.

My father went to Garry's office nearly every day as if he worked there. I think he used the phone. I'm sure he wanted to get away from my mother. He wasn't used to spending time with her. Garry said he could work for Compass, but the management company shut down before that happened. All their actors went with Pat McQueeney, and Herbie Molina took the writers. The only one without a place to go was my father, and it annoyed the hell out of my mother. "I'm not his slave, Pen," she said. "He doesn't even look for a job."

· · ·

I spent a lot of time with my mother. If I was free, I met her for breakfast or lunch, and when she couldn't get ahold of me, or when I didn't
call as planned, she left a message on my service asking where I was.
She needed someone to tell about the minutia in her life, and that
was me. She told me what she made for dinner, how much money
the managers of her building had in their saving accounts (compared
to her and my father, who had nothing), and even whether she was
having "loose movements" that day or nothing at all.

"It's this unpredictable, hectic life I lead," she said one day with a
sigh. "If only I had my suicide jar."

She babysat for Garry's children, and told me how Gary's wife, Barbara, slipped her cash—but never in front of my father. It was her
mad money, she said, and it kept her in cheap dresses and visits to
the hairdresser. She also helped take care of Tracy, who was now five
and spent summers with me. She was better off with Mickey, who
was remarried and had the more stable home.

Look, my mothering skills didn't suddenly materialize between
June and August. If Tracy woke up early, I sent her to the corner store
to pick up breakfast—a Fudgsicle for her and cigarettes for me. My
mother hadn't been June Cleaver, and I wasn't Mrs. Brady.

My grandmother grew harder to manage. We once picked her up
for a doctor's appointment and she got in the front of the car, except
she stepped on the seat and sat on top of the head rest, not realizing her head was pressing against the roof. My mother grabbed her
ankles and yanked her down until she was properly seated.

At least my mother's sense of humor remained intact. She needed
it. Once, after buying my grandmother a bright, new housecoat, she
came back to find Nanny had cut off the sleeves, made pockets, and
sewn them onto four other dresses. At one time she would've railed
about the waste of money. Now, she laughed. "The gray background
with pink and green flowers on her yellow, blue, and white checked
dresses looks stunning," she told me.

For all of her complaining, she enjoyed L.A. One night she saw a preview of *Easy Rider* at the Directors Guild and sat next to a woman she recognized from Alexander's. Then she got into a conversation with a man who mistook her for Jean Stapleton. When he told her that Jean was very funny, my mother replied, "Well, I'm funny, too. Would you like to give me a job?"

As I recall, we were supposed to go shopping the next day, but I showed up late after getting a callback for a commercial. When I walked in, she was typing a letter to Ronny — she was still always typing. I read over her shoulder and saw she was catching my sister up on the latest events, including my love life. "She's still sleeping with the guy from William Morris," she wrote. "He's among a few others, but I can't say anything. Did I tell you she goes to his beach house in Malibu? I'm sure the neighbors tell his wife, but Pen doesn't care."

"Ma!" I exclaimed. "Why are you telling Ronny all about my personal life?"

"What?" she said, perplexed. "It's true, isn't it?"

CHAPTER 16

I Made Him Sick

Penny and Rob Reiner in 1973

Marshall personal collection

WHEN ROB REINER and I were children, we lived across the street from each other in the Bronx. We never met because the Grand Concourse was a busy street and we were too young to cross it. One time I saw his father, Carl, in the tiny grocery store in our building. Then one of the stars on *Your Show of Shows,* he was the most famous person in our neighborhood. He was also known for giving out the best Halloween candy.

In 1963, my brother and Jerry Belson worked for Carl as staff writers on *The Dick Van Dyke Show,* and I knew about Rob from hanging out with comedy people. The name Reiner stood out in Hollywood. There was one degree of separation between us for so many years that when we finally met, it felt like destiny was completing a circle that had been drawn years earlier.

It was a summer night, and I left Just in Time's acting class. I crossed Santa Monica Boulevard and walked into Barney's Beanery, a late-night bar and restaurant popular with actors, writers, and musicians. I spotted some people from The Committee at a table, and Rob was among them. Someone invited me to sit down, and Rob and I immediately looked at each other.

"So you're Garry's sister," he said.

"So you're Carl's kid," I replied, not missing a beat.

Rob and I were instant friends. I hung out at the house on King's Road he shared with what seemed like half of The Committee: Chris Ross, Carl Gottlieb, Larry Hankin, and John Brent. They were all creative — and nuts! John, who had made the comedy album *How to Speak Hip* with Del Close, kept an array of pills in a large flashlight. Every so often he dumped them out on the coffee table and said, "Let's see, two of these are equal to one Nembutal."

I liked Rob because he wore pajamas and didn't do drugs. He had already gone through his wild period and now focused on his work. He wanted to write and direct. His closest friends included his high school buddies Albert Brooks and Richard Dreyfuss and his writing partner, Phil Mishkin. They cranked out TV and movie scripts, as well as a play, *The Howie Rubin Story*, which won an L.A. Drama Critics Circle Award in 1970.

They were funny. Together, they would trade stories and twist them until they had spun them into comedy gold. I remember laughing one night as they recalled how they got out of the Vietnam draft. Albert had a bad shoulder and he did a whole bit on how that would have been bad for the war effort. Ricky Dreyfuss was a conscientious objector. Rob had a letter from his doctor saying he wasn't fit for military service, and then when he filled out his draft papers he checked every possible box on the page, including the one that indicated that he was a homosexual — which earned him a warning from the draft board that he would never act or write in Hollywood.

We would have dinner with Rob's family, including his younger siblings, Annie and Lucas. These were warm occasions that Carl livened up with games. I remember him once handing out kazoos for all of us to play. He would call everyone a genius when of course he was the only real genius at the table. One night, as Rob and I walked across the old railroad tracks in Hollywood, he made a surprising confession.

"You're the first Jewish girl that I've liked," he said.

I looked at him like he was missing the obvious.

"That's because I'm not Jewish," I said.

Then, all of a sudden, our relationship was put on hold. Rob had a nervous breakdown. He moved back in with his parents and dropped out of sight. I thought it was because I'd told him that I'd liked him, too. It might have been too much for him to handle. As time went on, though, I understood this wasn't about me. Although he had written for *The Glen Campbell Goodtime Hour* and *The Smothers Brothers*, and his play had won an award, none of that was enough. He was under extraordinary pressure to succeed and make a name for himself, separate from his father, and I thought perhaps he had buckled under the weight of his own expectations.

I stayed in contact with him as best I could. I got updates from Carl Gottlieb and spoke fairly often with Rob's parents. They were mystified. He couldn't work. At first he felt too much of everything, and then he went through a phase where he felt nothing. Literally. If he hit his arm against a tree, he didn't have any pain. He didn't have any sensation whatsoever.

Then, a few months later, I checked in with his father and things had improved. "He shaved today!" Carl said. It was the breakthrough all of us had been hoping for. From that point on, Rob improved slowly but steadily. Soon we were hanging out again. He would call and ask if I wanted to get something to eat or go to a movie and I always made myself available.

I was now living in a one-bedroom, ground-floor apartment on Palm, just off Sunset Boulevard. Barry Levinson, who was then writing comedy with Craig T. Nelson, had helped me move. I decorated the walls with jigsaw puzzles that I glued together after completing them. Jerry Belson came over one day and warned that that was a sign of sickness, not art. I disagreed. I thought it was a sign that I didn't have enough money to afford anything else.

Those were tough times. I spent three days on a Jack in the Box commercial shoot, playing a pregnant woman whose husband stops for a burger on the way to the hospital. George Furth, who was collaborating with Stephen Sondheim on the play *Company*, was my husband. I expected to make enough from the commercial to pay my rent for several months. But the ad was pulled at the last minute. Apparently you weren't supposed to show a pregnant woman detouring from the hospital. I guess someone at the FCC feared that thousands of babies would be born in the drive-through line.

I was also in an episode of *Love, American Style*, playing opposite actor Mike Farrell in a segment titled "Love and the Pickup." The script described my part as the "homely girl at a bar." Was I? Apparently. After I saw myself, I cried for three days. Reading those parts could send you to a psychiatrist for years. (Note to future scriptwriters: Don't describe girls as ugly, fat, or homely. You can tell the director quietly, in private. But it's not nice.)

Then I hit a new low point when someone tried to break into my apartment. It was late at night, and I was in bed. I had the window open a crack because it was hot. I had just put my book down and turned off the light when the lamp on my nightstand fell over with a crash. Startled, I noticed a large hand reaching through the Levolor windows next to me, searching for something to grab onto. I leapt out of bed and screamed.

My neighbor, Jesse Pearson, the actor who had played Conrad Birdie in *Bye Bye Birdie*, raced over from next door as soon as he heard my frightened scream. From behind the door where I was hiding, I pointed toward the window. Jesse yanked up the blinds and standing there was a guy holding his shoes in his hand. He looked as startled as we were.

"Don't get upset," he said, waving his hands. "I'm a cop."

The real police came quickly and took him away. Morgan Upton from The Committee stayed with me the rest of the night, and Rob, who I hadn't been able to reach, took over the next day. Our relationship progressed without incident until Tracy visited. Before I could even introduce them, Rob blurted, "That's all I need is a kid." His comment surprised me. He was thinking ahead. We hadn't even slept together yet, though it wasn't from a lack of interest on my part. Whenever we got to my door Rob either had a headache or a sore throat or an upset stomach. I thought I made him sick.

One night in December I decided to save him from any future ailments. After seeing Robert Redford's new movie *Downhill Racer,* Rob brought me back home and walked me to the front door. I told him that I wanted to give back his Nichols and May records as well as all the other albums that I'd borrowed from him. He didn't understand. I explained that I was breaking up with him. I felt like we had to move on — for his sake and mine.

"No, I want to come in," he said. "I really want to."

"Do you feel okay?" I said. "You aren't nauseous? No sore throat?"

He shook his head and followed me inside. The next morning, Rob made it clear that our relationship had moved to a more serious place.

"I just want to tell you that I'm going to fart in front of you," he said.

"All right," I said.

And we were together from then on.

CHAPTER 17

All in the Family

Penny and Rob cutting the cake at their 1971 backyard Hollywood wedding

Marshall personal collection

*B*EING WITH ROB meant being with his friends, especially Albert. They were like Rob's father and Mel Brooks: best friends who made each other even funnier. I would go to Rob's house up in Benedict Canyon with my little suitcase and Albert would listen to us, waiting for the right moment before asking if we wanted to get something to eat at the deli in the Beverly Wilshire Hotel.

When Rob and I finally moved in together, it was without Albert. I didn't want him listening anymore. Our place was a funky cottage in Laurel Canyon. We had a tree growing through the second bedroom and some artistic crap the previous residents had done on the ceiling. We also had two cats, Howie Rubin and Rhoda Kleinman, both named after the lead characters in Rob's play. Friends were reluctant to come over since our narrow street didn't have parking and anyone who did visit got a ticket.

My father couldn't understand our relationship. "So what do you say to people — 'We live together'?" he asked.

Soon the point was moot. We told people that we were going to get married. We looked at dates in November and December. Then we put our plans on hold indefinitely. Although it might have looked like there was a problem, the reason was actually good news, Rob was cast as Archie Bunker's liberal son-in-law Michael Stivic on *All in the Family*. I had also gone up for the part of Archie and Edith's daughter Gloria, but the show's executive producer, Norman Lear, chose Sally Struthers. She looked more like Carroll O'Connor's daughter , while I looked more like Jean Stapleton's. I thought it was for the best. Working together would have killed us.

Rob never thought *All in the Family* would continue past the initial thirteen episodes CBS ordered. It seemed like he might be right, too. The show's January 12, 1971, premiere finished behind the competition on ABC and NBC, and ratings remained sluggish the following weeks. Rob wasn't concerned whether it was a hit or not. His real goal was to write and direct, not act.

We set April 10 as our wedding date. It was the first break in Rob's schedule. The ceremony took place in his parents' Beverly Hills backyard. The 150 guests included our parents and siblings, as well as Neil Simon, Norman Lear, Bud Yorkin, and Marilyn and Alan Bergman. It was different than my first backyard wedding. Rob wore a leather suit and blue suede shoes, and I walked down the aisle in a blue dress that made me look like Robin Hood's Maid Marian.

During the brief, nonreligious ceremony, Rob said, "I'll love you and be your best friend." I replied, "I'll love you and try not to make you nervous." The justice of the peace marrying us then turned us around and said, "Presenting Mr. and Mrs. Rob Reiner." Rob had instructed him to refrain from any unnecessary comments, which that was considered to be. So he cursed under his breath all the way down the aisle. He had already fought with his mother about what to serve for dinner before settling on Chinese takeout from Ah Fong's. So that was nice.

We partied well into the night. Harry Shearer's girlfriend played a song on the guitar. Albert made a toast that was more like a stand-up routine. And actor Martin Landau, a close Reiner family friend, read a charming fairy tale he had written about two people who had lived across the street as children but didn't meet until they were adults. Around midnight, our friends followed us back to our suite at the Beverly Hills Hotel, where we kept the festivities going until Rob and I left the next day for our honeymoon at the Kona Village on the Big Island in Hawaii.

Somehow, we managed to keep that to just the two of us.

A month later, *All in the Family* won several Emmy Awards, including Best Comedy, and all of a sudden the series caught fire. Viewers discovered Archie, Edith, Gloria, and Michael. The Bunkers's living room became a flash point for the country's take on politics, race, sex, and culture. For the next five years, it was America's number one rated TV series. Rob was surprised but proud. Having grown up around famous people, he was largely unaffected by the attention. If anything, success made him work harder.

I did my bit, too. I went to every dress rehearsal and taping for *All in the Family.* I sat with Carroll's and Norman's wives and did needlepoint. I even hooked a rug there. And after each show I told Rob that he was good, which he was.

My career trickled along. I appeared on two Dick Clark–produced music-variety series, played Cinderella opposite Don Adams in a Hertz commercial, and had a small role as a bank teller in my brother's very funny TV movie *Evil Roy Slade.* I was also in an episode of pop star Bobby Sherman's series *Getting It Together,* directed by Jerry Belson, who also cast Rob and Carl Gottlieb as old rock 'n' rollers in a band called Mona and the Moonbeams.

My break came when Garry gave me a recurring role on *The Odd Couple* as Oscar Madison's whiny secretary, Myrna Turner. The series had premiered on ABC in September 1970 with Tony Randall and Jack Klugman as mismatched friends and roommates Felix Unger and Oscar Madison. They shot the first season with a single camera, but for season two they switched to three cameras and an audience and added more characters, including Myrna.

When it came time to cast her, Jack went to my brother and said, "Why don't you get your sister? She's the one who made me do this in the first place."

"Do you think I can get her by Tony?" Garry asked.

Tony Randall was an actor's actor, as well as a perfectionist. He expected the same from his fellow cast and crew.

"No," Jack said. "But *we* can get her by Tony."

As it turned out, I got myself by Tony. All I had to do was prove I was funny, and the way I laughed as Myrna cinched the deal. The way it came out was an accident. During a run-through, I was reading the script and it said, "Myrna laughs." So I pretended to laugh: "Heh-heh-heh." I didn't know how to laugh yet. Cindy Williams would teach me later. I sounded like an injured goose. But everyone cracked up. So that became Myrna's laugh — and I had a job.

Still, I had no idea what to do on a three-camera show where actors were always in the scene unless they exited. Seeing that I was petrified, Jack took me under his wing. He made sure I always knew where my mark was and had something to do. He was very kind and generous. Even so, I developed my own method of calming my nerves. Right before I entered a scene, I would take a deep breath, say the dirtiest words I could string together — "fuck, shit, piss!" — and then walk through the door and calmly whine, "Hi, Mr. M."

Jack and Tony were pros. Like their on-camera personalities, they were complete opposites off-camera. Tony adored opera, and Jack was always making bets on the horses. The writing staff might have been funnier than the show. Veteran comedy writer Harvey Miller, who also directed some of the episodes, would sit at the table and crack jokes as Jackie Hitler, Adolf's stand-up comic brother. Jackie was one of Harvey's go-to characters. Jerry Belson was also hilarious. But the show was never a ratings hit and my brother had to fight with the network for a pickup every one of its five seasons.

With steady incomes, Rob and I bought a house on Hesby Street in North Hollywood. It had better parking, more room, and a swimming pool. We brought our cats, Howie and Rhoda, and added a dog, Barney Google, who liked to take money out of my purse and eat it. When Rob closed our bedroom door, he stood outside and growled. He reminded me of Albert in that way.

After we settled in, Tracy also joined us. Mickey had moved to Colorado and had another daughter, and I think there might have been a little rivalry there. Tracy gave a more practical reason for the change. We had more TV channels. We adjusted in our own ways. Rob bought himself a Mercedes, and soon after Tracy used the cigarette lighter to burn a design of holes in the carpeted floor mats. My therapist at the time said she might be angry.

"About what?" I said. "She's away from her stepsister and she has her own color TV."

She joined a busy household. In addition to *The Odd Couple*, I did an episode of *The Bob Newhart Show*, where I met director Jay Sandrich, who put me in his TV movie *The Crooked Hearts*. Jerry Paris also found a role for me in his TV movie *The Couple Take a Wife*. As for Rob, he wrote a handful of *All in the Family* episodes and launched *The Super*, a sitcom he created with Phil Mishkin. Its ten episodes aired in 1972. I worked on one of those, too.

Rob took up tennis and decided he wanted to be Hollywood's number one celebrity player. He also put a sauna in the backyard, where he and Albert and Ricky would disappear for a *schvitz*. They were from Beverly Hills, but once in the sauna, they turned into eighty-year-olds with thick Jewish accents. Success changes some people. They aged.

As the stable couple, our house became a hangout for comedy's elite. In addition to Albert, Phil, and Ricky, regulars included Harvey Miller, Jerry Belson, Charles Grodin, Billy Crystal, Ted Bessell, and Jim Brooks. These were the pot-smoking years, and a lot of it was smoked at our house. I cleaned the seeds and stems in a shoebox top. It was a skill, and I was good at it.

Some of the guys occasionally brought a girlfriend, but this was mostly a guys-only atmosphere, as was comedy in general, and they didn't care what women had to say. If a woman tried to make conversation, they just glared at her. They were a bit hostile.

The only woman they were sort of impressed with was Louise Lasser, but only because she'd been married to Woody Allen and starred in *Take the Money and Run* and *Bananas*, movies they respected. I was also allowed to talk. But it was hard for anyone to get a word in with quick wits like Jerry Belson and Harvey Miller telling stories. "When I went to Emerson College, it was new and desperate for students," Harvey said. "My father took me, and in the bookstore he wrote a twenty-five-dollar check. They put him on the board."

Albert was always breaking in new material, too. If he was in the mood, he could do twenty minutes easily. Sometimes he didn't stop until Jerry interrupted. "Can we take a break to smoke a joint?"

Albert was notorious for getting the munchies, drifting into the kitchen, and eating the brown bag lunch I had prepared for Tracy to take to school the next day. She resented him for years. What were you going to do? Jim Brooks had created *Room 222* and *The Mary Tyler Moore Show*. Ricky Dreyfuss was a standout in the movie *American Graffiti*, along with my friend Cindy Williams, who had also appeared in *Travels with My Aunt* and *The Conversation*. Ted Bessell was beloved as Donald Hollinger on *That Girl*. This was a special group of people coming into their own and our house was where they let down their guard.

But it wasn't just our living room. Carl Gottlieb organized The Celanese Players, a group of actors and writers that included Steve Martin, Valerie Curtin, Larry Hankin, Richard Stahl, Howard Hesseman, Murphy Dunn, myself, and others. We made more than 150 sixty-second, improv-style commercials for the Celanese Fiber Company, manufacturers of double-knit pants and dresses. They paid what was then a record sum of $3 million to air a completely new, unique, and hopefully funny ad on *The Tonight Show Starring Johnny Carson* every night all through 1973.

We wrote and shot them on the weekends in San Diego, driving back and forth every Thursday and Sunday. Sometime during this period Albert had some kind of breakdown on our couch and stayed there for a long time. I went away one weekend and he was fine. When I came home he was comatose.

"Albert, do you want something to eat?"

"Eh."

"Can I get you anything?"

"Eh."

Okay. I didn't pass judgment. Who doesn't want to lie down for a month or two?

CHAPTER 18

Funny Business

Penny with Jim Brooks, who gave Penny one of her first starring
television roles, in *Paul Sand in Friends and Lovers*

Ted Bessell

D URING A BREAK from *All in the Family,* Rob and I went to New York and saw the *National Lampoon's Lemmings,* a sketch comedy show at the Village Gate. Rob was a huge fan of Tony Hendra, the Cambridge-educated British humorist who had written, directed, and produced the show and cast it with then-unknowns Chevy Chase, John Belushi, and Christopher Guest, who Rob knew.

It was brilliant. After the show, Rob and I took John and his wife, Judy, out to dinner. Something about John drew both of us to him. At the table, Rob and John spent two hours doing Marlon Brando impressions, and I began a lifelong friendship with John and Judy. He was my naughty, relentlessly funny, unpredictable friend. I told him how, after I moved to L.A., my mother had predicted that I was going to take acid and jump off a roof.

I expected him to say, "What a nut!" Instead, he leaned forward, furrowed his eyebrows, and asked, "So have you?"

He showed up at Hesby a few times. My brother recalls me introducing him to John and saying, "Garry, this guy's going to be big." Garry said, "Hi, how're you doing?" Apparently John couldn't put sentences together too well at that moment, and Garry thought he was mixed up. I explained this was the off-hours version. I knew John was special, and I was right.

I had a simple rule for navigating Hollywood's confusing roads: Stick with the most talented people you know. I was lucky. I knew a lot of them. But that didn't prevent frustrations or failures. When Paramount refused to give me a $100-an-episode raise on *The Odd Couple,* I asked my brother what to do. "One day you'll get even," he said. He had started *Happy Days,* so I took Jim Brooks up on his offer to costar on his new series, *Paul Sand in Friends and Lovers.*

It starred actor Paul Sand as a musician with the Boston Symphony who had endless problems with his girlfriend; his brother, played by Michael Pataki; and his sister-in-law, played by me. I knew that Jim was an exceptional writer, and along with his partner, Alan Burns, I trusted him implicitly. He had the magic touch, and listening to him talk about the characters made me feel like it had a shot.

Then the problems started. During rehearsals, I discovered that I was allergic to Michael. Every time I kissed him, I broke out in a rash. The same thing happened later with Michael McKean. It was something about their skin. Or else I'm allergic to guys named Michael. Before production started, the pretty blonde who played Paul's girlfriend had a nose job, and that was the end of her. Once you get your nose fixed, you're no longer as funny.

They changed the show's premise to Paul's date of the week, and unfortunately Paul wasn't a date-of-the-week kind of guy. Then Jim left for reasons that were never clear to me. His parting words to me were to watch and observe everything. What I saw was that without Jim at the typewriter the show had a different sensibility. It was no longer the same show.

They brought in Jerry Belson's sister, Monica Johnson, to write. Monica was nuts but funny as shit. She wanted to marry a dentist, she said, because she didn't have the self-esteem for an M.D. In reality, she had already married and divorced the first two of her eventual seven husbands. We became fast friends. Like me, she acknowledged that nepotism had been her get-into-show-business-free card. Her brother had hired her to type *The Odd Couple* scripts, and she added jokes as she typed. Three years later, she won an Emmy.

Even with Monica onboard, *Paul Sand* struggled. The characters didn't have any chemistry. It was like forcing puzzle pieces to fit. My mother said she thought Marvin Hamlisch should take over for Paul. The series was canceled after fifteen weeks. What made one series work and another not? What was the difference between a hit and one that was merely well done?

Those questions dominated conversations among those in our living room. Everyone wanted to figure out the magic formula. Even though Jim and my brother clearly had the touch, they had their hits and misses. After I appeared on *The Mary Tyler Moore Show* several times as Mary's neighbor, Paula, Jim briefly mulled over creating a spinoff with me and Mary's other neighbor, Sally Jo, who was played by Mary Kay Place. But our on-screen chemistry wasn't right.

In the meantime, *Happy Days* was a smash for my brother. With his own kids at TV-watching age, he had wanted to create a show his whole family could enjoy, and everything he did on that series worked. The lesson that I observed, and that I think my brother and others would agree with, is that while no one really knows how to make a hit, the people running the studios know even less. Every fall TV season offers proof, but let me tell a specific story.

I was on an episode of *Chico and the Man*. I played a waitress named Anita Coffee. The show was a hit, and so one day Paramount's head of TV, Michael Eisner, called my brother to his office and told him to add some Puerto Ricans to *Happy Days*.

"Is there a need for them?" Garry asked.

No, but Eisner wanted them. My brother disagreed. They had a heated discussion, and my brother, who has no sense of direction and to this day only makes right turns when he drives, walked out of the meeting, with Eisner right behind him. Not knowing where he was going, my brother led the executive straight into a boiler room, where they continued to argue.

Eisner showed up at the next *Happy Days* run-through. Afterward, he and Garry met again.

"Where are the Puerto Ricans?" Eisner asked.

"They were there," my brother said.

"Where?" Eisner asked.

"They were working in the back," Garry said.

That's comedy.

CHAPTER 19

Out with a Laugh

Penny and her grandmother, "Nanny," at Ronny's 1958 wedding

Marshall personal collection

ME: When did Nanny die?

RONNY: I was already out here. I got divorced and moved here in 1971, and it was a few years after that.

ME: What do you know about it?

RONNY: We're not big on funerals.

ME: We had her cremated, right?

RONNY: Yeah. No one wanted a funeral and a burial. We didn't do that. And she wouldn't know the difference. She was dead.

ME: But I remember we did have some kind of service.

RONNY: We went to Pierce Brothers Mortuary. It was Mom and Dad, Garry, Barbara, Penny, and Rob. We were put outside in a spot with a big wall in front of us. All of us sat down in a row of seats. The seats were canvass and connected to each other.

ME: If one person moved, the other person went up.

RONNY: Right.

ME: I remember we were standing up and sitting down when the minister came in. I mean I guess he was a minister.

RONNY: He just appeared. We didn't know who he was. He

could've been anyone.

ME: He didn't know my grandmother. He had no idea.

RONNY: But he rambled on about her.

ME: Without ever saying she was a pain in the ass.

RONNY: The cement wall behind him had square cutouts with a box in each one, nine boxes in all. There were three rows of three. And Nan's urn was in what looked like a gift-wrapped box in the middle.

ME: And Rob leaned over and said, "Look, she's got the center square."

RONNY: So we all started to laugh, and the minister kept talking about her even though none of us was paying attention because we were laughing so hard.

ME: Then Garry and our mother stood up and shifted all the rest of us in our seats because if one person moved everyone else did, too.

RONNY: We laughed even harder.

ME: But Nanny always had a good sense of humor.

CHAPTER 20
Live from New York

Dan Aykroyd, Penny, and John Belushi in 1980

*I*T'S HARD TO IMAGINE a time when Saturday nights didn't include the phrase "Live from New York, it's Saturday night." *Saturday Night Live* is such an institution that you can forget or may not know that tuning in at 11:30 p.m. was once an adventure into the unknown, a true television event. George Carlin, Richard Pryor, Lily Tomlin, Peter Cook, and Dudley Moore were among those who gave name recognition to John Belushi, Danny Aykroyd, Gilda Radner, and other cast regulars, although it wasn't long before *SNL* writers such as Anne Beatts, Tom Schiller, Herb Sargent, Alan Zweibel, now-Senator Al Franken, and Michael O'Donoghue had their own fans. They were brilliant, stoned, fearless, and fucking funny, and word went out that this show was hot even before it aired.

Lorne Michaels was the show's creator and executive producer, the calm head in the middle of the storm. He came out to L.A. before *SNL*'s October premiere, wanting Rob to guest host. He had signed up George Carlin and Paul Simon for the first two shows, and he asked Rob to do the third. He also asked me to do it with him. I wondered about his judgment.

"Why? I'm nobody," I said.

"I've seen your work," he said.

Lorne is one of those people who knows what he wants — and more important, he knows how to get it. Although I had just met him, I learned within five minutes of trying to wiggle out of *SNL* that there's not much point to arguing with him. So Rob and I went back for the week. It was packed with meetings with writers, rehearsals, dinners, and late nights with Lorne, who was a welcoming, entertaining host still trying to sell his show.

I was already sold, but I still had no idea why I was there. I kept saying, "I don't know why I'm here. You aren't writing for the girls to begin with." Lorne replied, "You're here because I paid for your ticket."

"I'll pay you back," I said.

We went back and forth like that all week. I had a great time. It was my kind of atmosphere. No one slept. Or if they did, they just dropped onto the floor and you stepped over the bodies. In one sketch I was supposed to play a Russian shopper in a shoe store, and I think the only reason it got as far as it did was because John and Danny wanted me to do an accent. The second I said I couldn't, they began trying like crazy to change my mind. It was a game. But I don't do accents, so they couldn't use that one. But they had more than enough.

As the clock ticked down on Saturday night, a different, more intense energy filled the studio. Rob opened the show as a Vegas lounge singer. The sketches that followed included John doing his Joe Cocker impression for the first time, singing "With a Little Help from My Friends." It was brilliant. After Laraine Newman played Squeaky Fromme pulling a gun on Jane Curtin, Andy Kaufman lip-synced to "Pop Goes the Weasel," and then Rob and I hosted a show of fashion mistakes.

Then there was a short film from Albert, who'd been hired to make films for the show. But his piece ran thirteen minutes, hardly short. When Lorne wanted to cut it, Rob defended his friend. Lorne compromised by putting a commercial in the middle of it. Everything else moved fast. The crew was involved in a ballet of set changes and movement that was impressive for only the third show. We square-danced in a piece where Danny was an evil hoedown caller and toward the end of the show Rob and I played a couple in deep conversation at an Italian restaurant when John, Danny, Jane, and others dressed as the Bees interrupted us.

"I don't want the damn Bees!" Rob shouted, pissed off.

"You don't have to be so hard on the Bees," I said. "They just did it because they thought it would help the show."

"They're NOT helping the show! They're ruining the show! I don't need Bees! I don't need Bees! I'm a major star! I'm on the number one television show in America!"

John then stepped forward as a spokesperson for all the Bees.

"I'm sorry if you think we're ruining your show, Mr. Reiner," he said. "But you don't understand. We didn't ask to be Bees. You see, you've got Norman Lear and a first-rate writing staff. But this is all they came up with for us."

John went on about how the Bees were in the same spot he had been in years earlier; they were a bunch of actors looking for a break. Rob felt guilty. I made him feel even worse by saying I was embarrassed. Then I tried to comfort him, saying, "It's all right, honey." But that appeared to add salt to the wound.

"Don't say 'honey,'" he said.

At the after-party, I thanked Lorne for allowing me to have a wonderful time even though I still didn't understand why I was included. Laughing, he asked what I thought of the week now that it was over. I reminded him of what I had said to him after our first night in New York. I said, "I think you're the most manipulative human being I've ever met, and you do it beautifully." Now that I had seen him in action, I admired him even more.

Lorne and I have been friends ever since.

CHAPTER 21

Ready for Prime Time

Penny and Cindy Williams in Fonzie's apartment, filming the 1975
pilot of *Laverne & Shirley*

Use of photo still from Laverne & Shirley *– Courtesy of CBS Television Studios*

I N NOVEMBER 1975, a *Happy Days* episode that Cindy Williams and I had taped finally aired. I was not expecting anything to come of it. About eight weeks earlier, my brother had called and asked what I was doing. I was working with Cindy on a Bicentennial-themed satire that Francis Ford Coppola wanted to produce. Carl Gottlieb had rounded up a bunch of people to write sketches, including Harry Shearer, Martin Mull, and us.

"Do you want to do a *Happy Days?*" my brother asked. "We need two fast girls who put out. If Cindy wants to do it, she can play opposite Ron. They were good together in *American Graffiti*. You can play opposite Fonzie. If she doesn't want to do it, you can play whichever part you want."

I asked Cindy. We were making $30 a week working at Zoetrope, Francis's studio. We both said yes.

In the episode, titled "A Date with Fonzie," we were two loose girls that Fonzie called to help Richie Cunningham out of a dating slump. Cindy was Shirley Feeney, and I was Laverne DeFazio. She knew Ron Howard from the movie, and Henry Winkler had worked with me in the *Paul Sand* pilot. After it aired, my brother was at a conference with ABC executives. Fred Silverman, the network's president, was looking for new sitcoms. He asked my brother if he had any spinoff ideas.

"I've got a couple of bottle cappers who work in a Milwaukee brewery," he said. "How about them?"

Fred liked the idea immediately. From then on, everything moved at an absurdly fast pace, especially for television. Along with Lowell Ganz and Mark Rothman, the writers responsible for the *Happy Days* script, my brother created a presentation for the network. ABC ordered the series immediately and put it on the midseason schedule for January. Everyone had the same reaction: Holy shit! We had barely two months to get the show written, cast, and taped. And that was just the first episode. The network ordered fifteen.

We couldn't afford any delays if we were going to deliver on time. But there was a major snag right away. Cindy wasn't sure she wanted to do TV. A trained actress, she was concerned that a TV series would sidetrack her film career. Today, it seems like a silly concern. Everyone does everything — TV, movies, commercials, infomercials, YouTube videos. At the time, though, people in the industry thought that if you did movies you couldn't do TV and vice versa. Cindy wanted to be a movie star. I didn't blame her.

But I was among a chorus of people, including my brother, who told her that *Laverne & Shirley* was a rare opportunity. We had something special. Everyone who saw our *Happy Days* episode agreed. She didn't have to give up movies, I told her. If we were a hit, she might become an even bigger star. She could make films between seasons.

I sensed that Cindy agreed. Her manager, Pat McQueeney, was the holdout. She didn't seem to know what to do. As a result, Cindy was indecisive. Until she made up her mind, I read with every actress who seemed like she might be able to play Shirley. We auditioned them in Fonzie's apartment. I spent so much time in that garage I should have just moved in. Frustrated, I called Gilda Radner in New

York, thinking she might be available. She wasn't, and she didn't even want to talk about leaving *SNL* only weeks after it had started.

An actress named Liberty Williams came closer than anyone to being cast as Shirley. Like Cindy, Liberty had short, dark hair and a cute, round face. But as soon as we called her back for a test, Cindy changed her mind. I was thrilled. In my mind, Cindy was the only one I could ever see as Shirley.

Once she was in, we worked out the fine details. We agreed to "equal but staggered" billing — my name would be first, but Cindy's would be higher. As for money, Cindy told a *TV Guide* reporter, our new salary was going to be "an amount of money I didn't know existed." She was openly worried that I might get preferential treatment since the show, as she told people, was something of a family business, with my brother in charge, my father one of the producers, and my sister, Ronny, in charge of casting.

You could see her point. But we made that concern a nonissue by agreeing to a most-favored-nations clause in our contracts. If one of us got something, the other one got it, too.

The rest of the pieces fell into place as if they had always been waiting for someone to put them together. Garry cast Phil Foster as my father. Way back when, Phil had given him his first break as a joke writer, as well as the best advice, telling him to stick with writing instead of stand-up, and this was my brother's payback. Garry is the most loyal person in the business. If you knew him in high school, college, or Korea, you've probably been in one of his movies.

Garry cast Eddie Mekka, a Tony-nominated Broadway veteran, as Cindy's boyfriend Carmine "The Big Ragoo" Ragusa. He thought one of us should have a boyfriend. Laverne would continue to play the field, but not as she was originally conceived. The girls were no longer loose. They were re-virginized, as I liked to say, for the family hour.

I pitched Michael McKean and David Lander. They were part of

122 · PENNY MARSHALL

the comedy group The Credibility Gap and regulars in Rob's and my living room. With little or no encouragement, they did these two characters, Leonard Kosnowski and Anthony Squiggliano, who were ridiculously funny. Squiggliano's name was later changed to Andrew Squiggman because we thought there were already too many Italians on the show. I thought they'd make good last-ditch dates for us.

Garry hired them as writers based on my recommendation, but then he warmed to the idea of them as characters after he saw them at our house. He nixed the idea of them as dates, though.

"There has to be somebody lower than the two of you," he said. "That's Lenny and Squiggy."

Back then you couldn't do better than having Fonzie usher you into living rooms across America, and that's the way my brother and ABC set us up. As the first script was written, Cindy and I ran next door to the *Happy Days* set and popped into scenes, trying to create familiarity with viewers. Then Henry came over to our set, on Stage 20, and guest-starred on our first show. At sixty pages, the script for that episode was double the normal show length. We did endless pick-ups — retakes of lines that were rewritten and tweaked until writers were carried out on stretchers. The taping turned into an endurance test.

But the effort paid off. *Laverne & Shirley* premiered on Tuesday, January 27, between *Happy Days* and *The Rookies,* and we woke up the next day as the stars of the number-one-rated show in the country. We hadn't even been home to watch the premiere because it was a Tuesday night and we taped new episodes on Tuesday nights. The feat was great for my career, not so good for my marriage. The show we pushed out of the top spot was Rob's, *All in the Family.*

Celebrations were postponed. We were behind schedule from the get-go. It seemed like we worked nonstop. We figured out our characters as we went along. Until the sixth episode, Cindy spoke with a New York accent. You couldn't blame her for being confused.

Between Phil, Eddie, David, Michael, my brother, and me, she was surrounded by people who sounded like they just stepped off the subway. Finally my brother told her to stop.

"You're in Milwaukee," he said.

At the beginning of any TV series you have to repeat who you are, where you're from, and what you do for a living so viewers will get to know you. The writers often need that help, too. Everybody is getting to know these characters. But I didn't want to have to constantly say we're two bottle cappers from Milwaukee. It's boring as shit. Nor did I want to hear Cindy say "Laverne" all the time. I thought if I put an *L* on my shirts and sweaters I would eliminate that part. I was wrong. We still had to say those lines. She still had to say my name.

The part people did remember from the start was the show's introduction. *Schlemiel! Schlimazel! Hasenpfeffer Incorporated!* It came about one day when my brother was working on the opening montage and asked me what that funny saying was that I used to do with my friends in the neighborhood. I had a lot of them, but he was remembering specifically "that schlemiel thing." Well, Ronny was on the set that day, too. I turned to my sister and said, "Do you remember it?" She did, and soon we were teaching Cindy the song: "One, two, three, four, five, six, seven, eight! Schlemiel! Schlimazel! Hasenpfeffer Incorporated!"

What did it mean?

I don't know. It's what we sang when we went to school. We had to walk seven blocks.

We constantly drew from our childhood. I put pictures of Julius La Rosa and Audie Murphy in Laverne's bedroom because I'd been a fan of theirs when I was a kid. All of Laverne's 45s were my actual 45s from childhood. Anytime we had to choose, we did One Potato, Two Potato. Every time we had to dance, we did something from my mother's school. And Laverne's milk and Pepsi? I actually drank that as a kid. At kosher camp, they couldn't drink milk with meat so they had Pepsi. I wanted Pepsi, too. But my mother made me drink milk first. Then she gave me the soda. Sometimes she didn't rinse out the glass. Sometimes it wasn't even empty. Eventually it became half and half.

When I did it on the show I knew it would get a reaction. And it did. People related to those little details.

They also liked the way we said "voh-de-oh-doh-doh" in place of anything related to sex. The word "sex" was off-limits. Even the word "it" was controversial. For instance, we couldn't say, "Did you do it?" Someone came up with the silly substitute voh-de-oh-doh-doh. It turned the whole issue into a bigger deal than it would've been, and made it much more humorous, like this classic exchange:

SHIRLEY: I do not voh-de-oh-doh-doh!
LAVERNE: Oh, you voh-de-oh-doh-doh.
SHIRLEY: I do *not* voh-de-oh-doh-doh.
LAVERNE: You voh di oh.
SHIRLEY: Once.

Almost everyone had a theory about why *Laverne & Shirley* took off. My brother said it was because we were doing Lucy. Cindy thought the show tapped into a nostalgia for simpler times. David and Michael had no clue; in fact, David says he never knew who Lenny and Squiggy were saying hello to when they came through the door. But once audiences laughed and applauded for them, they didn't care. I didn't overanalyze our success, either. I thought it was simply because Laverne and Shirley were poor and there were no poor people on TV, but there were plenty of them sitting at home and watching TV. What mattered most, of course, was that the show was funny.

CHAPTER 22

Chick Fight

Penny behind bars during the 1976 *Laverne & Shirley* episode
"Guilty Until Proven Innocent"

Use of photo still from Laverne & Shirley *– Courtesy of CBS Television Studios*

W E MADE *LAVERNE & SHIRLEY* on Stage 20. This was home to America's favorite family show. Yet my brother wouldn't allow his children to go inside. They could visit the *Happy Days* set on Stage 19. But we were off-limits. Garry told them that it was because some of the people working there used bad words. "Even Aunt Penny?" his daughter asked. Garry nodded somberly. "Yes, even Aunt Penny."

But screw it, we worked hard and, yes, sometimes it got contentious and bad words were tossed around, though honestly, bad words were the least of anyone's problems. What Cindy and I wanted — and in fact insisted upon — were funny words. Our first season had set the bar very high. When we came back for season two, we were determined to keep it there, if not take it even higher.

We knew what we were doing. Although some would say we thought we knew more than we actually did, I think it evened out very quickly. One of my best shows of the entire run was the season's second episode, "Angels of Mercy." It was when I came into my comedic own. Laverne and Shirley were volunteering as candy stripers in a hospital. In the key scene, Laverne had to make a bed with a patient still in it. The script contained descriptions of things the writers thought would be funny for Laverne to try. But they weren't logical. They only made sense to a guy sitting in front of a typewriter, not a real person trying to do the job.

During rehearsal, instead of following the script, I simply tried to make the bed. At one point, I tugged on the sheets, lost my footing and slipped under the bed. A light went off in my head. I realized that I could take the bit even further. The next time I practiced it I asked the prop man to powder the floor. When I did it again, I slid almost all the way under the bed. I heard the crew laughing, and even better, I saw my brother wiping tears from his eyes. I knew I couldn't get a bigger compliment.

Within a few weeks, I would also realize this marked a point in the show's young history when the writers had basically given up on expository scripts in favor of more traditional three-camera block comedy. In a block comedy, you write to a big scene — or a block. Like *I Love Lucy,* everything builds to a big moment. If it's not funny, it hurts the entire script. We weren't shy about telling our writers what we thought of their scripts. That's why my brother wouldn't bring his children onto the set.

We were tough. Not just Cindy and me. All of us. David Lander and Michael McKean, originally hired as writers, were kicked out of the writers' table because they were very critical. David once threw a script into the garbage and that earned all of us a reputation for throwing scripts. The truth was, the script he threw was printed on pink paper, meaning it was a first draft, and everyone knows that pink stinks. But we didn't throw scripts. We did swear. And sometimes we yelled. I would question things. I was a stickler for logic. I believed things should make sense. So the writers didn't want me around. Cindy would go off on her Boo Boo Kitty tangents about inserting animal rights messages or this or that, whatever kick she was on that week, and so they didn't want her, either.

If the dialogue sucked in read-through, Lowell, who sat next to me, could hear it in my voice and he would sound the alarm. "Uh-oh, we lost Penny on page fifteen." If the writers didn't fix it by rehearsal,

I showed my displeasure in various ways. Once, I tossed popcorn into Cindy's mouth. Other times we wore stupid hats. Sometimes the tension between us and the writers was like an undeclared war. However, that determination to make each show as entertaining as possible was where a lot of the great jokes came from, as well as business like the milk and Pepsi. I would try to figure out something that was funny.

My brother, who went back and forth between shows, played peacemaker, writer, chief negotiator, psychiatrist, older brother, and boss. He scratched his head a lot. He didn't like confrontation. When one of us did something wrong, he would talk to the other person. If I messed up, he told Cindy. I could hear it. Cindy and I would look at each other, wondering if we had lost our minds.

From the beginning, Cindy worried that I would receive preferential treatment because it was my brother's show. She would point out that I called one of the producers Dad. She was right, in a way. I was treated differently than the rest of the cast and crew. I was treated worse. One week my father got mad at me and locked my paycheck in his desk drawer.

He told my brother that I had been "fresh" to him and he wasn't going to give it to me until I apologized. Garry said, "Listen, Pop, that's not the way it works." It wasn't an allowance. He made him give it to me.

Cindy didn't see it that way. The problem was her insecurity and her manager, Pat McQueeney. Pat was always on the set, conferring with Cindy. She counted lines and kept track of laughs. From the time I got that reaction in the hospital scene, she insisted that I was getting more screen time than her client. Also better lines, more jokes, and all that. She said it was due to my family connections. She constructed a whole conspiracy theory — everyone was out to get Cindy — none of which was true. But that didn't matter. It was her leverage with her client. And basically she drove Cindy nuts. She made her insecure about a job that she was doing extremely well.

We're all insecure. I'm insecure. I wanted to be prettier. I hated my posture. My self-esteem fluctuated more than the stock market. But I didn't have a manager telling me all that shit every day.

I would have been perfectly happy if Cindy had all the lines. I didn't like memorizing lines. I was content to make milk and Pepsi or add whipped cream to something. I did props very well. She dated David briefly, so I had to move over and stand with Michael in our two-shots. Then when she and David broke up, I moved back into two-shots with Cindy. I had to put up with that shit. I didn't care. I tried talking to her about the shit Pat was putting in her heard. It was wrong, and besides that, it was stupid and missed the point. To me, we were like *The Odd Couple,* which had taped on our same stage. Jack Klugman got the laughs, but it was only because Tony Randall could go to the moon and back. He was the real actor and everybody knew it. We were the same. I may have gotten the laughs, but so did she, and everyone knew it was Cindy's acting talent that made it possible.

In early November, Pat pushed Cindy over the edge. We were on our eleventh show, an episode titled "Guilty Until Proven Innocent." In it, Shirley tries to get Laverne out of jail after she's wrongly arrested for shoplifting. Jim Burrows was directing, and the veteran comic Louis Nye was a guest star. In the middle of the week, work suddenly stopped. Cindy had apparently reached her breaking point, and Pat had stormed into my brother's office demanding changes, immediately.

The next thing we knew, writers were fired, including Lowell Ganz and his partner, Mark Rothman, and word spread that Cindy was bringing in her own writer-producer, someone more sensitive to her needs as an actress. Then in walked Monica Johnson, one of my best friends. She was Cindy's writer.

As this went down, Pat and Cindy came into my dressing room. Monica followed. She wanted to shut down production for a week to get a sense of the situation, talk with Cindy, and write new material.

Pat also wanted to shut down. She claimed it was for the good of the show, but it was really about her exercising control. Cindy was simply upset. As I recall, she was about to throw a bottle against the wall when David and Michael walked in wanting to know what was going on. It was like a scene out of the show. *Hello.*

Their timing couldn't have been worse — or more perfect. It shut Pat up and let me take control of the conversation. I kicked everyone out except Cindy. I wanted to talk to her alone. I told her that I was a fan of Monica's and if having her on the show made her happier, I was all for it. But we couldn't stop work. It was a waste of money, it would create bad press, especially for her as the one who stormed off the set, and I didn't want to come back to the episode.

"None of us do," I said. "I mean, do you want to take a week off and come back to this?"

Cindy agreed. Then I spoke to Monica, who also understood why we couldn't shut down, and why, by finishing the episode, she would look like a hero, someone who came on the set and solved the problem rather than creating an even bigger one. We had the next week off anyway. She could get acclimated then and write new material.

I had one last point, my own stipulation: Lowell Ganz had to stay. I needed someone I trusted, someone I could look at in run-throughs and know whether it was funny, and for me, that was Lowell.

Monica always said she hated producing the show because it meant she had to be someplace on time. That was evident. She arrived on the set wearing a nightgown and bathrobe, with her hair in curlers. Like her brother, Jerry Belson, she knew funny. However, she had no idea how to produce a TV show. If my brother hadn't saved her life by writing a how-to manual, we might still be there, hearing her soft, feathery voice ask, "Now what do we do?"

CHAPTER 23

From Suds to Stardom

Penny and Toni Basil in the 1978 *Laverne & Shirley* episode "A Chorus Line"

Use of photo still from Laverne & Shirley *– Courtesy of CBS Television Studios*

WHILE MONICA RETOOLED the show, Cindy and I went on our first publicity tour. It was November, and the show was red hot. We were also plugging our *Laverne & Shirley Sing* album, a collection of oldies we had recorded the previous summer. (Cindy had taken it very seriously while I was happy to just say, "One . . ." "Two . . ." on "Sixteen Candles." And oh boy was John Belushi mad that I hadn't let him be on the album.) In Milwaukee, a crowd of screaming fans greeted us at the airport and more waited at a local radio station.

Then we went to Philadelphia for *The Mike Douglas Show* and were mobbed again at a record store.

We were shocked. This was our first time out in public as Laverne and Shirley, and although we weren't naïve about fame, neither of us had the self-esteem that let us understand why thousands of people would get excited to see us. What we needed was an instruction book like the one my brother wrote for Monica. No one tells you how to be famous, and it confuses the shit out of you when it happens. I remember Rob getting mobbed by his fans and I got pushed down the block. They didn't know who I was. After *Laverne & Shirley* hit, Rob liked my fans better because they were kids.

After Philadelphia, Cindy and I went to New York for the Macy's Thanksgiving Day Parade. We drove there in a limo. It was our first time in a stretch limo. We didn't even know how to open the sun-roof—or the moon roof, as it was called then. In Manhattan, cops pulled our car over in Central Park. Our driver did something wrong. However, as soon as the cops saw us in the back, they let us go. *Hey, it's Laverne and Shirley! How you doin'?* We were big with cops.

We got the star treatment at the Plaza Hotel, too. The first thing Cindy and I did was compare rooms, flowers, and gifts from the net-work, and blah, blah, blah. We couldn't help ourselves. We turned into twelve-year-olds again. On the night before the parade, Cindy and I had a party in our rooms. John Belushi, Dan Aykroyd, *Saturday Night Live* writer Herb Sargent, and Beach Boys drummer Dennis Wilson were among those who partied with us while I made signs for us to hold during the parade that said "Happy Thanksgiving Rob and Tracy."

In the morning, Cindy and I got up early and rode in a car amid the giant helium balloons and marching bands. We waved at the crowds lining the streets and shouting our names as we passed them. Cindy and I elbowed each other every block or two, as if to say, "Can you believe this?" At one point, part of the crowd broke through the barricades and rushed toward us. Even the cops pushing them back wanted autographs. It was insane.

Our lives were never the same afterward. How could they be, when suddenly everyone in the world recognized us? Although my brother has told me that we came back from that visit on a power trip, I dis-agree. It was an eye-opener without question. But there's a difference between being recognized and really knowing someone, and while I can't speak for Cindy, I knew how I looked and felt when I crawled out of bed in the morning, and not even Rob cheered when he saw that pretty picture.

Now, with even more perspective on the phenomena, I can pro-vide the lowdown on fame that I wish had been there for me. For starters, it's scary. I remember Farrah Fawcett coming up to me when we were both on *Celebrity Challenge of the Sexes*. Her famous poster had turned her into an overnight sex symbol and she was petrified by the way people were reacting to her. "They're making me out to be something I'm not," she confided.

I understood. But what was frightening to Farrah was intoxicating to others. One night John Belushi called me and exclaimed, "Penny, I can sleep with models now. They want me!" I said, "John, it's not because you're suddenly more attractive. You're famous."

I like the way Louise Lasser and I handled it. We bumped into each other at a party. I congratulated her on the success of her new series *Mary Hartman, Mary Hartman*, and she said the same to me about *Laverne & Shirley*. We were very mature and professional. Then we slipped into the bathroom and jumped up and down, screaming, "We're famous! We're famous!"

Then there was Princess Grace of Monaco. She had the best perspective that I ever encountered. Rob and I were on the celebrity tennis circuit, and Merv Griffin invited us to his first annual Merv Griffin Money Tennis Classic in Monte Carlo. Bill Cosby and Wayne Rogers were among the group. We flew on a chartered plane and played tennis on beautiful red clay courts. At night, we dined in the palace, where, as I did years later at the White House, I made sure to use the bathroom. Why not? You have to check it out, right? Anyway, before leaving, I chatted with the Princess, who was as gorgeous as I remembered her in movies when she was Grace Kelly, the star from Philadelphia. When I asked if she missed acting, she smiled and said, "What do you think I'm doing now?"

CHAPTER 24

Live from New Orleans

Penny's mother, Marjorie, dancing with Frances Williams, makes
a special appearance in the 1977 *Laverne & Shirley* episode
"The Second Almost Annual Shotz Talent Show"

Use of photo still from Laverne & Shirley *– Courtesy of CBS Television Studios*

*C*INDY WANTED TO DO *Saturday Night Live.* I had already done the show and didn't care whether I was on it again. But Lorne didn't know Cindy, and he asked, "Why would I want her without you?"

It was 1977. The two of us had agreed to be princesses in the Endymion Parade, the largest and rowdiest of New Orleans' Mardi Gras parades, and Henry Winkler had accepted an invitation to put on the crown as Bacchus and lead the Sunday-night parade that ended the weeklong celebration. Somehow these events coincided with Lorne's decision to produce a Mardi Gras special from New Orleans. He had convinced NBC to fill a hole in its Sunday-night schedule with a live show from the French Quarter, featuring the *SNL* cast plus guests Eric Idle, Buck Henry, Randy Newman, Henry Winkler, Cindy, and me.

He approached it with the confidence of a general leading his seasoned troops on their first major campaign across the continent. But you didn't have to be Einstein or a network censor to foresee the potential for disaster in unleashing John and Danny and new cast member Bill Murray, as well as writers like Michael O'Donoghue, on the Big Easy.

I was too preoccupied to realize what I was getting into. Cindy and I were working on our second-to-last episode of the season, and immediately after the last run-through of the week, we hopped on a redeye flight for New Orleans. Cindy brought Pat and some assistants; I was by myself. We landed and went straight to our hotel. Exhausted, I took a Valium and got into bed. I guess Cindy changed her room a few times. She wasn't my responsibility. Then, as I dozed off, the phone rang.

"Penny, it's Lorne."

"Uh-huh."

I was out of it.

"We can't find Cindy," he said.

"I just saw her," I said.

"We can't find her."

"So."

"You have to come rehearse," he said.

"I can't."

"And you have to do her scenes, too."

"Lorne, I can't," I said. "I have enough problems on my own show."

"Penny."

"Do you hear me, Lorne? I'm slurring my words."

"I'll send someone to get you," he said.

Soon Danny Aykroyd and John Belushi roared up in front of the hotel on their motorcycles. They were at their best when on a mission, either from God or Lorne, though many would attest they were the same. They knocked on my door. After I opened it a crack, they pushed past me as if they were cops. When I told them I couldn't go to rehearsal because I'd flown all night and had recently taken Valium, John pulled out a vial of coke and gave me a hit.

A few minutes later I was riding through the French Quarter on the back of John's bike. He had a cast on his leg for some reason. During rehearsals of John and Danny's Wild Bees sketch, I woke up. It didn't take long. As I looked around, I got the impression that Lorne and his crew were prepared. The show was planned as a mix of reportage from parades and parties across the city, as well as skits and musical performances, starting with Danny in the cold open as President Carter addressing the nation about tough economic times, the energy crisis, and his commitment to carry his own garment bag as well as his drunk brother, Billy.

Most of the rehearsal was spent discussing and coordinating coverage of the Bacchus parade route. Buck and Jane were assigned color commentary on the parade. Gilda was going to interview King of Bacchus, Henry Winkler. And Cindy and I were given the job of doing on-the-scene reporting from the Krewe of Apollo Ball, essentially a beauty pageant for drag queens. But we were not supposed to mention that viewers would be seeing men dressed as women. The show was airing in prime time, not late night.

While it would have been nice if Cindy had been at rehearsal to hear those instructions, she did turn up for the Endymion Parade. But she went missing again on Sunday when the show went on the air live. Only a few people paid attention, like me. The rest had bigger problems. Like the Bacchus Parade, the main part of the show. Buck and Jane were in a booth prepared to provide commentary as it passed in front of them. However, when the cameras cut to them, they were still waiting for the parade, which was nowhere in sight.

Instead, viewers saw mayhem. They were bombarded with beads. A little rubber ball bounced off Jane's head. People tried to douse them with drinks. "It's an incredible thing to realize that hundreds of thousands of Americans have traveled thousands of miles just to come here to New Orleans to visit Bourbon Street and to throw up," Buck said.

The show didn't get any smoother. Gilda was pawed and groped as she did her Emily Litella sketch. I was set up at the Krewe of Apollo Ball, still waiting for Cindy to show up. Every so often I heard a voice in my earpiece say, "Get ready, Penny." "We're coming to you soon, Penny." "Have we found Cindy yet?" At one point, I did hear Randy perform, which was nice. Then it was back to them talking to me: "We're coming to you next. Has anyone located Cindy?"

Buck and Jane had no clue Cindy was not there when they threw to us — er, when they threw to me. Similarly, I had no idea they had passed the baton, so to speak. At the time, I had just borrowed lipstick from some guy, who viewers had to think was a woman. My confusion was evident as I waited, and waited, on live TV, until I sensed that I might be on the air — at which point I very articulately said, "Now?"

When no one answered, I took that as an affirmative and began to describe the club and the setting. "Doesn't she look beautiful?" "And she's wearing baby's breath. It's lovely." It was endless filler. "That's a lovely satin gown." Finally, I said, "We will be coming back to this *wonderful* ball in a few minutes. I hope Cindy will, too."

Miraculously, she did turn up in time for our second and last segment. She said that she had changed hotel rooms and the producers couldn't find her. By this point, I didn't care about her reasons for showing up late. I was overjoyed to have her next to me when they threw to us to describe the crowning of the new Queen of the Krewe of Apollo.

"Isn't he something?" Cindy said. "He's something, isn't he?"

"What?" I said, surprised by the secret she was revealing to viewers.

But why would she know that was off-limits? She hadn't been to the briefing. Who gave a shit? As soon as we finished, I tossed back to Jane and Buck and lit up a cigarette. They never did see the parade. It had been diverted after someone along the route was accidentally run over and killed. In the show's closing moments, Jane explained, "The parade has not been delayed. It doesn't exist. It never did. 'Mardi Gras' is just a French word meaning 'No Parade.' Good night."

In the meantime, I didn't have a ride back to the postshow dinner from the ball. No one had been designated as my driver. Nor had I been assigned a security guard, an intern, or even a helper. A guy in the crowd saw me looking around and asked if I wanted a ride on his motorcycle. He could've been a murderer for all I knew. I didn't care. I said okay and got on the back of his bike.

Thank God, he dropped me off at a restaurant where I recognized people. I left with Herb Sargent and went back to his hotel, with Tom Schiller in the background saying, "He's too old for you." I didn't care. After the trauma of the show, I didn't want to be alone. But Tom was right. Herb fell asleep in the middle of the night.

Still awake, I had no idea where I was or how to get back to my hotel. I called downstairs for a cab, but the concierge said that wouldn't be possible. The streets were still too crowded. Yes, I realized that half-naked drunken people were continuing to walk around down there. That's why I had wanted a cab. I called the police instead.

"Laverne, is that you?" the desk sergeant asked.

"It is," I said.

Two cop cars showed up and took me to my hotel. Then Cindy and I flew back to L.A. I didn't do *Saturday Night Live* again until I was promoting *The Preacher's Wife* with Whitney Houston in 1996. Why so long? I needed those twenty years to recover from what had happened in New Orleans.

CHAPTER 25

Where's Mom?

Penny and her mother celebrating Easter in 1978

Garry Marshall

SOMETIMES I HEARD a tone in Tracy's voice that reminded me of the way I had sounded when I spoke to my mother. It would make me cringe. I knew what it was like to have a mother who not only worked but was more interested in her work than doing traditional mother things. Also, I remember Tracy bringing kids home after school to play, and then they would leave. I'd ask where so-and-so went, and she would say, "They didn't really want to be friends. They just wanted to see you and Rob." My heart ached.

Every so often I would try to make it up to her. In June 1977, for instance, she was going through what I called her Patty Hearst phase, whining that I never took her anywhere. Well, she had been to Monte Carlo and Venice, among other places, but instead of arguing, I took her to the Plaza Hotel in New York and showed her where I had grown up.

It was my version of a trip to the old country. I took her to Rob's building. We walked up Jerome Avenue. I pointed out the store where I had bought my 45s as well as the Jade Garden, the Chinese restaurant where we ordered takeout if my father didn't come home for Sunday dinner. It was underneath the el, and I explained how we would wait after placing an order and couldn't hear shit when they called your number because of the passing train.

For me, though, the highlight of our trip was when we stood outside my old apartment building and I showed Tracy the windows on the ramp leading down to my mother's dance school. There were three of them. She noticed that someone had spray-painted the word FONZIE on one of them. I liked seeing that a touch of Marshall creativity was still attached to the building, and Tracy was eager to tell her grandmother.

If only my mother had been able to fully appreciate it. She was still as much of a pain in the ass as ever — meddling, complaining about my father, or offering an opinion on work. "Why does your brother dress you so silly?" Rob could tell from the sound of my voice when I was talking to her on the phone. At family gatherings at our house, she took the grandchildren outside and taught them tap in our driveway. We would hear the scraping on the cement.

But we had begun to notice a problem. Her feistiness was turning into forgetfulness. It was first apparent in late 1977, during *Laverne & Shirley*'s third season, when we taped an episode titled "The Second Almost Annual Shotz Talent Show." Cindy's and my mothers were both in it. Her mother, Frances, sang and mine danced. In many ways, the episode was a tribute to my mother, starting with the person who wrote the script, Paula Roth. Paula was the daughter of my mother's partner in the dance school, Mildred Roth.

In the second season, after the show was a hit, Garry had told me that I could give someone a life, meaning I could give someone who needed a break a job on *Laverne & Shirley*. I chose Paula. Although I had been mean to her as a kid, those days were behind us. I took her to plays and events when I was in New York. She was usually available. She was a key-punch operator going with a married guy. I didn't think that constituted a life.

She jumped at the chance to work on the show. Garry gave her the same manual he'd given to Monica, and Paula picked up writing quickly. I did the same thing with Marty Nadler, a friend's brother.

Garry also let Cindy give two people a life. It was easy to open the door and, in a way, it was necessary to pay it forward if you wanted to stay real amid all the hoopla of show business.

Once the door was opened, it was up to others to prove they belonged. Like Paula, whose "Second Almost Annual Talent Show" brought all of us back together for the first time since we'd been children. During rehearsals, we reminisced about how my mother had taught us how to entertain. Now, here we were at Paramount Studios, Garry, Ronny, Paula, and me, all of us influenced in some way by her. Even more remarkable was my mother's ability to tap. She danced effortlessly, picking up steps wherever Garry instructed. She delighted all of us.

But she couldn't remember any of her lines, not even a single short one. That was worrisome.

As we puzzled over it, Garry remembered that she'd had trouble on her previous TV appearances. The first was the "Oscar's Birthday" episode of *The Odd Couple* in 1972. No one had told her it was lunchtime and she was found hiding on the set. The second was a *Happy Days* in 1976. She had one line — "When do we eat lunch?" — and she repeatedly said, "When do we go to the airport?"

After the talent show episode, we took my mother to the doctor. She was diagnosed with dementia or what we have since come to know as Alzheimer's disease. I tried to make light of it. "Maybe it's good — maybe she won't know who I am and will like me better," I said. But she didn't forget me — or her sense of humor. A short time later, a reporter doing a story on our family was allowed to sit next to her during a *Laverne & Shirley* rehearsal. "It has too much sameness," my mother said. Then she added, "You know, my son did all this for the money."

Gradually, as the disease took hold, she would occasionally forget our names and call us whatever name popped into her head. She had done the same thing when I was a kid. She would call me Gertrude or Gladys and say, "Don't you get tired of always being called Penny?" Despite her Alzheimer's, she still hated my father. Their conversations were hilarious. One day she was looking in her purse for her checkbook. She couldn't find it or remember what it was called. She kept asking for the "long brown thing."

My father, good with numbers but not the sharpest tack, said, "A salami?"

"A salami?" she exclaimed. "What would I do with a salami in my purse?"

At that point, we took her car away. She and my father were living in Studio City so they could be closer to Garry, Ronny, and me. She still got around on the bus, but she would forget where to get off. Several times she went to the end of the line and wandered around. Once, a cop picked her up and called my sister-in-law. They had my mother in the downtown jail, where she was regaling hookers with stories about teaching dance. They loved her.

Years later, after the disease had rendered her bed-bound and helpless, I took a Polaroid of her lying in bed. I knew she was nearing the end of her life and I wanted to remember her. I showed the picture to Jimmy Belushi, who was living in a spare room at my house. He grabbed the photo from my hand and threw it in the fireplace. "That's not your mother," he said.

He was right. My mother dressed in a blouse and slacks and spent her days in the cellar — or rather the ballroom — sitting at an upright piano, smoking cigarettes, drinking Yoo-hoo, and making sure her 360 students knew what it felt like to entertain.

Even though she drove me nuts, I would never forget her.

CHAPTER 26
The Remodel

Penny and close friend Carrie Fisher,
who were introduced by Lorne Michaels

Michael O'Donoghue / Tracy Reiner

Penny and Carrie blowing out the candles in 1986
at one of their legendary joint birthday parties

Marshall personal collection

RIGHT BEFORE ROB quit *All in the Family* at the end of the 1977–78 season, we bought a home in Encino with a tennis court, a swimming pool, ample parking for friends, and a guest house. It was supposed to be our dream house, the place that said we had made it. We called it "the house that yuks built." Jerry Belson came over one day and said, "Wow, this is a great house — if life was worth living."

Before long we were agreeing with him. We wanted to add a master bedroom and update the kitchen. We hired an architect and a contractor, who told us the job would take six months max. So we moved into the guest house: Rob, Tracy, me, our two dogs, Barney Google and Joey, and a white cat we referred to as The Ghost of Howie for the way he coughed and wheezed like our old cat, Howie. We thought we could handle the close quarters for a while.

But two years later we were still living there. Somewhere in that time span we lost our sense of humor. Our contractor and architect would assure us that the job was coming along and then something would happen. The wrong materials arrived or they weren't shipped at all. Or the wood we wanted to use was too heavy for the floor.

When I complained, the contractor said, "You can go ahead with that flooring. But you might have a cave-in. Your call."

To get through the annoyances, Rob and I relied on our ability to turn even hardship into humor. Without *All in the Family,* he worked hard. In June 1978, he and his partner, Phil Mishkin, wrote and produced *Free Country,* a period sitcom about Lithuanian immigrants in turn-of-the-century New York. Rob also starred in it. I think he wanted to do the Eastern European version of *Roots.* But the network canceled it after only five episodes. He tried a variety series the next summer, and despite contributions from Billy Crystal and Martin Mull, and the debut of *This Is Spinal Tap,* it also had a short run.

Rob was unaccustomed to failure. Frustrated, he struggled and second-guessed himself into a place of self-loathing. Once he was in that state of mind, there was no getting through to him. If you liked him, you were a fool, and if you didn't like him, you were an idiot.

I knew we had problems when I got out of bed one morning and he asked where I was going. I reminded him that I had a show. He drifted and stewed about the little things that we had always tried to ignore, including my paycheck, which was now bigger than his. What did it matter? Well, apparently it did. We were out of sync. He was fiercely ambitious, and I didn't give a shit. While he worked, Albert and I would take mushrooms and watch *Family Feud.* Then he would come home and find us laughing at "Show me 'banana'!"

Egos were fragile. With our house in disarray, friends didn't hang out as much. We had people over to swim and play tennis, but it wasn't like the old days. I would go to New York to hang out with my *SNL* friends. One day I went to The Sherry-Netherland Hotel to say hi to Jerry Belson, who was working on a rewrite of *Close Encounters of the Third Kind,* and Steven Spielberg was there.

"So you're the *Jaws* of TV?" he said.

Steven and I became instant friends. He gave me a small part in his movie *1941,* his action comedy starring John Belushi and Danny Aykroyd about a feared Japanese attack on Los Angeles during World War II. It was a high-concept, big-budget film, and as Hollywood's wunderkind filmmaker, he knew many in the business were looking for him to fail. When you get too successful, people want to see that you're fallible, like everyone else.

He understood. When he offered me a couple days work on the movie, he joked, "I have a hundred and seventy-one speaking parts. If this dies, I'm going to need someone to talk to." He covered a lot of bases because it was hard to find someone who wasn't in the movie. Even Michael McKean and David Lander were in it; they played machine gunners defending the coast.

My scene took one day and then I spent another day on the set watching Steven work. I didn't know shit about cameras or directing, and he knew everything. He was experimenting with a Louma crane, which was this long expandable, extendable arm with a camera at the end that could snake through crowds and fly overhead while being operated from a seated position far away.

When he filmed me, Steven was literally around the corner. I made him stick his picture on the end of the camera. I was used to talking to another person. I think I amused him. We watched movies together and discussed changes we would have made in scenes and different endings. I was endlessly fascinated. I don't know that everyone at our place was as enamored by him. Some were intimidated. Others were jealous. Steven didn't do drugs. He was a straight arrow, and that made some people uncomfortable.

I tried to get a Quaalude in him. They were my drug of choice. I constantly joked about wanting to know what he would be like if he relaxed.

"I want to know what's inside you," I would say.

"Celluloid," he would say, laughing at me.

Carl Gottlieb had cowritten the screenplay for *Jaws*, and he called me one day when I was in New York with a request. He was thinking about buying the house on Martha's Vineyard where they all had stayed while making the movie, and he asked me to go with his then-wife Allison to look at the house. He trusted my taste. Once Steven heard that I was going there, he called me with another favor. He had left his favorite pillow there and wanted me to try to find it.

"How am I going to find it?" I asked.

"It smells a little like celery," he said.

"Celery?" I paused. "Never mind."

The house was a large log cabin that hadn't been occupied since they had used it as their home base. As Allison looked around, I went through each bedroom and smelled the pillows. I inhaled a lot of dust without finding a hint of celery anywhere. Carl didn't end up buying the house, either.

Back in New York, Lorne arranged for me to meet Carrie Fisher at her place in the Eldorado on Central Park West. He was pals with singer-songwriter Paul Simon, who was dating Carrie, and they thought we'd hit it off. They were right. We've been best friends ever since. She and Paul were heading to St. Hip, her name for some island in the Caribbean. I helped her pack and listened to her bitch about whether she was able to keep up with Paul.

A high school dropout, she thought everyone was smarter than she was, especially Paul. In reality, she was smarter than everyone. She was brilliant. Everyone knew it. Steven, Lorne, and if you asked him at the right moment, Paul would've agreed, too. Carrie read voraciously. She was funny and clever. She wrote and provided nonstop, hysterical commentary on people, movies, books, and Hollywood, where she grew up the daughter of Debbie Reynolds and Eddie Fisher. She was a one-woman show thirty-five years before she did one.

There was a reason I was glad to have a new best friend: I was gradually losing my old one. The remodel cost more than we paid for our house. It also cost us our marriage. Two years in the guest house took a toll. When Rob and I finally moved in, we saw a report on TV that we were breaking up. It wasn't a good welcome. We made a stab at normalcy, opening our doors again to friends. We welcomed back the old crowd, including Albert, Jim Brooks, and Ricky Dreyfuss, who took over the guest house. Added new faces, like Ed Begley Jr., John Landis, Jimmy Belushi, Tim Matheson, and Steven Spielberg. One night Cindy arrived with Andy Kaufman, who she dated briefly. He wanted to wrestle us.

"I don't think so," I said. Then I turned to Cindy and added, "Please take him home."

I wasn't into fighting in any way, not even with Rob. Our marriage continued to head in the wrong direction, and it wasn't helped when we worked together on his TV movie *More Than Friends*. The movie was a charming romance — underrated if you ask me — that Rob wrote with Phil Mishkin about two longtime friends who debate over a couple decades whether to become lovers. Originally titled *I'll Love You and Be Your Best Friend,* it was loosely inspired by our relationship. In fact, ABC promoted it as a "like story."

Rob and I starred with Howard Hesseman, Carl Gottlieb, Michael McKean, and other friends. We shot in our old Bronx neighborhood and reconnected with past acquaintances. Jim Burrows directed, but the film was Rob's. He often yelled cut. Our problems arose because he immersed himself in every aspect of the movie and expected me to do the same. But I didn't want to go to dailies and watch myself. I didn't like doing that. Nor did I want to run lines at night. I knew my lines.

New York was my playground, and I wanted to play. Rob and I got into an argument when I insisted on going to the *Animal House* premiere rather than staying at the hotel and rehearsing with him. I had friends there: John Belushi, Stephen Bishop, John Landis, and Tim Matheson. I was making up for the fun I'd missed as a young mother. Rob was interested in making movies.

Back home, as Rob put together the movie, he began talking about wanting a beach house in Malibu. We had never gone to Malibu. We weren't beach people. He also kept referring to it as *his* house. I realized what was going on. There weren't other people. Neither of us had cheated. We just weren't making each other happy anymore.

In March 1979, we decided to split, but then we stayed together another six months because Ricky Dreyfuss, who was living in our guest house with his Best Actor Academy Award for *The Goodbye Girl,* couldn't handle us breaking up. He cried. The three of us probably should have gone to therapy together.

Finally, in August, Rob moved to the beach house. I stayed in Encino so Tracy could continue going to the same junior high school. We didn't rush to split everything or sign divorce papers. We remained friendly. I think both of us felt guilty. Maybe, though, in the end, I did make him sick.

I had a harder time than I let on. As this went down, Cindy and I were shooting the two-part *Laverne & Shirley* episode "You're in the Army Now." It aired early in the fifth season. I completely fell apart during a scene when we parachuted down from a helicopter. All of a sudden I went blind. As we dangled on ropes above the set, I told Cindy that I was having a breakdown.

"I know my lines," I said. "Just make sure I get on my mark."

With her pushing me from one spot to another, I made it through. I don't shut down for nothing. But a few nights later, I looked and sounded like I was ready to fall apart. I arranged to have dinner with my brother. I wanted to tell him about Rob's and my decision to divorce. We met at a restaurant near my house. I had never been there. It looked okay from the outside. I thought he would find something that agreed with him.

What we found instead were waiters who came to the table and talked with puppets on their hands. *What's your order?* Oblivious to my tears, they were auditioning for us, hoping to get a job. It was absurd. I laughed and cried at the same time.

Carrie helped me through the roughest patches. In addition to being available on the phone or in person, she played matchmaker, introducing me to Art Garfunkel, the singer. He was in town and staying at an out-of-the-way hotel on Hollywood Boulevard. She was having a fight with Paul that day, and who better to complain to about Paul Simon than his on-again, off-again partner Art Garfunkel?

We went to Artie's hotel, and although Carrie consumed most of the attention, Artie and I hit it off. He was still depressed following the suicide of his longtime girlfriend, Laurie Bird, the year before, and I was depressed, too. It was perfect. We were proof of the cliché that misery loved company.

CHAPTER 27

Tripping

Penny playing in the snow on the way from Salzburg to Siena in 1981

Tracy Reiner

M Y FIRST BIG NIGHT out was the premiere for *1941*. It was December 1979. I went with Danny Aykroyd, John Belushi, and his wife, Judy. The four of us raided the wardrobe department at Paramount for period outfits and then, as long as we were there, we borrowed an antique car. When we rolled up to the theater, John hollered at me to turn away from the window. He wanted to be recognized before me.

I was happy to stay out of the spotlight. With the holidays approaching, I was still nursing the pain from splitting with Rob and was not in a great state of mind. Carrie Fisher suggested spending Christmas in Switzerland. I thought that was a good idea. We put together a group that included Tracy, Phil Mishkin's daughter, Heidi, and *Saturday Night Live* writer Michael O'Donoghue, and flew to Geneva. I was amazed at what was possible when I said yes.

After recovering from jet lag in Lausanne, we went on to Gstaad, the famous ski resort in the Alps known as a playground for the rich. On our first day there, we turned it into a playground by taking mushrooms and then going to lunch at a restaurant, where seeing turtle soup on the menu triggered fits of uncontrollable laughter.

After lunch, we decided to go skiing. It made no difference that Carrie was the only one who actually knew how to ski. The rest of us were gung-ho. Tracy and Heidi took off on the bunny slope; that was the last we saw of them for a while. But Michael and I had a problem. We couldn't even get on the T-bars — thin metal bars that you're supposed to lean on as they take you up the mountain. We would hold on, aim our butts, and go flying backward, head over heels onto the snowy ground, where we'd stay for another ten minutes, paralyzed by hysterical laughter.

Everyone there was annoyed. They didn't seem to have much of a sense of humor. Several people tried showing us the correct way to get on. "Make like you're an ironing board. Be very straight and stiff." This actually inspired an episode of *Laverne & Shirley* titled "The Ski Show," where we found it impossible to get on the ski lift. Once Michael and I eventually got to the top, the rest was anticlimactic. We snowplowed back down the mountain. Was that it?

The whole thing was ridiculous. *Let's learn to ski in the Alps. And we'll do it on mushrooms.*

From Gstaad, we traveled to Zermatt, the village next to the Matterhorn. Inspired by the storybook scenery, we bought a Christmas tree. Don't ask. We had so much luggage, and now we had to carry around the tree. Michael also got sick. Undeterred, we toured the village's streets in a horse-drawn buggy with our tree sticking out the back.

Before we left Zermatt, my attorney Gary Hendler called. He had been speaking with another client, Arnon Milchan, a wealthy Israeli entrepreneur who was getting into the movie business, and mentioned that we were on our way to Paris. Arnon, who became one of the most successful independent producers in movie history, offered us his home outside of Paris. He insisted it would be nicer than a hotel — and it was.

Arnon's driver met us at the train station in Paris at 2 a.m. and drove us and our thirty pieces of luggage to Arnon's country estate. We had no idea where we were headed. We drove forever into the middle of the French countryside, which was pitch-black. All we heard was the sound of the tires on the gravel roads. I don't know how the driver navigated.

Finally, we pulled up in front of Arnon's house. Inside, we picked bedrooms and went to sleep. When I woke up the next day, I found myself in a gorgeous home decorated tastefully with what I'm sure was expensive art, including a sculpture made out of coins. After making it to the kitchen, I looked out the window and saw Tracy riding across the yard on a horse. Beyond her was a lake. I could have been looking at a painting of a French landscape.

In another room I found Michael trying to decapitate R2D2. Somehow Arnon had gotten ahold of what appeared to be the real astromech droid from *Star Wars*. When the real Princess Leia appeared with her morning coffee, I laughed at the surreal intersection of reality and make-believe. It was clear that what passed for normal life could no longer be considered normal.

Carrie and I went hiking through the woods without realizing we were among hunters who could have shot us. On New Year's Eve, we went into Paris to celebrate and got a little lost. I don't even know where we went. Playwright Israel Horovitz, who I'd gone out with for five seconds years earlier, was living there at the time. He found us and took us to his apartment. I don't think we were his wife's idea of a fun night. We were a little wacked.

In 1980, I received my third and last nomination for a Golden Globe as the Best Actress in a Musical/Comedy. I didn't win. I never win those things. But that's not the story I want to tell. I needed a date for the event. I called Steven Spielberg, whose marriage, like mine, had recently ended. We had cried on each other's shoulders. Why not party together, too? When he picked me up, he referred to himself as "the big-time director escort service."

After the Globes ceremony, we went to John Belushi's birthday party. John had rented Candice Bergen's home. Inside, the first person we saw was Michael O'Donoghue, who was wearing a button that said: *Born 1949/Died 1941.* It was a reference to John's latest movie, then considered a flop. I cringed, as it was also Steven's movie. But Steven had a sense of humor about it.

He needed one at this party. People were out of control. At one point, I walked into the bathroom as a famous British rocker and another guy were cooking up cocaine and inhaling the smoke. Free-basing. I had never seen that before.

"What are you doing?" I asked.

"Oh, hey Penny," the rocker said. "How are you doing?"

"I'm doing pretty good," I said, watching them fix up all their little things. "So what does that do?"

"Makes it way more intense," the other guy said.

I tried one hit and immediately knew freebasing wasn't for me. My neck and chest froze. I left the bathroom with my upper body temporarily paralyzed. That was fun?

Later that evening, Hunter Thompson kicked me. I had no idea who he was. He was in the kitchen, trying to smoke opium. I watched as he sucked the life out of what looked like a Tootsie Roll. It seemed like a lot of effort, almost funny — until he leapt up from the table and kicked me.

"What the fuck is your story?" I said.

He cursed me out with a string of colorful words that caused me to stop and stare even more intensely, not out of fear or anger but rather amazement at his vocabulary. That was when someone mentioned that he was the famous gonzo journalist and warned it was best not to rile him up any more because he carried a gun and didn't hesitate to pull it out and start shooting.

At the end of the night, I thanked Steven for getting me home safely.

I stayed on the move. I met Carrie in Chicago, where we hung out with John Belushi and Danny Aykroyd. They were shooting *The Blues Brothers* movie. One night Carrie, Judy Belushi, and I took acid. It was my first time taking LSD; same with Carrie. It seemed like the thing to do. We played pool for hours and took pictures of ourselves with a Polaroid camera at a hole-in-the-wall bar that the guys called the Blues Bar. We thought the cops there were extras from the movie and so made no effort to hide our silliness; but they turned out to be real police officers.

After several hours, Carrie and I went back to the Ritz-Carlton Hotel and gave ourselves facials. Laughing at everything we saw, we rode up and down on the hotel's elevator, lying on the floor so we could stare up at the pretty deco ceiling. I can't say how long we did that, but it was a while. Only once did the elevator stop and the doors open, and then Eric Idle, of all people, stepped in. We laughed too hard to even say hello. He understood.

I broke the spell by going out to get some more Polaroid film. Being outside in the lights and around other people wasn't so good for me. I went back to my room and had an anxiety attack. Danny tried talking me through it. He put on some heavy metal music. That didn't help. Upset, I called my brother, who didn't know from acid. His drug of choice was still Benadryl.

But Carrie and I were supposed to fly to Albuquerque the next day and play baseball in a *Happy Days* charity event, and I felt an overwhelming need to tell him that I was freaking out on acid and might have gotten too high. I didn't know what to do or how long it was going to last — hopefully not forever.

"Is anyone there?" my brother asked.

"Yeah," I said. "But not at the moment. I'm in my room. Carrie's here, though."

"Well, I think you just need to go through it," he said.

He was right. I got to Albuquerque and saw him on the baseball field. He rubbed my back.

"So tell me, that was fun for you?" he asked.

Fun enough.

· · ·

Undeterred, I dropped acid again the next time I was in New York. I was with Carrie and Paul, and we were shopping for folk art. Before leaving Paul's apartment, Carrie and I took acid once more. There was a reason behind our madness: It was fun. I'm not going to apologize. We laughed our asses off. It added a touch of adventure and unpredictability that we enjoyed. The only fallout in this case was transportation. We changed limo drivers fifteen times. At the tiniest hint of something out of the ordinary, we called for a new car and driver.

A little paranoia was nothing. In fact, we took it in stride when Carrie accidentally lit her fur coat on fire instead of her cigarette. By that afternoon, we had ditched the folk art and gone in search of the city's best marzipan. When we finally staggered back into Paul's apartment, I remembered that I had a date with Artie. I had forgotten all about it, as happens when you're on acid all day.

We were supposed to double-date with Stephen Bishop and Karen Allen. I called Artie and told him to pick me up at Paul's.

"I can't just come over to Paul's," he said.

"Why not?" I asked.

I knew nothing about their long history together other than that they had made some of the most popular and enduring music of the '60s and '70s, including "The Sound of Silence" and "Bridge Over Troubled Water." I wasn't aware of their very complicated, touchy relationship. They had known each other since grade school. Sometimes they were friends. Sometimes they weren't. I didn't know they would sometimes go years without speaking to each other. I had more than enough of my own issues.

Eventually, Artie explained why he couldn't just come over to Paul's. He had to be invited, he said. *Invited schmited,* I said. I didn't care. I couldn't follow what he was saying. I had been tripping, and as a result, I couldn't leave Paul's by myself. Finally, he understood and agreed to pick me up.

Once he was there, everything seemed fine. He and Paul were friendly to each other. I gave Artie a tab of acid. "Here, join me."

We invited Carrie and Paul to come to dinner, too. They declined. I offered to bring them something back if they wanted. Looking back, it was funny. Here I was, totally ignorant of one of the most strained partnerships in pop music history, arranging a social date with these two guys who have wanted nothing to do with each other for God only knew how long.

Outside, Artie and I got into a cab, and now, thanks to the acid, we were glued to each other. We walked in the restaurant, but couldn't find Stephen and Karen. After fifteen minutes, we realized that we were in the wrong restaurant. We were supposed to be in the one next door. So we went there, had a nice time, and went back to Paul's, where the good times continued. As conversation flowed, I innocently said, "Why don't you guys sing something?"

After an awkward silence, Paul and Artie shrugged. I guess they couldn't think of a reason why not or just didn't want to go into years of slights and bickering in front of Carrie and me. Paul got up and walked slowly to his guitar closet. Then he and Artie carefully searched the room for a spot with the best echo, the best sound, and they started to sing. They played oldies in lieu of their own songs, but it was, quite frankly, the most thrilling night of my life.

Artie and I spent the night at Ricky Dreyfuss's apartment. He was out of town and left the keys for me. We floated inside, knowing we'd had a sensational evening. I wouldn't have guessed it could get better, but it did when Artie serenaded me with an absolutely beautiful rendition of "There's a Place for Us." He filled that song with emotion and meaning from both of our lives — his grief, my new life, the fact we'd found each other — indeed, at that moment, it was about us.

How could you not fall in love with that?

CHAPTER 28

Dirty Laundry

Penny and Art Garfunkel on their motorcycle trip through France and Italy

Penny Marshall/Art Garfunkel

ONE OF THE FUNNIEST *Laverne & Shirley* episodes we ever did was "Not Quite South of the Border." Our one hundredth show, it had the girls going on a vacation somewhere *near* Mexico (we weren't allowed to insult Mexico) where everything went wrong. They checked into a bungalow that was missing two walls (it was literally a hole in the wall). They had to share it with a stranger with Montezuma's revenge. Their luggage was lost. And then a hurricane hit.

The hurricane itself was one of the most spectacular scenes we had ever attempted, and we'd done a lot of physical bits over the years. When we shot it, Ron Howard, Henry Winkler, and Steven Spielberg came to watch. My brother was nervous with Steven there, especially afterward, when Steven was silent.

"What's the matter?" my brother said. "You didn't like it?"

"No," Steven said. "The opposite. It would take me eleven days to do what you just did in a couple hours."

Early on, the studio had given us small apartments in an area known as Lucy Park where Cindy, David, Michael, and I gathered every Tuesday night after we finishing taping and unwound while watching a tape of the show that had aired on the network that night and commenting about what had been cut. David and I had the same conversation every week for eight years.

It was these late nights that put an end to my driving. I would find myself driving back to Encino on the freeway, thinking I was speeding, when in reality I was only going twenty miles per hour. I asked for a driver and got one, as did Cindy, thanks to the most-favored-nations clause in our contracts. After Tracy graduated from junior high school, Rob and I sold our Encino house and I rented Gore Vidal's house in the Hollywood Hills. I kept the driver even though I lived much closer to Paramount.

It simplified my life.

That in turn left more time for something closer to my heart: Art Garfunkel. Artie came back to town to guest on "The Beatnik Show," a fun episode in which the girls went to a coffee house after Shirley wanted to become a beatnik. In it, Cindy did a strange dance, I played the bongos, and Artie was a poet playing a tree. Teri Garr and Carol Kane sat at tables, too. At that point, Artie and I — to quote the show — welcomed each other into our lives as "ham welcomes cheese to the rye bread of friendship."

He was just the distraction I needed. After five years of *Laverne & Shirley,* we had burned through nearly every comedy writer in town. The same was true for actors. We brought them in, said can you lift me? Can you kiss me? Can you come back in three weeks? We ended the season with our lowest ratings since going on the air. We didn't face cancelation, but changes had to be made.

As soon as we went on hiatus, Cindy and I flew to the South of France for an international TV festival in Cannes. Once a series completed five years, there were enough shows for a big syndication sale, and our job was to drum up excitement. But neither of us looked like cheerleaders as we checked into the Hôtel du Cap, the famous old resort in Cap Ferret. We were jet-lagged, and the gray skies and chilly temperatures sapped whatever enthusiasm we had left.

The hotel was empty. Although we probably weren't the only

people there, it felt like it. As we wandered from the front desk and down the cavernous hallways, the former nineteenth-century mansion reminded me of *The Shining*. I turned to Cindy and chanted, "Redrum, redrum." She gave me a dirty look. She was sensitive about such things and didn't want me to mess with her.

I suggested taking a walk around hotel's expansive grounds before we faced meetings with international TV buyers and reporters at the convention. We followed a path along flowerbeds revealing the first colors of spring and past clusters of thick trees. Then we turned a corner and found ourselves standing at the entrance to a graveyard. But this was no ordinary graveyard. The headstones all were very small. We didn't know what to make of it.

"Redrum," I said.

"Shut up," Cindy said.

I thought they might be for the hotel staff. Or perhaps some of the hotel's guests.

"Don't say that," said Cindy.

She figured out the graves were for the hotel's pets. As an animal lover, she thought that was sweet.

The walk re-energized us through most of the press conference, though I had trouble with a Dutch journalist who said his people didn't think *Laverne & Shirley* was funny. "I don't think the Dutch are known for their sense of humor," I snapped. Later, at dinner with some TV executives from Belgium, Cindy and I crashed, literally, head first onto our plates, sound asleep. We blamed it on the time change. I suppose we did our job anyway. *Laverne & Shirley* broke new syndication records.

Back home, as I recounted the trip to Artie, his eyes lit up at my description of the South of France. Well-traveled, he had been through the South of France many times before, including the Hôtel du Cap, and my enthusiasm for Europe inspired him to suggest another type of trip: motorcycling across Europe. Just the two of us. Going wherever our mood and the road took us.

I had never done anything remotely like that in my life. Who lived that kind of life outside of characters in novels? Artie did. To me, it was one more reason to fall in love with this man. His father had been a traveling salesman, and Artie liked to rack up the miles, too. In the short time I had known him, he had periodically called and said, "How about Austria?" "How about Istanbul?" I was employed Monday through Friday. He, on the other hand, picked up and left for two or three months on a whim.

I said yes. The motorcycle adventure was something I would have done in my early 20s but I already was a mother then. However, now was even better. I had the time, the money, and the perfect traveling companion. Artie and I flew to Paris, where we spent a week with Jim Brooks and his then-wife, Holly, and Lorne and his girlfriend, Susan, who all happened to be there at the same time. It was a party.

Then, one morning, after bidding good-bye to our friends, Artie and I stood in front of the Hôtel Plaza Athénée, secured two small suitcases to the back of his rented BMW motorcycle, and took off. Someone asked where we were headed and Artie simply said, "South."

The ensuing days were wonderful, amazing. Avoiding highways, we drove at a leisurely pace on back roads through small villages and gorgeous countryside. I had a Michelin guide, but we stayed in whatever charming place we found, whether it was a five-star hotel or an inexpensive pension. Every four or five days, we boxed up our dirty clothes and sent them to his place in New York. Artie preferred to buy a new T-shirt and underwear rather than do laundry.

After nearly two weeks, we parked the bike in Avignon so I could fly to Boston for an event that nearly qualified as a family get-together. My brother and Jerry Belson were workshopping *The Roast*, a play they had written about an old comedian whose tribute dinner is spoiled when dark secrets are revealed. It starred Rob and Peter Boyle, and Rob's father, Carl, directed. Was it odd that we were all still working together? Not to me. That's show business.

I watched from the back of the theater and gave notes. I don't think they helped. In May, the play went to Broadway and closed after three days. (As it closed, the sign for *Cats* went up.) My brother blamed his and Jerry's inability to agree on an ending. I'm sure he was right. Onstage, you have to tie up the loose ends neatly and send the audience home with a resolution they like. In real life, as was evident, that's not as easy. I was familiar with indecision. My life was a play in the midst of a rewrite. But was that bad? I didn't think so. In fact, I had asked my therapist why I had left a marriage that was comfortable and predictable for a great big question mark.

"Were you happy?" he asked.

"No," I said.

He shrugged.

That cost me a fortune, but he was right. Sometimes the most complicated questions have simple answers.

Were you happy?

I was learning that I didn't have to have everything figured out. Often the point was to live and see what happened. Artie was a great person with whom to discuss such matters. He thought about the big questions and read deep books. My approach was far simpler. I remember once laughing at our differences when I noticed the books we were carrying through an airport. He had Stendhal's *The Red and the Black* and I had Xaviera Hollander's *The Happy Hooker*.

After Boston, Artie and I flew to Washington, D.C., and met up with Carrie and Harrison Ford for the premiere of *The Empire Strikes Back*. The dressy event was a benefit for the Special Olympics, a favorite organization of mine. My first husband worked for the Special Olympics in Albuquerque, and I had once volunteered as a "hugger" at the finish line during one of his events. I recommend the experience to everyone.

The D.C. premiere was a hit with everyone except, ironically, the Special Olympics kids. The spaceships and Wookiees traumatized them. Artie and I tagged along with Carrie, Paul, and Harrison to

London, where they attended a royal screening of the movie. Not among the invitees, we stayed at our hotel, where Artie left the bathtub running while we went out for dinner. When we returned, the place was flooded. We spent the night on our hands and knees, cleaning the goddamn hotel room. It was very *Laverne & Garfunkel.*

Carrie and Paul and Artie and I then traveled to Portugal, where we were engulfed by a dense fog that never lifted. When Carrie and Paul began grating on each other, Artie and I broke away and found a hotel that had been a monastery four or five centuries earlier. The rooms were small, austere, and claustrophobic — perfect for decades of meditative silence. Artie liked that, but I didn't. Late at night, we got into an argument and decided to leave. But locating the monk or night manager — whatever he was — at that hour to check us out was next to impossible. I think we ended up finding it humorous.

By the time we picked up the motorcycle in Avignon, we had patched things up. Our bike broke down on the way to Eric and Tanya Idle's house in Cotignac and all I could talk about after we arrived was how I had fixed it. Again, another life lesson for which I had Artie to thank.

We also visited my friend Carol Caldwell in a one-horse village in the French countryside where, it seemed, only two things happened: In the morning the sheep were herded out over a hill and at night they were brought back. They wore bells around their necks. We would hear them coming and going like a rustic symphony.

From Carol's, we drove south to Nice and into Italy. As we crossed the border, Artie and I were struck by some of the contrasts: how well the French roads had been marked, the silence of the French countryside, and then the noise in Italy, where people honked and screamed at one another. We knew we were among Italians.

Then the best scenery of all: We climbed through the Great St. Bernard Pass in the Alps and crossed into Switzerland. Inspired by the majesty of the views and unable to contain myself, I burst into songs from *The Sound of Music.* Artie reminded me that I wasn't Julie Andrews.

"Please don't sing," he said.

I wasn't insulted.

We rendezvoused with Tracy and my niece Wendy in Geneva. We picked them up at the airport, rented a car, and resumed our travels with one girl on the back of the bike and the other in the car with me. I taught both girls, recently turned sixteen, to drive on the country roads in France. Why take lessons in the San Fernando Valley when you could practice finding sixteenth-century cathedrals in Annecy?

As we headed back to Paris, we ate lunch on the side of the road. At dinner, Artie harmonized with the girls. In Paris, we showed them Notre-Dame and walked along the Seine. I was living a dream, yet it was my life, and when it was time to go home, I felt recharged and ready, sort of. Tracy admired me for being adventurous, but really, Artie deserved the credit. He had given me a gift. He had opened my eyes to travel and exposed me to a new approach to life.

The rest was up to me.

CHAPTER 29

Taking Direction

Penny playing the tambourine onstage with Paul Simon and
Mayor Ed Koch at New York's Palladium Theater in 1980

Marshall personal collection

WITH THE HIGHS came lows. It was fall 1980, and I had flown into New York to see Paul Simon perform at the Palladium. I arrived in the grip of a deep depression. Sometimes the feeling is beyond control. This was like a strong current that took me out to sea. Deep down, I knew that the stuff I had run away from by going to Europe was catching up to me. Luckily, my friends were sympathetic. Paul suffered from bouts of darkness, and Carrie had a whole wardrobe of mood swings hanging in her closet. Before the show, Paul said, "Why don't you come onstage and sing at the end when I play 'Amazing Grace'?"

"No thanks," I said. "I'm not a singer."

"Penny, we'll have a large gospel choir backing you up — as well as Mayor Koch," he said. "No one will hear you."

"They won't know who I am," I said, sounding depressed.

"What are you, nuts?" he said. "Come on out and see what it feels like," he said.

After turning in an amazing two-hour-plus show, Paul got to "Amazing Grace" and motioned to me on the side. Reluctantly, I walked out and stood next to him, and I will forever be glad I did. As we sang, the cheering from the audience was like a gust of wind that blew away some of my depression.

I wasn't cured, but it made dealing with the stuff that had depressed me a little easier when I got back to L.A. I was still a little sad about Rob. Every so often feelings of remorse would sneak up on me. My mother was also fading, and that was not so nice. And then there was the show.

While I had been off motorcycling with Artie, my brother had huddled with the show's producers and studio executives and decided to give *Laverne & Shirley* a reboot. For its sixth season, they reset the show in 1964 — just after the Kennedy assassination and just in time for the Beatles — and moved everyone to Los Angeles. They also added Ed Marinaro as stuntman Sonny St. Jacques and Leslie Easterbrook as our wannabe actress neighbor.

I thought the whole thing was a mistake. L.A. didn't make sense to me. Even poor people there have a house with a lawn and a couple of trees. They dress like they're on vacation. They don't look poor.

Laverne and Shirley were poor. That was part of their appeal. They were regular folks. I thought they should go to New York, where they would face new struggles and we could use different actors. But my opinion counted not so much. In the season's opening episode, titled "Not Quite New York," Laverne and Shirley lost their bottle-capping jobs to machines and moved to Burbank, California, as did everyone else.

Despite my criticism, we still did some excellent work, including the episode "I Do, I Do." In it, two British rockers try to marry Laverne and Shirley so they can stay in the United States and escape the high British taxes. Eric Idle and Peter Noone from Herman's Hermits played the rockers, and I added songwriter Stephen Bishop to their band for authenticity. Lenny and Squiggy arrived dressed as Simon and Garfunkel and went looking for Mary Jane in the bedroom. Numerous other drug jokes kept this show from being re-run again.

At one point, I was supposed to play the intro to the Rolling Stones' classic "Satisfaction" on the guitar. I got lessons from Crosby, Stills & Nash's Stephen Stills and Snuffy Walden, a rocker who was becoming one of TV's leading composers. Stephen Bishop also tried to teach me. I never got it right. Finally, Eric Idle said, "Forget the fingering and just pretend you mean it."

That worked.

That season I also directed two episodes: "The Dating Game" and "But Seriously Folks." It wasn't my first time behind the camera. I had directed "The Duke of Squiggman" the previous season. I didn't think it was a big deal. By this time, everyone had directed — Cindy, Michael, the first assistant director, the camera coordinator, and even the script girl. So when they looked in my direction, I said, "Sure, I'll do it."

Why not? It was easy. After a hundred-plus episodes, everyone knew their characters. How many doors can you walk through? "Go do what you're supposed to do," I told everyone. "I'll tell you if it's wrong."

Laverne & Shirley writer-producers Marc Sotkin and Arthur Silver also asked me to direct the pilot for their new sitcom, *Working Stiffs,* starring Jimmy Belushi and Michael Keaton. "Well you're down at the bottom of the barrel, aren't you?" I said. After it sold, though, John Belushi yelled at me. "What are you doing putting my brother on television?" he said. "He's a better actor than I am."

This was an exciting time to be at Paramount. In addition to *Laverne & Shirley* and *Happy Days, Bosom Buddies, Mork & Mindy,* and *Taxi* were among the shows produced there. On any given day, Tom Hanks, Danny DeVito, Henry Winkler, Robin Williams, and I were poking our heads into one another's sets or grabbing lunch together in the commissary.

I didn't like the studio's commissary. It was new, and it blocked the straight path we had taken for years to our parking spaces. All of a sudden we had to walk all the way around to Poughkeepsie, you know, and it took forty minutes because of the little decorative squares of grass they put in the cement. Jim Brooks got tired of hearing me bitch about it.

"Why complain to me?" he said. "Call Barry Diller and tell him we need the Gower Gate open."

"Okay," I said. "Give me his number."

What he failed to mention was that Barry was the chairman and chief executive officer of Paramount; he'd been appointed to the position in 1974, at age thirty-two. He was brilliant, demanding, and tough. But I didn't know who he was. For all I knew, Jim said to call him because he was in charge of parking lots — which, I guess, he sort of was.

I got on the phone and asked for Barry Diller. His assistant picked up and for some reason put me through.

"Hi, this is Penny Marshall," I said. "I work on the show *Laverne & Shirley.*"

"Hello," he said.

"Are you Barry Diller?"

"Yes."

"You know that new commissary you built?" I said.

"Yes, isn't it lovely?"

"Well, yeah, it's sort of nice," I said. "The secretary's heels get stuck in the grass but that's another thing. Look, I work on Stage 20 and we can't get to the parking space because of the commissary and your little squares of cement. So could you please open Gower Gate?"

"Hmmm."

"Look, the TV department is carrying the studio right now, and you're wasting money by making us take so much time to walk. We all could work longer if we could get to our cars quicker."

At the end of the day Barry opened the gate and left it open for about a year. He couldn't figure out who I was and why I mattered, and furthermore why or how I knew all the same people he knew: Warren Beatty, Jack Nicholson, and even David Geffen. Later, we became friends. I loved and trusted him. He's the most honest person I've ever met. And like me, he's committed to the work.

When the season ended, Artie was off on his own someplace, as periodically happened with my peripatetic friend, but now I had the travel bug. I asked one of our producers, Chris Thompson, to meet me in Athens, after he dropped off his grandmother in Yugoslavia. We saw the sights there, then went to Mykonos, and then on to Italy, including Lake Como. Finally, I told Tracy to come to London, where, now bored with Chris, I pointed him toward Paris and Tracy and her friend Mark Getty and I caught a flight to Salzburg and then drove back to Rome before venturing to outlying cities in search of our Italian ancestors.

We ended up on a Sunday morning in a little town called San Martino sulla Marricina, where we asked locals if they knew anyone named Masciarelli. Everyone there said they were Masciarelli. It was like the scene in *Spartacus.* They broke into the hall of records, but didn't find any close relatives of mine.

Later that summer, I rafted down the Grand Canyon with a group that included Jeffrey Katzenberg, producers Don Simpson and Craig Baumgarten, Tony Danza, and some of their wives and girlfriends. Director Tony Scott arrived late, walked into the canyon, and bodysurfed down the river until he caught up. On our way out, Don sprinted the nine miles to the top, whereas I huffed and puffed, stopped for a cigarette, and then started up again. Other vacationers on the trail were stunned to see me.

"Hey, Laverne, what are you doing here?" one guy said.

"Trying to get the fuck out," I replied.

In truth, I enjoyed myself. It was like I was back in junior high or camp. I had always liked hanging around with the guys, and they liked me, too.

CHAPTER 30

Old Friends

Penny with her close friend John Belushi in New York in 1976.
John passed away in 1982.

Jack Winter / Judy Belushi

*T*HE END OF THE SUMMER was always bittersweet. As a child, it meant going home after camp, saying good-bye to friends, and starting school. For the past six years, my life had followed a similar pattern. I had to dial back on the fun and return to ten-hour days on Paramount's Stage 20. But thanks to good friends Paul Simon and Art Garfunkel, I managed to squeeze a little extra fun into my calendar before starting the seventh season of *Laverne & Shirley*. Who could blame me?

Paul and Artie were reuniting for a free concert in Central Park. Except for two songs on *Saturday Night Live* in 1975, they hadn't performed together in concert since 1972. Well, there was that night in Paul's apartment when I asked them to sing. Maybe that contributed to them getting back together. I don't know. Whatever the reason, I wasn't going to miss it. I told *Laverne & Shirley*'s producers to write me light in early September because I wanted to see the concert and spend at least a week there getting ready.

By that time, I had left Gore's place and was renting Tommy Chong's house in Bel Air. It was large and airy and, best of all, directly across the street from my friend Ted Bessell, who told me to have fun at the concert. It was a night to envy. I hung out with Carrie while the guys rehearsed after negotiating for months about what they'd play and who would back them. The concert was the night of September 21, 1981. We had a police escort through the park and directly to the stage, where we looked out on a crowd estimated at more than five hundred thousand. It was a sea of people as far as one could see.

Both guys were tense. Paul made Artie wear a hairpiece, which he didn't like. From the side of the stage where Carrie and I watched, I never saw Paul and Artie look at each other. But those were minor details that didn't affect the concert. They sounded magnificent. They played twenty songs in total, and from the opening notes of "Mrs. Robinson" to the closing refrain of "The Sound of Silence" at the end, I had chills. Everyone did.

Except for Artie. When it was all over, we got in our separate town cars. Paul and Carrie went to his place, three blocks away on Central Park West, and Artie and I headed toward his building on Fifth Avenue. Artie liked to give everything a grade. A trip was an A–, a meal would be a B+, and so on. He was impossibly analytic and self-critical. In the car I asked what he had thought of the performance. He thought about it for a moment and said, "A C–."

"You're crazy," I said. "It was sensational. People are still singing the songs as they're leaving the park." I rolled down the window. "Can you hear them? Don't you hear? They loved it!"

You never know what goes on behind the scenes.

In early 1982, I participated in the *Night of 100 Stars,* a fund-raiser for the Actors' Fund of America. Taped for TV, it was a clusterfuck of confusion once Warren Beatty, Elizabeth Taylor, Diane Keaton, Dudley Moore, Liza Minnelli, and others descended on New York's Radio City Music Hall. I went with *Saturday Night Live* writer Tom Schiller, and we were there all day and some of the night. I saw Gina Lollobrigida sleeping against a coat rack, and the producers forgot a frail and aged James Cagney was waiting beneath the stage in his wheelchair.

Afterward, a bunch of us went to a club where Cher sang and

Robin Williams entertained. Following hours of standing around and taking direction, we all let loose and partied. I went to the bathroom and overheard Bobby De Niro and Al Pacino outside the men's room, saying, "So who's taking Liz [Taylor] home?"

I kept thinking one major star was missing from the festivities: my friend John Belushi. John had dropped off my radar — and most everyone else's — after making Larry Kasdan's movie *Continental Divide*. I heard he was bored. I wasn't at my best when I was bored, and John was worse. Merely walking down the street with him was an experience. People gave him drugs. They pressed it into his hand or shoved it into his pocket — and he'd do it.

With John, there was no such thing as casual drug use. I knew John Landis had fought with him on *The Blues Brothers* about the amount of coke he did. I had witnessed him in action myself. We were once at a party where he led me into the bathroom and pulled out a bindle of heroin. He said I could try some, too. I flushed it down the toilet.

"Don't fuck with that stuff," I said.

I had tried heroin once. It made me carsick. The person who gave it to me said it was an acquired taste. I didn't need to acquire that taste. Artie didn't like it, either, thank God. When others were chipping on weekends, he was my ally in not doing it, and I will always be grateful to him for giving me the wherewithal to keep saying no.

I wish John had done the same. Around this time, Paramount-based producer Don Simpson asked me to direct *The Joy of Sex,* an adaptation of the bestselling how-to book by Dr. Alex Comfort. He showed me a script from John Hughes, the first one from the prolific screenwriter who went on to write *Sixteen Candles* and *Home Alone.* It was done as a series of vignettes, and it was funny. I thought the parts that didn't work could be easily fixed.

With *Laverne & Shirley* going into its eighth season, I liked the idea of a new challenge. I received encouragement from friends, including Jim Brooks and Steven Spielberg. Steven compared directing to babysitting. He jokingly pointed out that I already sat on the phone with half of Hollywood at night, dispensing advice. Why not get paid for it?

I asked Barry Diller what he thought I should do. Even though *The Joy of Sex* wasn't his kind of picture — he made *Reds,* after all — I knew he would tell me the truth — and he did.

"Penny, you have a lot of friends, and they're very smart and very funny," he said. "But when it comes to directing a movie, and committing your life to making a movie, you cannot listen to any of them. You have to see if there is something in there that you identify with, something that makes you *need* to do it. And remember, we are the studio. We are not your friends."

The message came through loud and clear. I still wanted to move forward. To ensure I had enough time, Mike Ovitz secured me a November 2 "out" date from *Laverne & Shirley*'s next season, meaning I would be finished three months earlier than usual. But I started right away. Wanting to get a feel for the script, I arranged a reading at my house that included Teri Garr, Danny DeVito, Carol Kane, and Jack Klugman. Steven Spielberg took pictures.

Unbeknownst to me, as I began to develop the project, Don and some of his colleagues at the studio decided they wanted John Belushi to star in the movie. They thought he would be funny in a diaper. When I finally heard about it, I didn't understand. There was no diaper mentioned in the entire script. Besides, I knew John wanted to do the movie *Noble Rot,* which he and Don Novello had adapted from a Jay Sandrich script. He was going to discuss all this at Paramount on March 6. But the meeting never happened.

On March 5, during a long night of partying at the Chateau Marmont hotel, John overdosed on a speedball, a combination of heroin and cocaine. Drug dealer Cathy Smith admitted to injecting him multiple times with the lethal combination of drugs. I once heard her name mentioned in connection with John. Someone said, "Watch out for her. She's bad news."

I was devastated when I heard about his death. The following days and nights were a blur. Tracy kept an eye on me while I talked end-lessly about it to friends on the phone, piecing together what had happened and trying to understand why. It didn't make sense. His death made me extremely angry. What kind of person would inject him with drugs? What if I had known the studio had wanted him to be in the movie? Would he have been at my house for the reading? Would he have avoided Cathy Smith?

There were too many what-ifs.

I tried to hold on to the good memories of John and Danny Ayk-royd crashing at Rob's and my house in North Hollywood. Later, John and his wife had stayed with us in Encino. John had been sweet with my daughter, who was in junior high. He had insisted on making her dinner and when I checked on them, they were laughing, but there were spaghetti sauce handprints all over the walls. He was irascible. In New York, he would refuse to leave my hotel room. He would come in and out of the bedroom as a different character. I couldn't not laugh. The phone would ring at 2 or 3 a.m. It would be Judy.

"Do you have him?"

"Yeah, I got him."

"Good. Keep him."

None of us could believe he was gone. John always said he was indestructible, and we believed him.

He was John.

CHAPTER 31

Good-bye Shirl

Penny filming the 1982 *Laverne & Shirley* episode "Lost in Spacesuit"

Use of photo still from Laverne & Shirley – *Courtesy of CBS Television Studios*

OVER THE YEARS I had seen Cindy in a number of relationships, but never one where she fell as fast or as hard as she did for Bill Hudson. Best known as one-third of the musical comedy trio The Hudson Brothers, he had split with Goldie Hawn following a brief marriage that produced two children, Oliver and Kate, before meeting Cindy at a celebrity softball game in 1981. In March 1982, Cindy got pregnant, and two months later, after Bill finalized his divorce from Goldie Hawn, they married. I went to the wedding. There was a lot of pink. Everything seemed good.

I was happy for Cindy and supportive. I thought, *She's pregnant; let her be healthy and happy, and we'll figure out a way to deal with her growing belly on the show.* At the time, we were headed into our eighth season. We had the show down. I didn't see why it had to be a big deal.

But it was. In May she told the studio about her pregnancy and began negotiating an out date of her own. I was in New York and followed the details long-distance. She was due in November and only wanted to act in thirteen episodes, insisting she finish in October so that she could rest through the end of her pregnancy. She also indicated a willingness to make small appearances after the first of the year if more episodes were ordered. In any event, whether she did thirteen or slightly more, she wanted to be paid for a full season of episodes, and she wanted her hours kept to a minimum.

Everyone said okay. A month later — the same month Tracy graduated from high school — Bill, now acting as her manager, delivered an additional set of demands, including more money, a Winnebago trailer, and shorter workdays not to exceed eight hours. I think Bill wanted credit, too. But Paramount balked. I guess they'd had their fill of demands the previous month. By the time we began shooting in July, Cindy was one very unhappy pregnant actress.

I thought I could talk sense to her the way I had years earlier, alone and logically. I said, "Take all the dialogue. Go home after four hours. Have them write all your scenes with you lying in bed. Be the biggest pain-in-the-ass pregnant person. I'll do the running around. Let's just do the work." But she deferred to Bill. She was in love and thought Bill was taking care of her. Whatever the reason, we managed to get through the first two episodes, "The Mummy's Bride" and "Window on Main Street," and then she was gone. It all just blew up.

I tried calling Cindy at home, thinking I could work out the problem. Bill refused to let me speak to her. I ended up not talking to her for years because Bill wouldn't let me. Soon lawyers got involved, allegations flew, and she went to the press, claiming the studio wanted to exclude her from the series or "drastically reduce her participation." She also told *TV Guide*, "What they want to do is axe me out of the show, and finally give it all to Penny."

It was all absurd. As this transpired, I realized that I had to get out of directing *The Joy of Sex*. I couldn't handle developing a movie at the same time the show was blowing up.

I jetted to New York, where I hid out at Lorne's house in Amagansett while the studio negotiated with Cindy. If she wasn't going to do the show, I didn't want to do it, either. It was *Laverne* AND *Shirley*. However, my agent said I had to come back. Mike Ovitz explained that walking out, or in my case, hiding out, was not an option.

"We did enough episodes," I said. "Let's just stop."

"That's not the way it works," he said. "It's not your call."

"I don't want to come back," I said.

"You have to," he said. "They'll sue you."

I flew back and met with Gary Nardino, Paramount's president of TV. I asked for double or nothing. I didn't even go to Ovitz. I said, "Since I'm here and it's *Laverne* AND *Shirley*, I get her money and her points. If she comes back, it reverts. But if I've got to do it alone and explain to the goddamn audience why she ain't here, it's got to be worth more money."

They gave me the money.

I went back to work, but the show was a mess. Although the show's title stayed the same, Shirley was edited out of the opening montage and her absence was explained in a note she left behind saying that she moved suddenly overseas with her husband. I recall the log in the *TV Guide* saying that Laverne was depressed and then angry that Shirley would only write a few words and not say good-bye. I felt the same way in real life. I was depressed, angry, and hurt.

The following week things went from bad to worse. I was injured on the set. In the episode, Laverne takes a job at an aerospace company. Bored, she slips into an antigravity suit. As we shot the big comedic scene, I was in a harness attached to wires and spun all over the room. During rehearsals, my brother and I had a to-do because I didn't wear a helmet. It was hot.

"I don't care," Garry said. "The next time you do it, you put on the damn helmet."

That was at the taping. I did as my brother said. I wore a helmet — and I was lucky I did. As I flew over the stage, one of the wires snapped and I fell to the floor with a thud that just stopped time. Everyone froze. Director Tom Trbovich yelled cut as my driver, Clarence, watching from the wings, raced over to me. I told him not to touch me. I stayed down and assessed the damage. My toes moved. My fingers moved. I was breathing. But my upper body hurt like hell.

Phil Foster was already entertaining the audience, distracting them with jokes that Garry had written for his act twenty-five years earlier. Ironically, my brother wasn't on the set that night. I heard someone say they were going to take me to the hospital. Then I could come back to finish. No, I didn't think so.

Slowly, I got up on one knee and said I wasn't going anywhere. I called the cast together and said I didn't want to come back and do this shit over again. Instead, I showed those who still had scenes with me where they could touch me (my head, the right side of my body) and where they couldn't (my left shoulder, the left side of my body). Then we finished the show. I could've sued, but I didn't want some prop guy to get reamed. Shit happens.

Later, I did go to the hospital. That was funny — trying to explain to the ER doc that I hurt myself while flying across the room in an astronaut suit. Luckily, nothing was broken. I'd heal. I went home, took a Quaalude, and reported to work the next day.

The rest of the season was simply painful. At least I still had my November "out" date from the movie. I wouldn't have to work through March. To get through the remaining episodes, I called friends, including Laraine Newman, Carol Kane, Louise Lasser, Anjelica Houston, Jimmy Belushi, and Larry Breeding, who I'd gone out with for about a month while Artie was off walking God knows where. Carrie also came on; she was a Playboy bunny with me.

We taped that episode (Laverne gets a job as a Playboy bunny) the same week Tracy left for Bennington College. My niece took her; I had to work. I was in a bunny costume as I hugged her good-bye in front of the soundstage. Carrie cracked, "Study hard and one day you can be as successful as your mother."

Finally, after 178 episodes, *Laverne & Shirley* taped its final episode ("Here Today, Hair Tomorrow"). The series went out with a whimper. The last show focused on Carmine (Eddie Mekka). I was barely in it, Michael had left to work with Rob on *This Is Spinal Tap,* and Cindy was long gone. Although lawsuits from her departure made the end more bitter than sweet, the memories from the eight seasons were positive. We had done more good episodes than bad ones and provided millions of people with laughs. I was proud. Between reruns and syndication around the world, I felt confident that *Laverne & Shirley* would always be best friends.

It turned out I was right.

CHAPTER 32

In the Event of My Death

Penny as a baby with Marjorie in the Bronx, 1943

Marshall personal collection

ONE DAY WHEN I WAS in high school, I found three envelopes in my mother's desk. They were addressed to Garry, Ronny, and me, and each one said, "In the Event of My Death." I opened the one for me, of course, and found a typewritten letter from my mother saying that she knew I stole her laundry quarters and used them to go to the movies with Marsha.

I had forgotten about those letters until one day in late December 1983. My brother was in Hawaii. I was in New York for the holiday with Artie and Carrie. Only Ronny was in L.A. She got the call from my parents' housekeeper, who was crying hysterically, "You've got to come! Right now. Hurry."

My mother had passed away. When Ronny got to their house, she saw our mother lying in bed, lifeless. She stood a few feet inside the room not knowing what to do or what to feel, sadness or relief. Dealing with my mother's Alzheimer's had been a challenge. We were fortunate to have the means to do it on our terms. We had moved my parents to a comfortable house in Toluca Lake so my father could be near his country club and my mother near her doctors. When she required specialized care, we put her in a facility. When that made her anxious, we brought her home and got round-the-clock care.

They had a Polish housekeeper who took wonderful care of her. My mother watched television a lot, and as long as she could laugh we felt like she was in a good place. She continued to hate my father until she faded further into the dementia. Then she thought he was her father, and she liked him.

She was aware that we were building a dance theater in her honor at Garry's and my sister's alma mater, Northwestern University. Garry had started the ball rolling in 1980, and we had shown my mother the architect's drawings. Construction took two years, though, and in that time her condition went steadily downhill. Like my brother and sister, I would sit by her bed and talk, reminisce, and give her progress reports on this very nice tribute to her.

Finally, in 1982, the Marjorie Ward Marshall Dance Center was completed. All of us went back for the dedication. We smiled, reminisced, and cried through the whole ceremony, wishing she could have been there with us. In a way, she was.

By then, however, she was in a coma and we knew time was running short. She lingered through the holidays, and that's when Ronny got the call. We had never talked about death or dying when we were growing up. As my mother would have said, it was an unhappy subject. Poor Ronny didn't know what she was supposed to do next. Since I wasn't there, I'll let her describe what happened:

> RONNY: We don't know shit. But I find a letter saying she has left her body to researchers at USC. I call the number on the thing. Well, it's the holiday, so nobody's there. What do I do with the body? I don't know. Meanwhile, Garry's housekeeper Maria is crying hysterically. She called her sister Lupe to come over. They cover the mirrors and are both wailing. I had my kids come over. And Tracy. Then my daughter and Tracy go in the bedroom and fight over my mother's necklace, which I think is a diamond.
>
> I still don't know what to do with her body. I keep calling the number at USC. Someone finally answers, but they transfer me, and then I get another person, a lady whose name was Mrs. De-Witt. I said, "I don't know what to do. She died and left her body to

science, but apparently science is closed for the holiday. What do I do?"

She put me in touch with her son who ran a mortuary. Soon two guys came in a station wagon, put her in the back, and off they went. I didn't get a name or a number. Then a few days later Garry and his family returned from Hawaii and he asked, "Where's Mom?" I didn't know. "Did you get a receipt?" No. "A name of who took her?" No.

Eventually someone called and said USC was open and they had taken her there. I thought that was that, they'd keep her. But a few months later they wrote a letter and said, All right, we're finished with her. Where do you want the remains sent? I had no idea. Now we were back to the same question as before: What do we do with her?

My sister left out a tiny part of the story. Mrs. DeWitt's son ran the Clinton Mortuary. Ronny heard DeWitt and Clinton together and thought it was a good omen since my brother had gone to DeWitt Clinton High School. I don't know. People make strange connections under stress.

We had my mother cremated and hosted a small service for family and friends. My brother scattered some of her ashes at the Marjorie Ward Marshall Dance Center at Northwestern, which was nice, and my father put some of her ashes in their front yard among the roses, which, as he knew, my mother hated.

That left one last request. Many years before she had let us know that she wanted her ashes thrown out over Broadway. I volunteered. I flew to New York with Tracy and my brother sent a candy tin to Artie's containing the ashes in a Ziploc baggie. Then Tracy and I went up to Lorne Michaels' seventeenth-floor office overlooking Broadway. I opened the window and removed the tin from my purse.

It was a chilly day out, as I recall. I felt a slight but steady wind as I stuck my hand out to gauge the direction my mother was going to blow. What did I know? I didn't want her blowing back at me or into

Lorne's office. And how was I supposed to do this? All at once? Little by little?

I grew sentimental about her life and the life she had given all of us, including me, the accident, the bad seed. I thought about the letter she had written me way back when, the one addressed "In the Event of My Death." She had known about the quarters I stole. I'm sure she had known much more than that about me. She was nuts. But she was also something else.

After a deep breath, I shook the baggie in the open air and watched as the ashes swirled in the sky over Broadway. It struck me that, once again, she was dancing. I turned to Tracy, then back toward the sky, and all of a sudden I felt the need to say something. I wanted to say good-bye to this quirky woman whose creativity and passion had brought joy to so many lives, including mine. But what was there to say?

She had wanted to entertain and she had been very entertaining. Then the ashes were gone. The dance was done. And you know what? At that moment the words came to me. My mother had written a song that we sang at the end of every recital, and this was the end of her show. So there in Lorne's office, as I dumped her ashes into the sky over Broadway, I sang the song again:

> *Remember the fun we had friends*
> *Remember the singers sweet*
> *Remember the dainty dancers*
> *And don't forget*
> *though we'll never meet*
> *That we like to entertain you*
> *And now that we are through*
> *We hope you'll remember us, friends*
> *As we will remember you.*
> — MARJORIE MARSHALL'S DANCE REVIEW

CHAPTER 33

Peggy Sue Blues

Art Garfunkel and Penny on vacation in Barbados

Carrie Fisher / Tracy Reiner

*I*T HAD BEEN ONE of those years. Tracy had dropped out of Bennington, fallen in love with Francis Ford Coppola's son, Gio, and run off to Europe with him. (Francis sent books, I sent money.) I finally bought a house of my own, a probate in the Hollywood Hills that Jim Belushi and Tracy's ex–musician boyfriend, Jonathan Melvoin, lived in while the wallpaper was taken off, new floors put in, and other work done.

I spent a week or so in London visiting director Miloš Forman, who was prepping his movie *Amadeus*. We had sat next to each other at an event in New York for dancer Mikhail Baryshnikov and choreographer Twyla Tharp. I thought he was funny, and he'd never heard of *Laverne & Shirley*. Once in London, I decided to quit smoking. It didn't make me the greatest houseguest. Miloš said, "Why don't you visit someone you hate?"

Well, I joined Artie on the Simon and Garfunkel tour in Australia and New Zealand. Jimmy and Jonathan sent me a postcard there: "Roses are red, violets are blue, wish you were here, glad you are not!" I dropped ecstasy in St. Bart's, rented a house for the summer in the Hamptons, drifted away from Artie, enjoyed a lovely relationship with *Saturday Night Live* bandleader Howard Shore (he bought me a bike and suggested I get healthy), and then I sort of got back together with Artie (but not really).

Paul and Carrie also got married, and I sailed up the Nile in Egypt with them on their honeymoon. And that was all before my mother died. Then, after saying good-bye to her, I stayed in New York, where my plans to do absolutely nothing for a while were interrupted by Lorne. He asked me to be on his new comedy series, *The New Show*. He asked everyone: Steve Martin, Gilda, Carrie, Buck Henry, John Candy. All of us said yes. No one refused Lorne.

Booked on the third show, I appeared in skits with Raul Julia and Randy Newman, who was also the musical guest. I also danced with the Dynamic Breakers, a group of street dancers, and surprised people with some unexpectedly slick moves, including kick-throughs, the Worm, and a head spin. At forty-one years old, I still had a lot of kid inside me.

I went home to L.A. where I still had a ton of work yet to do on my new house. Tracy helped me unpack the boxes that had been in storage since we had moved out of Encino. I puttered around. I loved the views that stretched from downtown L.A. to the ocean. But as I put down roots, I found myself asking an unfamiliar question: "Now what?"

Randy Newman, knowing I was best when I was busy, pushed me to work with John Ritter in the TV movie *Love Thy Neighbor*. "You should do *something*," he said. "John is funny." Suddenly Randy was my guidance counselor. As things turned out, though, I needed more advice than he could provide.

In March, producer Larry Gordon called and asked me to go to the Academy Awards with him. He had produced *Terms of Endearment* with Jim, and he needed a date for Hollywood's biggest night. I accepted. I had visited Jim on the set of *Terms*. Even though I can't think of anything more boring than being on someone else's set, I was interested in watching Jim work. It was his first movie, and he was on his game. I knew that I'd learn something.

At night we went to Jack Nicholson's, and Debra Winger was there.

Jack was always entertaining. After a few hours, some cheerleaders for the Houston Rockets basketball team came over, which pissed off Debra, who in turn pissed off Jack, and it ended as one of those nights.

Terms of Endearment dominated the Academy Awards, winning five Oscars, including Jack for Best Actor, Shirley for Best Actress, and Jim for Best Director, Best Picture, and Best Adapted Screenplay. It was extraordinary and well deserved, especially for Jim. Later, following the Governor's Ball, I went to a party at On the Rox, the private club above the Roxy on Sunset, and I saw Debra there. She had been nominated for Best Supporting Actress but didn't win. Others from *Terms* had also been nominated and not won, including John Lithgow and Polly Platt. But you're only human, you know?

I sat down with Debra, knowing she must have felt like shit, and we talked and smoked for what seemed like the rest of the night. She told me about the next movie she was going to make, a romance called *Peggy Sue Got Married.* Somehow I had already read the script about this woman who goes back in time and falls in love with her husband again. I liked movies with themes that gave them universal appeal like *Peggy Sue*'s main question: "If only I could go back in time, would I do the same things?" People could easily identify with those kind of stories.

"Why don't you direct it?" Debra said.

Her question surprised me.

"I don't direct," I said.

"Well, maybe you will," she said.

Debra went to Ray Stark, whose company was producing the movie, and said she wanted me to direct. They were a group of hard-nosed movie veterans with their own definite views, but because they wanted Debra, they agreed to let me direct. But make no mistake about it, they never wanted me. Unfortunately I was too unsophisticated about the business to know that.

I started to work up ideas. I got out pictures from my junior high reunion and compared them to those in the yearbook. Some people looked similar. Others were totally different. I entertained the idea of double casting to make the stars stand out even more. I spoke to Tom Hanks and Sean Penn. I had access to practically everyone thanks to the joint birthday parties that Carrie and I had started to host a few years earlier. We had done two or three of them by this time and they quickly became A-list events.

I also had deep contacts with the people who worked behind the camera. I spoke with Oscar-winning cinematographer Gordon Wills, who was shooting *Perfect*. I'd heard he sometimes took over for the director, which was fine by me. I was going to need help. I also talked to production designer Dean Tavoularis, whom I knew through Francis. He'd won an Oscar for *The Godfather II* and received four other nominations. Not too shabby.

Like a coach, I began to put together a team, and as I did a vision began to emerge. I read the script with actors and met with the writers. Debra was there with her dog, who she loved very much. I remember they kissed each other and were very affectionate. I don't ask.

But three weeks into pre-production I was summoned to a meeting with the producers at the studio. I had no idea why, and it turned into an unfriendly inquisition. I was completely unprepared for such a turn. It was like being in front of the KGB. Did you talk to Dean? Did you talk to Gordon? Did you have a meeting with so-and-so? Did you let Debra kiss her dog? The questions went on and on. I felt like I was being accused of a crime. I had no idea what was happening.

I was officially fired a few days later. I met Howard Koch at his office. He was a large man with a long face and silver hair combed to the side. He got straight to the point. They thought the movie was too big for a first-time director. They would find me another movie, he said. Something family-friendly, like *Annie*.

I didn't want another movie. "You knew I was a first-time director three weeks ago," I said. "What changed?"

I went home and retreated to my bedroom. David Geffen and a few other influential friends called on my behalf. My brother sat on the edge of my bed and tried to cheer me up, but as he said, "There's nothing to cheer about. I can't even say you'll get even. You were fired."

I did get paid, though I didn't understand why. "I didn't do anything," I told my brother's partner, Jerry Belson.

He told me to stop complaining. "That's my dream in show business," he said. "To get hired, fired, and paid for doing nothing."

In the aftermath Debra Winger dropped out, Kathleen Turner stepped in, and Francis Ford Coppola took over and used Dean Tavoularis as his production designer after I'd been given the third degree for merely talking to him.

"What happened?" Francis asked later.

"I don't know," I said.

And I didn't.

The whole thing just hurt.

At the end of December, I went to see *A Passage to India* with Jack Nicholson and Anjelica Huston. The state of California had just passed a law prohibiting smoking in movie theaters. Jack and I smoked anyway.

Jack and Anjelica and I decided we wanted to have a New Year's party. None of us, it turned out, had plans, though actually organizing it was a careful negotiation as we were all a little territorial. Jack wanted it at his house, Anjelica wanted it at hers, and I wanted it at mine.

Finally, Jack got producer Lou Adler to open his Sunset Strip nightclub, On the Rox, and we had a party there.

It quickly became *the* party. Jim Brooks, Deborah Winters, Warren Beatty, Debra Winger, Harry Dean Stanton, Tim Hutton ... everyone came. I was surprised at how many famous people had nothing to do on New Year's. We stayed up late and then a bunch of us went to Canter's deli in the morning for breakfast. As I recall, Sean Penn and I were the last to get dropped off there.

My New Year's resolution was to get out of town. I needed a new backdrop, a change of scenery. I found a willing accomplice in Joe Pesci. I knew Joe through Robert De Niro, whom I'd met years earlier in Hawaii when I was with Rob. Joe had come to Carrie's and my birthday parties. He was living in the Mayflower Hotel in New York but needed to be in L.A. for a movie. It was perfect. We swapped places — sort of. He ended up staying at my house for three years.

I'm serious. He overlapped with Jim Belushi. My niece Penny Lee also lived there. Others camped out, too. One morning she walked into the kitchen and found Joe and ballet great Mikhail Baryshnikov eating breakfast. Baryshnikov made her eggs. Once, Joe called to tell me the toilet was broken. I said, "Are your fingers broken? Call someone to get it fixed." I think that's when he began to think of it as his house. He still does.

He wasn't alone. At another point, Louise Lasser and Michael O'Donoghue occupied different guest rooms. Michael and Mitch Glaser wrote the Bill Murray movie *Scrooged* there. Friends knew my door was always open.

New York turned out to be the refresher I wanted. I did a reading of *Eden Court,* a light comedy about two couples living in a trailer park. Melanie Griffith, John Goodman, and Guy Boyd were already committed to the Off-Broadway production, with Barnet Kellman as the director. Following the reading, they asked me to be in it, too, and I said sure, why not? I hadn't done a play since I lived in Albuquerque. I thought it would be fun to work in front of an audience and be around people who stayed up late and smoked, like me.

Before rehearsals started, though, Melanie got pregnant and dropped out, and John jumped ship to the Broadway musical *Big River.* Ben Masters replaced John, and Ellen Barkin stepped in for Melanie. As we got ready for previews, the play's author, Murphy

Guyer, hated one of us each week. The play was at the Promenade Theater on the Upper West Side. I was excited about getting in front of an audience. Having come from three cameras, I knew the audience would tell you whether the material worked and exactly where the problems were. You didn't need tons of previews; all you had to do was listen the first night.

I liked hanging out in the theater. I was reminded of my days with the Civic Light Opera in Albuquerque. Developing the piece onstage exercised new muscles and let me apply the experience I had in a new way. Since I wasn't in the opening scene, I would listen from the dressing room and tell Ellen where she was walking through her laughs. "That's a joke," I said. "Let the audience laugh. Take the butter dish, put it in the refrigerator, and then go on to the next." She has credited me for teaching her comedy.

My own entrance was a challenge that I worked on. I came in from nowhere, with no warning, and had to get the audience's attention without angering them, as I went into a long speech. I played it as if I were out of breath and struggled to get the words out. "You're not going to believe . . . what happened . . ." Gradually, I crossed over to Ellen and, as I did, I brought the theater with me. Later, Ellen told me that she hadn't ever seen a performer direct an audience like that. She hadn't spent eight years doing a three-camera sitcom.

The *New York Times* critic Frank Rich singled out Ellen's performance ("If it were possible to give the kiss of life to a corpse, the actress Ellen Barkin would be the one to do it") and praised the rest of us, including Barnet's direction. The problem, he said, was with the script. I knew that was the case. During previews, I had brought in friends to help fix it — Jim Brooks, my brother, everyone in the world. I was like, *Why do you think they call Neil* Doc *Simon? If something doesn't work, you fix it.* But the writer wouldn't change a word.

In the meantime, I starred in an off-stage drama of my own. Backstage one afternoon, Ellen noticed that my breasts were larger and my clothes seemed more snug. "Are you pregnant?" she asked. It turned out I was. I hadn't been thinking about it because I wasn't with anyone at the time. I thought it might be Artie's, but I wasn't seeing him anymore. It must have been Immaculate Conception, I told myself. I didn't know what to do.

What I did was talk to everyone who I trusted or who might have been involved. Those who had children said, "You did it already." Others pointed out that I could afford to raise another child. Money wasn't the point. I barely had five dollars when Tracy was born. I debated the issues. Did I want Artie in my life forever? Did he want a child? Did I want a child? Would I be able to live with myself if I didn't have the baby?

Joe Pesci touched me by offering to be the child's father. As much as I loved Joe, I said no thanks. I sat with my brother and his wife Barbara and made a list of pros and cons. I asked my daughter, who confessed to some experiences of her own that I didn't know anything about. I was shocked. But it didn't sway me one way or another.

Ultimately, we all live our own lives and make decisions based on many factors, including whether we can live with them, right or wrong. Who knows what's right or wrong? There's no one-size-fits-all answer. It comes down to the individual. I had never had an abortion, and I didn't want to be that person who did. But . . . I just didn't know until I had to know.

The play didn't run that much longer. After it closed, I decided to terminate the pregnancy. I did it with a heavy heart. My friend Carol took me. My shrink, who I'd also been talking to, came with us. I was the one person who always said I hadn't had an abortion, and then I was one of those people. It's the one thing I've regretted most. It fit that difficult time of my life. I guess everyone goes through a blue period. This was mine.

CHAPTER 34

Jumpin' Jack Flash

Penny providing direction to star Whoopi Goldberg on the set of
Jumpin' Jack Flash in 1986

RECOVERY TOOK LONGER emotionally than physically. Strangely, I found comfort being in New York and decided I should get a place of my own there. I looked on Central Park West, but I didn't want to pay a fortune to press my nose against a window when I wanted to look out. As I scoured the upper West Side, I crossed paths with Debra Winger on the block where she was filming her new movie *Legal Eagles*. A few days later, I bumped into Whoopi Goldberg, who had just started production on *Jumpin' Jack Flash*.

It was her birthday, in fact, and she invited me to have dinner with her that night. It felt good to reconnect with these smart women.

In between seeing both of them, I found an apartment on West End Avenue with a large terrace. My brother happened to be in town, and I asked for his opinion. Although not crazy about heights, he gave his blessing and said, "Congratulations. You're one of the first people I know who's bicoastal."

I put a down payment on it immediately and went back to L.A. to get warm clothes. I had high hopes for spending winter in the city and began thinking about how I wanted to furnish my new place.

Then those plans changed unexpectedly. While in L.A., I received a call from producers Larry Gordon and Joel Silver. *Jumpin' Jack Flash* was their movie. Somehow they'd heard that I'd had dinner with Whoopi. They had just parted ways with the movie's creative team, including the director, Howard Zieff. They wanted me to take over.

"We're already shooting," Joel said.

"But we can't shut down for pre-production," Larry said.

I didn't understand what pre-production was. It sounded to me like I'd be cutting a class. But why did they want me? That was the real question. I figured it was likely because they knew that I was a reliable human being *and* I got along with Whoopi. I guessed that was a short list.

"Can I read the script?" I asked.

"What do you need to do that for?" Joel said jokingly.

There were forty thousand versions of the script, including the Nancy Meyer and Charles Shyer version originally written for Shelley Long, and also one from David Mamet where everything was fuck or motherfucker. But I liked the basic story about a woman (Terry Dolittle) who was bored at work. She was too smart for her job. Then one day a guy hacks into her computer. He needs her help, and everything changes. Suddenly her life is on the line.

As I told people at the time, I had responded to the script starting at that moment when the guy says, "I'm in trouble. I need you." Joel had called me out of the blue and asked for help. I said yes, and my life changed.

Whether or not I should do it was another question. And could I do it? That was a more pertinent question. I didn't think so. I knew three cameras, not one camera. But my brother said, "It's a strange business. They pay you to learn. Just don't fall down. And finish." Jim Brooks said, "It's not your movie, so it doesn't matter. Finish it, you're a hero. If it fails, it's not your fault." Finally, Steven Spielberg added, "Do it — and remember to take the lens cap off to camera."

It was a Thursday when I called Larry and Joel back and said I'd do it. The next day I met with director of photography Matt Leonetti and asked if he had anything against first-time directors or a problem working with a female director. After he said no to both questions, I whimpered, "Will you please help me?" We hugged and then spent the rest of the weekend blocking out shots. He drew the scenes on pieces of paper and showed me where the cameras went. It was like taking a graduate-level filmmaking course in three days. We kept that process going throughout the whole picture.

They moved the production from New York to L.A., and shooting began on Monday. On day one, I realized that directing, as I always say, was a dog's job. I arrived on the set at 5 a.m. — not my best time of day. My hair was a mess, and my eyes were red and tired. Before anything I gathered the crew — they were predominantly male and all experienced — and introduced myself. I let them know how I was feeling and where I stood.

"I need your help, and I'm open to suggestions," I said. "I ask only one thing. When I make mistakes — and I will make them — please don't go behind my back and make faces. Just come up and tell me."

The first scene I shot was of the Russian exercise instructor who shows up on Terry's computer screen. Bodybuilder Teagan Clive played the overbuilt Soviet fitness chick with the large shoulders and the nick on her leg. It was simple, and we made it up on the spot. I added a janitor in the background just to give the scene some additional business. The next scene was Whoopi walking down an alley, searching the garbage for a frying pan.

Whoopi was already in a cranky mood for any number of reasons, not the least of which was that she had a new director who had never directed, never mind that I came from TV. But that was her problem. I had my own. Things moved so slowly I thought I'd die. I mean it was the slowest fucking medium I'd seen in my life. They had to light, and they had to get the master, and then they had to go sideways, and then this way and that way. I thought, *Kill me now.*

On the second day, Whoopi pulled me into the makeup trailer. I guess she didn't want to look at me the way I looked at that hour. I appreciated the gesture. But Joel walked in a few minutes later, looking for me, and asked what the fuck I was doing there.

"I'm getting made up," I said.

"You're the director," he said.

"I can still look good," I said.

One of the smartest things I did was to call everyone I knew and ask if they wanted to be in a movie. I brought in Jon Lovitz, Phil Hartman, Lynn Marie Stewart, Carol Kane, Jim Belushi, and my brother, who played a detective. I cast my daughter, Tracy, as the boss's assistant. Movies are only written for the two people talking to each other, but you need other things going on, especially in a film like *Jumpin' Jack Flash*, which took place mostly in this one big office in the bank. Things have to happen to keep it interesting, and I knew my friends could improvise and say something funny.

And they did. Lovitz was brilliant in the opening scene. His ad-libbed chatter gave Whoopi and Carol Kane something to play off of. Phil Hartman did the same, chiming in as soon as the Russian exerciser appears on Terry's screen. Suddenly, there was a whole world of interesting personalities. It's like real life. It makes you want to watch. I kept adding friends, too. One day I called Michael McKean. I needed him to move Whoopi to her mark sometimes. Tracey Ullman, who was pregnant, also came in for that scene and played his wife.

I had learned how vital this is from my brother's first movie, *Young Doctors in Love*. In it, he has a scene with two doctors talking about a diagnosis. A phone rings in the background. A midget answers it, says, "No, he's not here," but then can't hang up the phone. And the whole scene becomes about his effort to hang up the phone. It's a masterful bit of business.

We needed that because Whoopi, who is mesmerizing to look at and holds the screen every time she appears, had done her dog-and-pony show for eight million writers, and so she was a little fed up with the whole deal. Matters weren't helped when *The Color Purple* opened during the middle of production and she became the toast of the town. The last thing the poor woman wanted to do was get up at 5 a.m. when the whole world was inviting her to parties at night.

I understood, and she knew I understood, and I knew she knew. Nonetheless, one day her frustration boiled over and she said, "Do you know what it's like doing something stupid over and over again?" Then she caught herself. "I'm sorry. I forgot who I was talking to," she said. "Of course you know what it's like."

All her lines were written on the computer, but some days she was cranky and in the afternoons she was a little crankier. As a result, I hired my poor niece Penny Lee to write down every line Whoopi said and then watch the dailies and count how many motherfuckers, assholes, shits, and fucks she said. I had to know where I could cut to ensure the final version had the least cursing.

We shot and rewrote and shot as we went along. Every day was a battle with someone or something. That's why I always say directing is a dog's job. I would ask myself, *How did I get here?* My brother called every week to offer encouragement. "You're still standing! That's good." Jim Brooks also came over. Even Rob took time out from making *Stand By Me* to visit the set. And Scott Rudin, who worked with Joel then, was also a support. The two of them and Larry used to bring deli food to my house on Saturdays, and we would eat and talk about the movie. I liked Scott, because he was the only one who read books or saw plays.

My days lasted twenty hours, and it was all I could do to keep up. We were doing a night shoot in San Pedro with actor Jeroen Krabbé, who flew into town from Belgium for his part as the spy Mark Van Meter. I had never met him or laid eyes on him, for that matter. He had been cast before I was brought on. When Jeroen arrived on the set, it was a chilly night and I was wearing a raccoon hat with flaps covering my ears and face. I said, "Hello, do you speak English?"

I had no idea. That's how it went sometimes. I trusted the crew to tell me what was funny. They were invaluable. Joel Silver came down periodically and yelled at them, which most of them, having worked with him before, were used to. He did action pictures. He wanted tons of explosions. He thought the movie ended when they shot up the office. I have to say, that part didn't make sense to me. Why would they create such a spectacle when they were spies?

As far as I was concerned, Whoopi's character had to meet Jack. That was the end of the movie. I cast Jonathan Pryce, a great actor, as Jack. He'd been doing Chekhov in London. He had only two lines onscreen (he had voiceovers through the whole movie). But I had to have someone who was believable. However, in terms of actual shooting, we finished with the scene where the cab crashed. Literally. The crash broke the A camera. I heard Matt say, "Well, that's a hun-dred-thousand-dollar shot." Joel wanted one more shot of Whoopi crawling over a roof. She refused. She hit him and walked off the set. So it was a wrap—an anticlimactic wrap. I guess I'm big with anticlimactic wraps.

CHAPTER 35

Keeping Things in Perspective

Garry, Penny, Stephen Collins, and Whoopi on the set of *Jumpin' Jack Flash*

AVING SPENT MONTHS piecing together different versions of the script and being told that I had way more than I needed, I didn't know what to expect when I watched the first cut of the movie. Honestly, it was quite good. I was impressed. It was a movie. But it was an action movie with *North by Northwest* music cut in. It didn't have the heart that I wanted. I like films to have a little heart.

I had the material to make the kinds of changes I wanted and when the original editor moved onto another picture, I took that as an opportunity to bring in Jim's editor, Richard Marks, as well as George Bowers. We talked it through, and they gave me a cut that I liked better. But even then I knew we still needed some pickups, or "wild lines," and a reshoot of a key scene toward the end. I also thought we might need some pickups in New York City as well.

I arranged to show the picture to Barry Diller, then the chairman of Fox, because I was going to need money for the reshoot and ultimately he had to give the OK. Why not go directly to him? I also called Tracy's ex-boyfriend, Gio Coppola, and asked if he might be able to shoot for me in Manhattan. He and Tracy had broken up, but they were still close even though he was with Tracy's good friend, Jacqui De La Fontaine, an aspiring fashion designer who had lived with us at Gore's house. It was a soap opera.

Tracy was the one who told me that Gio was in the D.C. area, working on his father's film, *Gardens of Stone.* He'd called her recently and said that Jacqui was pregnant. Tracy was pissed at Jacqui for doing that. But Gio sounded enthusiastic the night I spoke with him. He was glad to hear from me, said things were going well for him on *Gardens,* and he was available to shoot in New York. Whatever I needed, he said. Just let him know.

The next day Tracy and I were in the kitchen. I was at the table while she got dinner ready. The phone rang. It was Sofia Coppola, and she was in tears.

"What's the matter, honey?" I asked.

"My mother's at the store," she said, "and they just called and said my brother—"

"Which brother?" I asked, already knowing that something terrible had happened.

"Gio," she said, before breaking down again.

"What happened?" I asked. "What's the matter with him?"

Between hysterical sobs, she told me that Gio had been killed in a boating accident in Annapolis. My heart dropped into the bottom of my stomach. They were still gathering details, she said, but he had been riding with actor Griffin O'Neal in a speedboat on the South River. Jacqui was waiting for them at the dock. They were having typical Memorial Day weekend fun until Griffin steered their boat between two others that had been connected with a rope. He ducked at the last minute, but Gio didn't see it and he died instantly.

I tried to calm Sofia down. I heard her mom, Ellie, come home. Then I hung up.

I stared at Tracy. I didn't know how to tell her. After I did, she went into shock. It was terrible—as terrible as terrible gets. The phone rang for days, and we debated whether Tracy should go to the funeral. Would it be awkward since she was Gio's ex-girlfriend? Would she feel like the other woman considering her friend was two months pregnant with his child? Would she be angry with herself if she didn't go and say good-bye to her friend?

Luckily, Anjelica Huston was also in *Gardens of Stone* and I knew her well enough to ask a favor. She went to the funeral and took care of Tracy.

Like my daughter, we all needed time to get over that tragedy. I ended up not needing a reshoot in New York, but Gio stayed in my thoughts and I thanked him in the credits. I did reshoot a scene in downtown L.A., the one with Whoopi being dragged in the phone booth. I also brought Jimmy Belushi back to life for that scene. He'd been killed earlier. I put a bandage on his head and said, "You're alive. Here are your lines."

If only real life were like the movies sometimes.

In October, the movie opened to mixed reviews and what I was told was mediocre box office. However, I didn't follow the box office. I didn't understand the poster, either. It said Whoopi saves the world. Her name was Terry Dolittle. It was confusing. I also thought the promo was wrong. But I didn't beat myself up. I didn't care what was said in the papers. I'd come on the movie at the last minute with no previous experience and finished the movie — and it had some good parts. To me, it was a success. You have to keep things in perspective.

CHAPTER 36

Getting Street Cred

Penny with Robert De Niro, who was in line to play
the starring role in *Big*

Marshall personal collection

*J*IM BROOKS AND I both had offices on the Fox lot and one day while I was in post-production on *Jumpin' Jack Flash* he came into my office and put a script on my desk. "This is your next movie," he said.

It was *Big*.

What he didn't tell me was that everyone in the world had turned it down. From Chuck Shyer to Steven Spielberg. Because I didn't read the trades or follow the business, I had no idea. Nor did I know there were three similar movies in the works: *Like Father, Like Son; Vice Versa;* and an Italian version.

But Jim was a mentor and friend. He knew that I had liked directing and making things up. He also knew that I wanted to do it again. I was grateful for his help because I probably wouldn't have known how to look for a project on my own. Luckily I didn't have to.

He had developed *Big* with writers Gary Ross and Anne Spielberg, Steven's sister. Steven had briefly thought of making it with Harrison Ford in the lead. But the project had been sitting on Jim's desk. I read the draft and liked the story. Twelve-year-old Josh Baskin can't get the girl he likes; she's interested in an older boy who can drive. He wishes he were bigger and wakes up the next morning as a thirty-year-old. He gets a job at FAO Schwarz, rises up the corporate ladder, and becomes the object of affection of a beautiful executive. It was a theme that everyone could identify with: *When I'm big I'm gonna . . .*

To make the high concept work, I wanted it to be real and believable. The biggest challenge would be casting the lead. I didn't have the luxury of pre-production in *Jumpin' Jack Flash* and now that I did, I wanted to get it right. I went straight to the three big box-office stars at the time: Tom Hanks, Kevin Costner, and Dennis Quaid. All of them passed. Everyone passed.

I tried a different approach. I looked for the kid who would be Josh's best friend, and I picked Jared Rushton. He had the most spunk of those I saw. He worked well as I brought in actors, including Sean Penn, who was terrific but too young, and Andy Garcia, who was also great, though one of the studio executives said, "We don't want to spend eighteen million on a kid who grows up to be Puerto Rican."

That was how they talked.

"He's Cuban," I said.

I also read Gary Busey, who had the energy of a child, but I didn't think he could pull off playing an adult. John Travolta was dying to do it, but at the time he was box office poison and the studio didn't want him. I started to get worried. Despite not having a lead actor, we were in pre-production in New York. I met with Robert Greenhut, one of our executive producers. This was our first film together. He was a slick line producer who had come up through the ranks and done all of Woody Allen's films.

I had an idea and asked him to think about working on a rewrite of a couple scenes. In TV, all the producers wrote. I assumed he did, too. He set me straight. He didn't write; he managed the production. I apologized, explaining that I was still learning about movies. But he still had excellent ideas, and he turned into an ally and confidant when I decided to take my search for a lead actor in a different direction.

I went to Robert De Niro. Bobby—or Bobby D. as I called him—was in the middle of making *The Untouchables*, playing Al Capone. Although I knew he didn't ordinarily read other material when he was in the middle of a project, I called him anyway. That's where I'm not at all shy or hesitant. I will call anyone. What's the worst they can say?

"Bobby, there's a script," I said. "I want you to read it, see if you like it."

I got him the material and called him back.

"Did you read it?"

"Yeah."

"What do you think?

"I like it."

It turned out that he wanted to make a commercial film. He had done all of Marty Scorsese's movies, but hadn't broken out in a film the whole family could watch. I told Jim and Scott Rudin, who was running production at the studio, that De Niro was interested. They were surprised and somewhat intrigued. They were also skeptical. Besides having a hard time envisioning him in the role, they'd heard stories about him. They told me to get him to commit. The way they said it was like a challenge.

I called Bobby.

"What do I tell them when they ask me?" I asked. "Do you want to do it or not? I've got to give them an answer."

"Yeah, tell them I'll do it," he said.

I hung up.

I had Bobby.

I told Jim and Scott, and I guess word spread. The next day I flew to Los Angeles to go to an event celebrating Paramount's seventy-fifth anniversary and posed for a photo with everyone who ever worked at the studio. Word had spread about Bobby D. and a handful of actors who had turned me down, including Kevin Costner, now asked about *Big*. Bobby had given me validity.

As work began on the script, Bobby told me to look at his movies and tell him what I wanted and didn't want. What I wanted was the energy he had in *Mean Streets* in the scene when he was first in the bar and coming out around the car. That's exactly what I got when he came to my house one day. I got him on tape with Jared. They skateboarded, shot baskets, and rode bicycles in my driveway. Bobby doesn't give you much until the cameras are on. Jared yelled, "Come on, De Niro. Move it!"

As word got out, actresses called to read with him. It was exciting. I didn't know exactly where the process was leading, in terms of the script, but it was moving in a good direction. I would have paid to see Bobby dance on piano keys.

Barry didn't want Bobby, though. I said, "Counter me." He said, "How about Warren Beatty?" To me, Warren was the same as De Niro, but different. He had already done something similar in *Heaven Can Wait*. But the two of us had dinner in New York and then we went up to my apartment. I asked if he would listen to me if I directed him. In the nicest way, he said no.

Well, that was thrilling. Why bother?

At least Warren was being honest. That's all I ever ask. Just tell me the truth. I'll deal with it. But I can't deal unless I know the truth.

Bobby was taken aback when I told him the studio had wanted me to meet with Warren. It's never easy to hear that you aren't someone's top choice, even at his level. But that was only a small part of what became an even bigger problem. An article came out in the papers about how much money Chevy Chase, John Candy, and other people were paid for movies, and all were getting a hell of a lot more than Fox was going to pay Bobby.

To be blunt, they were going to pay him shit and they weren't budging. They just didn't want him. Jim Brooks suggested I give Bobby my salary. I offered. Bobby didn't want it.

"We're working together," he said. "You and me, you know? I'll take Jim's."

However, he had second thoughts and called the next day. Apologetic, he explained he couldn't do the movie anymore. He'd be too angry. I understood. But now I was back to square one. Sort of.

CHAPTER 37

Heart and Soul

The cast and crew of *Big* celebrated when the movie grossed over $100 million. Left to right: Rita Wilson and Tom Hanks, Tracy, Penny, Sarah Colleton, and Jim and Holly Brooks.

Marshall personal collection

OTH TOM HANKS AND Jeff Bridges now wanted to be in *Big*. It was a nice problem to have. Tom was making *Dragnet*, and Jeff had done *Starman*, which I thought had the same kind of innocence I needed in *Big*. It came down to choosing between them, and I went with my gut. I decided to wait for Tom.

I had known Tom for years and we'd always liked each other. He was one of the nicest guys in the business. I felt good about the decision. When we finally met about *Big*, I asked with raised eyebrows what he'd been doing with Danny Aykroyd in *Dragnet*, and he said, "Having fun." As for playing Josh, he asked whether I wanted *The Nutty Professor* or *Being There*, and I said the latter. The movie was high concept, but in order to for it to work it had to be played with total honesty.

As we waited for Tom, casting director Juliet Taylor worked on filling out the movie's other parts. She brought in the world. I read them all. In fact, I was reading actresses for the part that went to Elizabeth Perkins when I saw John Heard waiting for his girlfriend to read. I asked if he would come in and read with her. I don't like to read with people; I'm not the character. He did, and he made me laugh more than anyone. I gave him the part.

When Tom was finally available, I heard from Bobby again. He had changed his mind and wanted to do the movie. Apologetic, I told him that we'd moved forward. By then Tom was reading with actresses for the part of Josh's mother, which went to Mercedes Ruehl. I remember telling her not to go in the sun. So what'd she do? She went in the sun. One day on the set, someone said, "Who's that Puerto Rican?" Well, that's Josh's Cliffside Park, New Jersey, mother.

As for the young Josh, I liked David Moscow. And once he was signed, I taped him doing all of Tom's scenes with the older actors so that Tom could use them as a guide for how an actual twelve-year-old boy would look and move and talk.

We shot in New Jersey and New York. Once production began, I developed a good rhythm with Tom. In his early thirties, he was confident, but still full of the eagerness of a young actor determined to own the part. I asked him to play innocent and shy but with a youthful energy. It was a challenge because the movie's high concept had to be honest, and there wasn't much variation in the script. Josh was either scared, happy, or confused.

I knew what it was like for an actor to find the right note, and I enjoyed watching Tom's process. He would try everything in rehearsals. "Just let me get it out of my system," he'd say. I'd wait him out. What's good about Tom, though, is that he's quick. We developed a shorthand. When I said "insh" — my own word — he knew it meant "be innocent and shy." All I needed to do was give him a word or a gesture and he'd run with it.

This was the first movie where I wore a headset so I could hear the actors through the sound system, and after certain takes I'd make little noises, depending on how they did. I wasn't aware of it. Then I must have groaned one too many times, and Tom finally said, "Penny, we can hear you." It didn't inhibit his performance. For the movie to work, he had to hit exactly the right note from the moment the audience first saw him as Josh waking up in the body of a thirty-year-old — and he nailed it.

We labored over the sequence following his transformation when he hides from his mother, checks himself out in the bathroom mirror, and takes clothes from his father's closet. It was key since the audience already knew Josh as a normal twelve-year-old boy, and Tom got better and better the more he did it. When he flees the house on his stingray bicycle, a grown up on a kid's bike, there's no doubt that he's Josh. The buy-in was complete.

I jokingly began referring to Tom as "Popo the Mute Boy" — or just "Popo" for short. It was because he was playing a kid and didn't drive any of the scenes as an adult would. He reacted to things. Luckily Tom has a terrific sense of humor, especially about himself, and didn't mind being Popo. But that lightness was part of the process. I think the secret to getting all that right was that we let ourselves play. I let Tom play. I let myself play, too. We always gave ourselves those precious five more minutes. It wouldn't have happened otherwise. Tom had to find the kid in him and let that out rather than simply act like a kid.

You can see that clearly in the scene at the office Christmas party. The table is full of adult food, including caviar, which Josh/Tom tries and spits out while coughing, sounding like a cat with something in its throat. That was in the script. But we did fifteen other bits. Tom put olives on each finger. He licked cream cheese out of celery. He *played* with the food. At one point, I spotted some baby corn in a salad on the prop table. I picked it up and mimed to Tom. He gave me a thumbs-up and knew exactly what to do.

I lacked the same shorthand with my director of photography, Barry Sonnenfeld. Talented and opinionated, he had worked with the Coen brothers on their stylized film *Blood Simple* and he wanted to shoot *Big* from similar angles. Movies bring together dozens of strong-willed people with a sense of how they want to make the film and every day is a collaborative effort. But at the end of the day, only one person is in charge, and that was me. Despite Barry's best intentions, I wanted the movie shot straight on and close up. The party scene was a good example. Barry didn't want to go in close when Tom ate the baby corn.

"You have to be in at least waist high," I said.

"I'm not going in," he said.

"It's too wide," I said.

"I disagree," he said.

I thought he was more interested in impressing the studio with his shot.

"Well, I'll do an insert of him picking up a piece of corn," he said. "Would you rather that?"

In the end, he went in, and the bit got a laugh as big as, if not bigger than, when Tom spit out the caviar. I don't want to be surrounded by people who only say yes. A good, healthy discussion creates new ways of looking at a scene or confirms initial thoughts, as it did in this case. As I told Barry, I wasn't a director who made shot lists, but I knew what I wanted.

For about seven weeks of the production I battled a nagging health issue that would have mattered only to a woman. I thought I had gotten my period, and then I didn't stop bleeding. It kept up forever. Every day my assistant, Amy Lemisch, would point me to the bathroom and tell me which stall she'd left the Kotex in. "Second one on the left." Finally, my body seized up on me. We were shooting the scene where Elizabeth takes care of Tom after he's had a fight. Right before lunch I turned to my associate producer Tim Bourne and asked him to drive me to a gynecologist my assistant had found. Poor Tim got an earful of what I thought was going on with me.

It turned out what I thought was an unusually long and heavy period was something else. After a brief exam, the doctor informed me that I'd actually had a miscarriage earlier. I was stunned. I had no idea that I was pregnant. Nor did I know who the father was. I supposed it could have been one of several guys, though I wasn't sure. I'd been on location for a while and it's easier to not worry about names. I know that sounds irresponsible, but I always took the proper precautions — or so I thought.

The doctor cauterized me and told me to rest for the next day or two. I turned down his prescription for a pain medication, explaining I was allergic. Then I had Tim take me back to the set, where I finished directing the scene while lying on the floor. I don't know if I was tough or stupid, but those who'd worked with me before knew I didn't stop for nothing.

Jim Brooks was in Washington, D.C., making *Broadcast News,* and he watched my footage and sent notes and suggestions. Sometimes I appreciated his input, and other times it seemed he was questioning my decisions. I was like, "Go do your own movie. You aren't here to know the circumstances."

As a result of Jim's comments, I reshot about ten scenes, though the film's memorable scene of Tom and Robert Loggia, who played Josh's boss, dancing on giant piano keys wasn't one of them. I handled that on one of the two days we shot inside FAO Schwarz, the landmark toy store on New York City's 5th Avenue. I had seen the piano months earlier, but it featured fewer keys than the one we used in the film, and the sounds that came out when you stepped on them didn't correspond to actual notes.

I found the piano's inventor and said I needed a version that was practical enough to play "Heart and Soul" and "Chopsticks." The first song was in the script; however, I knew enough about playing the piano to think that the second one would be better visually. I also needed the keyboard made longer — long enough for two people to dance on it.

As we waited for him to build it, I had cardboard facsimiles of the keyboard made and sent one to Robert, who was in France, and one to Tom, so they could practice. He rehearsed with intensity, and it made me laugh.

We shot that scene from numerous angles. Greenhut hocked me to use dance doubles. I repeatedly said no. If I could do it — and I did do it — Tom and Robert could, too. What I should have used was a click track, which keeps the actors in the same tempo. It would have made life a lot easier for my poor editor, Barry Malkin. But each take was slightly different. In the end, though, Tom and Robert were happy with the way it came out, and so was I.

After we finished, Tom asked me where to go on vacation with his then-girlfriend, Rita Wilson. I suggested St. Bart's. They went there and he proposed to her at Maya's, my friend's restaurant. They got married a few months later in a big Greek wedding, which I attended, and the rest is one of Hollywood's happiest marriages.

Big was an education. The scene when Tom and Elizabeth (Susan) are in the back of the limo after the Christmas party is an example of where I screwed myself because I didn't know shit. Someone convinced me that we could carry it on the back of a flatbed and shoot into it, which we did. But the way it was configured only let us shoot toward the back of the limo, and all the good stuff and gadgets, like the TV, were in the front part. What was Tom going to play with? He found the windows, the locks, the radio and the phone, but my lack of knowledge had limited my options. I learned from those mistakes.

For as much as I shot, I was always asking, "Do we really need this scene?" If I said no, then I would move on. But I liked making things up. Take the scene when Josh shows Susan his apartment. That was crucial to the story's progression. He is still innocent and oblivious to what's on her mind as they get out of the limo and go upstairs. He's twelve and she's older. Even when she says flat out she wants to spend the night, he thinks she wants to have a sleepover.

He invites her to jump on his trampoline. It's fun. She didn't know how to have fun yet. Again, it was this idea of play that I was constantly thinking about, that shaped me as a kid and influenced the rest of my life. As we did it, I wanted to also go outside and shoot from across the street and see them through the windows. I needed a transition between Tom coming out of the bathroom and Elizabeth already in bed. If I had stayed in the room, I'd have to deal with the question: When did they change?

I also thought the shot from outside was a way to convey fun and innocence, too. It signified a larger transition.

But Bobby Greenhut didn't want to go outside. He didn't want to spend money lighting up the whole street. Why would we have to light up the whole street? I didn't understand. We battled over that as we worked into the night. Determined to get my shot, I waited till he took a catnap. He wasn't good late at night. Around 4 a.m., he was asleep. Barry and I stepped over him, took a camera into the building next door, and pointed it at the windows.

I directed Tom and Elizabeth from the walkie-talkie. *To your left. Okay, sit down. Now Elizabeth, jump. Sit. Jump sitting up.* I was pleased with that effort.

Toward the end of production I lost my assistant director, prop man, and a bunch of others. They all went to Woody's picture because Bob Greenhut did Woody's movies. I showed up one day and asked where is So-and-so? They were gone. Luckily we didn't have much left. We were basically at the end where Josh, having decided he wants to go back home, is at the Zoltar machine, making his wish, and Susan finds him. The script had four lines, something like, "I'm sorry. I didn't know. Don't go." And they both had to cry. It wasn't right.

Jim got on the phone with Bob and me and we rewrote it. In our version, Josh says there are a million reasons to go back but only one to stay. Hearing that she's the one reason, they hug and she asks, "So how old are you anyway? Fifteen or sixteen?" When he says thirteen, she groans. I groaned, too. And that was the reaction I wanted — that bittersweet ache in the heart.

I kept the cameras rolling after she offered to drive him home and they turned and walked away. Later, we wild-lined in that same scene when she muses, "Ten years. Who knows? Maybe you should hold on to my number." I was always thinking ahead. Maybe there was hope. Then she drives him home, they wave, and you hear scrape, scrape, scrape, and there's David Moscow in the suit and the shoes. No special effects. It was all done in cuts.

Someone at the studio wanted Susan/Elizabeth to go back with him. I said no. Who says she's from the same neighborhood? Is his mother going to allow her to sleep in the house? Sorry. But in the end you heard how happy Josh's mother was that he'd returned. Somebody had to be happy at the end.

I watched the editor's assemblage in Los Angeles with a few trusted people, including my brother, Jim Brooks, and Randy Newman, plus the editor, Barry Malkin, and Howard Shore, who I had hired to write the score. Barry had used jazz tunes for temp music, but it changed the feel of the picture from what I had imagined, and I was a little sour when the lights came back on. I turned to Howard and said, "You don't have to do this if you don't want to."

Howard saw past my reaction and insisted he knew what to do, and he turned out to be right. In the meantime, Randy introduced me to Battle Davis, a talented music editor who redid the temp music, and it worked, allowing me to see the movie the way I had imagined. Battle had a dry sense of humor like Randy's and became one of my dear friends.

Soon I showed another cut to my sister. She gave me comments and a few more scenes came out. After several more cuts, we started showing the movie to audiences. Their reactions were good and confirmed most of my thoughts. Unfortunately, I wasn't satisfied with the footage at the end when Josh goes back to look at his old neighborhood. Seeing Tom in a rain coat staring wistfully at children playing made me think of a pedophile. It didn't work for me. Nor did Howard's music in that part.

I was responsible for the problem, and I tried to fix it by putting in Artie's very pretty rendition of Percy Sledge's classic "When a Man Loves a Woman." Artie had a sweet voice, and I thought that and the lyrics made up for whatever was missing. But the next screening we had of the movie turned into a disaster when the film caught on fire. The screen filled with the orange flair of celluloid frying. I heard the three editors there — Barry, Richie (Marks), and George Bowers — exclaim, "Fuck," and then run to the booth. It kills everyone to see that happen.

They got it back up and the movie finished. Everyone loved it. But Jim and I had a fight over the music. He thought I had used Artie's song because I had dated him, and I argued that it was there solely because it fit the story. We got a little heated and personal before arriving at the real issue, which was whether there should be a song with lyrics or no lyrics. Eventually, I cut in music from David Pomeranz's pretty song "It's In Every One of Us." It swelled at the right time.

I had many similar conversations with Howard about the music he composed. For some reason, it was tough to get it right in each scene. But those are only some of the thousands of little details that you have to get right if a movie is going to work.

Between the long hours and the endless decisions that had to be made, I had no other life. It's either return calls or eat and take a bath. I was too tired for both. That's why I always say directing is a dog's life.

In June, the studio threw a carnival-themed premiere party on the Fox lot and that was followed by a wide opening. The reviews were overwhelmingly positive, but I didn't bother to read them. What was the point? Some people liked me or it was all about Tom or this or that. By then, it was out of my hands and all I wanted to do was get the fuck away.

I planned a trip to Moscow with Allyn Stewart, a friend from Warner Brothers, and on the way I stopped in New York, where Greenhut persuaded me to sneak into a theater on Broadway with him. I stayed a couple minutes. I got too nervous. "I need to get out of the country where no one knows who the fuck I am," I said as we caught a cab.

A week later, I was in Red Square at midnight and spotted a kid wearing a *Big* T-shirt. It turned out the executive in charge of foreign distribution for the studio was there with his family. Otherwise, I spent a blissful two weeks seeing the sights without anyone staring back at me. We were at the American Embassy meeting with Russian filmmakers on the day when a U.S. warship mistakenly shot down Iran Air Flight 655, thinking it was a fighter jet, and there were momentary fears of a response that could involve the Russians. It made for some tense hours. But I supposed we were at the safest place in Moscow.

From there, we went to Leningrad. After a few days there, I cut short the rest of our trip, including a couple days in Georgia. I was tired of speaking through an interpreter and wanted to get back to people who spoke English. I had learned Russian cab drivers will stop immediately if they see you waving a pack of Marlboros, and so I got us to the airport pretty quick.

They served caviar on the plane ride back to London. For some reason, there were a lot of American students in first class who asked for my autograph. I traded them a signature for their caviar and had a filling flight. Once in London, I saw my hysterically funny friend Nona Summers and hung out with Jack Nicholson, who was there getting fitted to play the Joker in Tim Burton's *Batman*. Jack was very appreciative when I shared the fifty-thousand-proof vodka I had brought back from Russia.

By the time I returned to L.A., *Big* was doing steady business. It wasn't number one, but it had legs. Tom and his wife, Rita Wilson, and I took the film to festivals in Deauville and Venice. The box office kept climbing. Eventually the total hit $100 million. My brother and others told me that it made me the first woman to direct a movie that reached and surpassed that magic milestone.

I was very happy for its success, but the box office was only one of the reasons and not even the most important. This may sound sappy, but I liked that the movie made people feel good. My mother had believed it was important to know what it was like to entertain people, and she was right. It felt great.

CHAPTER 38

A Medical Mystery Tour

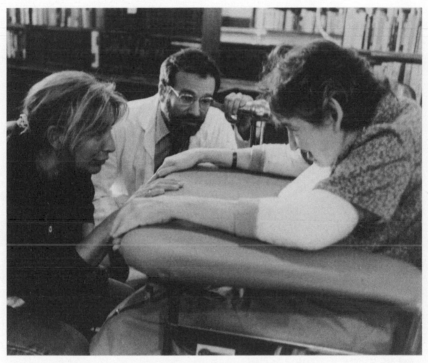

Penny on the set of 1989's *Awakenings* with Robin Williams and a patient

"Awakenings" © 1990 Columbia Pictures Industries, Inc. All Rights Reserved.
Courtesy of Columbia Pictures.

*A*FTER BECOMING A $100 million director, I was given a little office at Fox, and it was there that someone gave me a documentary on the All-American Girls Professional Baseball League, a professional league of women ballplayers that started in 1943 as a diversion while men were in the service and lasted until 1954. I had never heard of the league before, and I was a sports fan. The studio suggested it could be a made-for-TV movie, but after watching the documentary I thought it was worthy of a feature film and set about getting a script.

My first instinct was to find a woman to write it, but none of the female writers I approached wanted to do it. Monica Johnson might have been good if she had known anything about sports. She was living in my house, having replaced Michael O'Donoghue and Louise Lasser. When she moved in, she brought her ex-boyfriend Greg's ashes. Greg, my assistant's brother, had overdosed on drugs. Technically, I guess she and Greg were still living together at my house. She would set his box on the table at dinner.

I had a group of friends who came over at night pretty regularly. They called themselves "Girls on Wheels" and included Lorne's now ex-wife Susan Forristal, Becky Johnson, Nona Summers, Lyndall

Hobbs, and Carol Caldwell. They drove me around since I hadn't gotten behind the wheel of a car in years. They were a worldly group, but the ashes were too much even for them. I told Monica that she couldn't bring the box to the table anymore.

"But it's Greg," she said, her soft voice sounding wounded.

"No!" I said firmly. "Greg can't come to dinner no more."

All that's a roundabout way of saying I finally asked Lowell Ganz to write the so-called "girls baseball" movie. Lowell and his writing partner, Babaloo Mandel, whose real name was Mark, were red hot. They had written *Night Shift, Splash, Spies Like Us,* and had recently turned in the script for Steve Martin's hit, *Parenthood.* They liked the idea and saw the same potential in the documentary. Even though they wrote guys better than girls, I had confidence in them.

But they took longer than I anticipated. As they wrote, I turned my attention instead to *Awakenings,* a script based on a 1973 memoir by Dr. Oliver Sacks, then a young British neurologist working in the Bronx, who had used the drug L-dopa to wake up patients who had been catatonic for decades. I don't remember how it got in front of me. It was a dead project at the studio, gathering dust. Producers Walter Parkes and Lawrence Lasker were attached, and the screenplay was from A-list writer Steve Zaillian. Everyone in the world had looked at it and passed — I think because the studio had fixated on turning it into a love story.

But I saw it as a medical mystery. I thought of my mother in her final years when she knew nothing and didn't respond to anything I said. I wondered if she could still hear me. I also liked that this story was about doctors treating sick people as human beings deserving of care and compassion even though they were ill.

I immediately thought of De Niro for the role of Dr. Sacks. I owed Bobby for giving me validity on *Big.* I went to him and explained that I wanted him to play the doctor. He was quirky and withdrawn. I saw the fit. But Bobby said, "No, I want the glitz." I understood. So then I had to find someone who would give me the energy the picture would need. As great as Bobby is, he's a solitary figure and self-contained, except with Marty. They are always in a Winnebago, making phone calls.

In the meantime, it was New Year's. After celebrating at the Hotel Bel-Air with Jim and Ed Weinberger, Ted Bessell, and their wives and others, I checked into the Pritikin Longevity Center in Santa Monica. This was my second or third year going there for two weeks in January to get healthy and clean and stop smoking. It was cheaper than the Canyon Ranch in Arizona, where I had gone a few times with Carrie, who would sneak in food and defeat the point of being there.

The food at Pritikin was much worse than at Canyon Ranch. It was all roughage, and dry. I ate jicama like crazy. I happen to like jicama so that was okay. But everything there gave you terrible gas. I was thinking about that because I had a meeting with Robert Redford about *Awakenings*. He had a place in Malibu and we arranged to meet there and walk and talk on the beach. But I was concerned about being around Robert Redford when I had a chronic flatulence issue.

I asked my friend Carol Caldwell to come over and take a practice walk with me on the beach. "All I do here is fart," I explained. "I sound like a duck. I want to know if I'm toward the water and he's up, can he hear?" It turned out he couldn't, nor did he work out for the movie.

Before my two weeks at Pritikin were up, Barry Diller called. Now, I wasn't taking phone calls while I was at the Center because I light up a cigarette as soon as the phone rings. It's an automatic thing with me. But I said, "Hi Barry, talk fast because I'm on the phone and I'm trying not to smoke."

"A friend of mine named Ronald Perelman is the head of Revlon and very wealthy—"

"Talk faster," I interrupted.

"He wants you to shoot a Revlon commercial campaign," he said.

"Okay, send me the stuff," I said. "Fax it or send it. I can't talk because I'm trying not to smoke."

A couple weeks after leaving Pritikin, I went to New York and met with Ronald, who I liked very much and who would become one of my dearest friends. But then it was business. I wasn't smoking and was still eating jicama. He and his marketing people explained they wanted to do a campaign with famous people answering the question: What makes a woman unforgettable? I returned to L.A., and they had a casting person and some marketing people who had certain names in mind, which was fine. But I also went through my phone book and shot Carrie, Sandra Bernhard, Harry Dean Stanton, Little Richard, and the Pointer Sisters, among others.

I went to meet Gregory Peck at his house. He had a three-legged dog, and we were told not to mention that the dog only had three legs. At his house, my assistant Jon-Michael and I saw a sign on the gate that said *Beware of Dog*. We had to drive around the block a couple times before we stopped laughing. Once we were inside, Gregory was wonderful. He told stories about old Hollywood and working with John Huston and the cowboy movies he did. The casting girl arrived late and during the first break in conversation immediately said, "Mr. Peck, what happened to your dog?"

I guess she didn't get the memo. Gregory skipped over it so I never found out what had happened to the dog, either. He was nice. I also used former Los Angeles Lakers coach Pat Riley and San Francisco 49ers quarterback Joe Montana. I tossed Joe a football to hold, to make him more comfortable. *Here, play with something while you talk.* Lauren Bacall was a pro. Grace Jones kept us waiting until I finally yelled, "If you want to do this, you must come out now. The crew is leaving!" Tony Curtis needed help.

"What makes a woman unforgettable?" I asked from behind the camera.

"Her smile," he said.

"Say it like you like her smile," I said.

We did another take:

Me: "What makes a woman unforgettable?"

Tony: "Like her smile."

So not everyone made it into the final cut of the commercials. Also, we didn't need as many people as we shot. They premiered on the Academy Awards. The *New York Times* noted the irony: "Penny Marshall, whose direction of the film *Big* was ignored by the Motion Picture Academy despite the movie's nomination for best picture, directed Revlon's spots." I watched the awards show at Jerry and Joanne Belson's house, but covered my eyes during the commercials. They weren't bad. I was just modest around my family and friends.

In the meantime, Barry Diller did not share my enthusiasm for *Awakenings*. Having Bobby De Niro and a script by Steve Zaillian didn't change his opinion. Without Barry's backing, the project was still dead at Fox. But I still wanted to make this movie. I met with Barry about taking it to another studio, even if there was another actor in it. The business term for that is "change of elements," but I didn't know that. I simply said, "Can I take it somewhere else? And if I do, are you going to change your mind?"

Barry gave me his blessing to shop it elsewhere. I called Dawn Steel, one of the most impressive people in the business. Only the second woman to head a film studio, Dawn was president of Columbia Pictures. She had brownish-red hair, a warm smile, and eyes that took in everything. She was at Columbia during a tumultuous time, and even then she managed to gain a reputation for supporting filmmakers, boosting confidence, and championing women.

I met with Dawn in a conference room full of studio executives. She and I were the only women in the room. I pitched the script and my vision, which included Bobby. I was halfway through my pitch when Dawn excused herself to go to the bathroom and told me to follow her.

"Don't trust any of these guys," she said when we were alone. "They will fuck you over."

"Do you want to do it?" I asked.

"Yes," she said.

"Are you going to be here still while I make it?" I asked, knowing studio heads changed every two and a half minutes. "Will you be here when I finish it?"

"I hope so," she said.

She wasn't. But she green-lit the film. Then I went after Robin Williams, who I had briefly spoken to about playing Dr. Sacks. I had watched *Dead Poets Society* and known him since my brother created *Mork & Mindy*. Ronny and I had actually brought Robin to my brother's attention. I called Peter Weir, who had directed *Dead Poets*, and asked how Robin was to work with.

"He'll do anything you want," he said.

Robin had costarred with Steve Martin in a production of *Waiting for Godot* that Mike Nichols did at Lincoln Center, and through various sources I'd heard his soon-to-be wife, Marcia Garces, had been giving notes. Okay, I thought, as long as he wasn't the problem, I could deal with her.

I told Bobby to watch *Dead Poets*. I said, forget the trailer. It's the one scene where Robin broke character. Just watch the movie. He did, and he agreed that Robin was the right guy for the role. When I spoke again with Robin, he had one concern — that Bobby would blow him off the screen. I said, "Look, it's my job to make sure that doesn't happen."

I arranged for them to meet. I took Bobby to Robin and Marcia's hotel. I knew Marcia was going to try to sit in on the meeting and worked out a plan with Bobby to keep her out. "I'll just say you're shy," I said, and that worked. The three of us had a productive, positive talk about the movie, their characters, and personal stuff, and I walked out with my two leads in place.

Then I met the real Oliver Sacks. We got together at the Botanical Gardens, his daily lunch spot. It was near Beth Abraham Hospital where he worked, in the Bronx. The food was terrible, but he was the fascinating, quirky character (he rode a motorcycle, misplaced his keys) I had come to know from reading the script and his book, as well as from talking about him with my therapist, who happened to have gone to school with him. He promised to be available on the set as often as I needed.

Production was about to begin on *Awakenings* when Fox green-lit *A League of Their Own.* Lowell and Babaloo had handed in their script and Joe Roth, who was running Fox that day (a minute earlier it had been Scott Rudin and Larry Gordon), wanted to do it. I wanted to do it, too, but I was about to leave for New York. We hired David Anspaugh to direct. We thought he would get to the heart of it, as he'd done on *Hoosiers*. I didn't think he'd get the comedy, but to me the heart was more important.

I moved to New York and began work in Brooklyn during one of the darkest, coldest winters ever. My friend Miloš Foreman introduced me to Miroslav Ondříček, the brilliant Czech who had worked on *Amadeus* and *Ragtime,* as well as *The World According to Garp* and *Silkwood*.

I adored Miroslav from the start. I could look in his eyes and know exactly what he thought, and if he didn't like a shot he walked in front of the camera. But his thick accent was impenetrable. I couldn't understand a single word he said. Miloš said he couldn't either — and he was Czech.

From what I could tell, the man spoke no known language, which made him a perfect complement to my equally brilliant production designer, Anton Furst, who had worked with Stanley Kubrick on *Full Metal Jacket* and won an Oscar for Tim Burton's *Batman*. His sets were un-fucking-believable. I had called him and asked if he'd like to do a smaller movie. "It's a little hospital setting," I said.

Anton spoke with a thick Cockney accent, and when we initially met to discuss the movie he kept talking about plinths and lintels, which I thought were beans. Both were actually different-size pieces of wood. Miroslav and I had no idea what he was talking about. Between all of our accents, though, I don't know if any of us ever understood one another.

We did a pre-shoot at Throgs Neck, the sliver of land dividing the Bronx and Manhattan. It was early morning, and we were working with the second unit, which meant we didn't have a still photographer. The AD kept looking at his watch as the crew built a platform to put the camera on. We were racing against the tide to get a shot of Bobby on a rock in the water while Robin stood on the dock saying, "Come in, Leonard." But the tide came in so fast some of the crew found themselves treading water. We got the shot. In a later take, it looked like Bobby was walking on water. Luckily someone on the crew had a Brownie and snapped a picture. That became our poster.

Our primary location was the Brooklyn Psychiatric Hospital, a working psychiatric hospital that treated patients with severe or long-term mental illnesses on the first and second floors. We shot on the third floor and used the fourth for dressing rooms. There was no shortage of atmosphere, screams wafting through the air ducts, or potential extras. Bobby likes to shoot in order, so the first part focused on Robin, who held the picture together as Dr. Malcolm Sayer, a research neurologist who steps gingerly into his first clinical position and finds himself wading through hallways filled with patients in wheelchairs who've been literally frozen in time for decades and essentially forgotten, except for Bobby's character, Leonard Lowe, a middle-aged man whose devoted mother still tends to him. For that role, actresses walked in with their Oscars. I was overwhelmed. They were amazing. We tested a few of them, including Theresa Wright, who had spunk, and an older woman, Ruth Nelson.

Ruth was a great lady. She was a New York stage actress in the 1930s who transitioned to movies but was blacklisted in the 1950s when her second husband was among those Senator Joseph McCarthy labeled a Communist. She was victimized by association and didn't work for three decades. When I met her, she was eighty-four and had battled a brain tumor and also had arthritis. I stared at her slender arms and gnarled hands. It looked like she had pushed her kid's arms and legs down for years. I liked her.

I couldn't get her insured, but I didn't care. Neither did she. She wanted to do it. To me, that's what the movie was about.

I also had an open call for people in wheelchairs. I needed them for background. Why not use real people? Everyone was shocked when they heard me audition them. *Okay, what happened to you?* One told me that he had been run over by a car while sleeping on the street. Others had similar tragedies. My directness shocked some people around me. But I had to ask. *Can you use a manual wheelchair? Because this takes place in 1969.*

If they said yes, they were in. We learned a lot about different afflictions from being around and watching these people. The patients in Dr. Sacks's real story had survived an early-twentieth-century outbreak of encephalitis lethargica.

There was one survivor from the group of original patients. We visited her in a hospital. It had been twenty-some years since Dr. Sacks had treated her. She was very sweet. We would be talking with her, though, and then suddenly she'd freeze. It was like a light switch had been flipped. I put her in the movie, but unfortunately she was cut out of the final version.

I cast Julie Kavner as the nurse because Steve Zaillian writes beautifully and very tight, but everyone spoke like Dr. Sayer. *When you wake up the next morning it twill be the next morning.* No one really speaks like that. At least Julie has a different sound. One day she asked how she would change Leonard's diaper. How would I know? I told her to go downstairs and ask actual nurses.

I tried as much as possible to utilize actual people dealing with diseases, including a couple of people with Tourette syndrome. It was nearly impossible for an actor to duplicate the reality and reactions of a mentally ill patient, especially when we saw what it was really like. Robin had a scene early in the picture where the simple act of pulling a pen out of his jacket to write on a woman's chart scared the shit out of her. I read numerous actresses, and they were all right. But then I tested five schizophrenics, including Waheeda Ahmed. I gave her the role. She screamed in a way that shook the walls like no actor could do because they didn't know what it was like to scream from deep inside your brain.

On camera, she was perfect, remarkable in fact, and she enjoyed the hell out it. After we finished the scene, I went to thank her. I found her sitting upstairs in one of the dressing rooms. She was all smiles. "I'm almost a star," she said.

Thursday was the night in the hospital when the patients on the floors below ours were taken off their meds so they could be checked by the doctors. And that was the night we shot the pivotal scenes where Leonard finally wakes up after Dr. Sayer has spent days giving him different amounts of L-dopa. It was late at night in the movie, too. Dr. Sayer wakes up and sees that Leonard has also woken up and gotten out of bed. He finds him in a nearby room.

"It's quiet," Leonard says.

"Yes, everyone is asleep," Dr. Sayer says.

However, as we shot, the patients from downstairs were screaming through the whole scene. It happened several times. What was I going to do? Tell crazy people not to be crazy?

There was another issue. Until this point, Bobby, like Leonard, had slept through the first part of the movie, and Robin became nervous with him suddenly alive and playing opposite him, reacting, changing the game. Bob is different when the camera is on him. He waits for it to find him. Before I said action, Miroslav asked if I wanted moonlight. I said sure, why not? We shot the scene and I thought it was great. Then I saw the dailies. Robin was blue. The following day when he asked how it had looked, I said, "Your acting is fine. But I have to reshoot your side of the table because the moonlight turned your face blue."

Indeed, I didn't know that moonlight turns people blue. You don't see it with your eye, but you see it on film. I didn't know until then. It was only my second full movie.

Robin and Bobby got along well, though they had different styles. Robin entertained the crew between takes, while Bobby disappeared into his dressing room. Everyone was afraid to get him. That job fell to me because I wasn't afraid. "What's going on? Are you ordering silverware patterns for the Tribeca Grill? Let's go."

Reports that he and Robin got into a fight on the set were false. In the scene where Dr. Sayer and Leonard argue, Bobby told Robin to actually hold his hands down and prevent him from moving. At the same time, Bobby was struggling to move. They were two opposing forces. And Bobby is strong. One time Robin's hands flew up and hit Bobby in the nose. Robin dropped to the floor while Bobby continued on with the scene. Afterward I said cut, wondering why Robin had overacted. It turned out he had broken Bobby's nose.

"Does it hurt?" I asked Bobby.

He shook his head. "It's numb."

"Well, do you want to go to the doctor?" I asked.

"No, let's finish it," he said.

After the scene, I asked how long it took him to heal. I wanted to know if he was going to be black and blue, would I have to shoot around him? He turned out to be a fast healer. It straightened his nose, actually. But the mishap was reported in the tabloids as a fight. Sometimes they said it was Bobby hitting Robin. Sometimes it was the other way around. It was all bullshit.

What went unreported was Bob's squeamishness in the scene when a cockroach walks across the table as Leonard freezes while writing. In real life, Bob hates cockroaches. Robin turned the moment into a stand-up routine, saying, "On my last job I was up for a cockroach in a Raid commercial." But Bobby was so scared that I ended up using one of the other patients to touch him on the shoulder and break Leonard's trance.

Then there was a minor interruption when Sony bought the studio. I remembered the conversation I'd had with Dawn Steele when

I asked if she'd still be the president when I finished shooting. Well, now she was gone — and so was Columbia Pictures. But it turned out good for us. The new Japanese owners loved Robin, and they just gave us more money.

We continued to shoot with a lighter attitude. I remember this scene where Dr. Sayer takes Leonard for a drive. We had the car up on a flatbed, and Miroslav and I were on the camera truck, watching. Bob had one line: "What a wonderful place the Bronx has become." He said it just as a bus rolled by so we couldn't hear him clearly. In fact, all we heard was Robin turn into Harvey Fierstein and say, "Well, Leonard, if you like the Bronx, wait till I take you to this place downtown. You're going to love it."

Robin made him laugh throughout the whole car scene. Every time we hit a red light or another car slowed us down he cracked a joke. Bobby would laugh and turn red. I had to wait until he went back to his natural pale color.

Bob was an equally powerful presence. Jazz great Dexter Gordon played a patient named Rolondo. The tenor saxophonist was ill at the time, battling cancer that took his life before the movie opened. He was 6'6" and rail-thin. He moved slowly. I had him play the piano after his character woke up. Despite needing a throat box to speak, Dexter kept asking, "Where's my scene with De Niro?"

I understood. When Bob walked out of Ward 5 following his speech there I instructed him to shake Dexter's hand. Then Julie moved in and helped Dexter walk away. But he got his scene with Bobby D.

To me, Bob's greatness as an actor was measured in the way he handled the parts that gave him the most trouble. There were three of them — speeches that weren't written in his rhythm, including the scene in Ward 5 where he goes a little crazy. He wouldn't let anyone in while he rehearsed, including Robin, who took me aside and said, "But I'm in this scene."

"Remember you got nervous the night Leonard woke up, the night you turned blue?" I said. "This is Bob's turn."

I worked with Bob privately and after a while I said, "Okay, Robin is coming in." The transition was smooth. Bob just had to go through his process. He acts within himself, and it's his restraint that makes him a ticking time bomb. He can say, "Did you fuck my wife?" and you don't know how he's going to react. In the same way, he surprised me in the scene where Leonard is in the bathroom shaving for the first time with an electric razor. I could see him thinking about what he was going to do as he held the razor in his hand. I went over to him — because you talk to Bob privately, not where everyone can hear — and I said, "Does it tickle? Leonard was twelve. This is all new to him."

He got it. His performance in that scene was layered with nuances that let you actually see this character's entire life start to come together. I liked the scenes with Leonard and Paula, the complicated sweetness of him having feelings and discovering the "gift and wonderment of life." Penelope Ann Miller was great as Paula. My favorite scene was when Leonard, his health rapidly deteriorating, tries to say good-bye to Paula, his love, in the cafeteria, and she gets up from the table, pulls him close, and they dance. You had Dexter playing the piano in the background. It was heartbreaking. I also liked the scene when Leonard's mother sees him awake for the first time. I thought everything in that worked.

My whole thing with Bobby was that I didn't want any *Raging Bull* in his performance. I wanted him to play against type, to play a sweet guy. As he said, it was the glitz.

We shot a whole back end of the movie that I knew I didn't even need, including a scene where Dr. Sayer sneaks Leonard out of the hospital and finds Paula ice skating at Rockefeller Center. It was so cold out that day, the Steadicam froze. None of it was necessary. I had been sneaking in shots of the patients and orderlies the whole time to use during Robin's final speech. I did make sure to get Dr. Sayer asking Eleanor out for a cup of coffee. That passed for a love story, which the studio had always wanted. But if not for all the extra shooting, we could've finished two months earlier.

Our wrap party, held at the Tribeca Grill, included a slide show of behind-the-scenes still photographs from the production letting us see our struggle against the cold weather. That wasn't the only challenge. The first assemblage of the movie ran five hours. My brother said, "I think you need to cater it." But the editor had put everything in, which is what I like to see. An hour came out like butter.

I walked away from that conversation with two additional editors, who began to cut heavily. I also called in Steve Zaillian and asked what he wanted out, and he basically agreed with my suggestions. We took out the subplot of Leonard building a library out of balsa wood. The whole back end came out then, too. The producers complained that I was ruining their movie, but Steve supported me and so did the studio. I liked the way it ended with a positive message. I was pleased when I saw it.

The studio loved that I got it down to two hours. They didn't believe I could do it. The movie premiered in New York at the end of 1990, shortly before its official opening in December — in time to qualify for awards. Barry Diller, bless him, was very proud of me. Although he had passed on the movie, he said, "You did a remarkable job." As was my habit, I was going away to avoid opening-weekend nerves. I was on my way to Phuket. I think Sean Penn had gone there and said it was beautiful. But Barry stopped me. "You can't go there," he said. He reminded me there was a war in the Gulf. "Terrorists are meeting in Bangkok."

Instead, he sent me and Tracy and my niece to Australia's Hayman Island, a ridiculously luxurious and beautiful haven in the midst of the Great Barrier Reef. No one was there, we had a butler, we ate phenomenal seafood, as you'd expect, and, of course, we played in the ocean. Relaxed, I returned to learn that *Awakenings* had received three Oscar nominations, including Bobby for Best Actor, Steve for

Best Screenplay, and the movie itself for Best Picture. Robin, who had held the movie together, should have been up for an Oscar. But he was nominated for a Golden Globe, Bobby won a New York Film Critics Circle Award, and Randy Newman, who scored the picture, earned a Grammy nomination.

Again, I was left out of the celebrations. Privately and publicly, people complained it was sexism. I don't know. I didn't dwell on it. I knew that people didn't expect me to make that kind of movie. It's not what I was known for. I hosted a non-nominee Oscar party at my house. As the awards show went on, though, and I saw that only Joe Pesci won from the pack of *Goodfellas* nominees, I realized I was going to be entertaining a bunch of depressed Italians. They knew about the food — fried chicken, macaroni and cheese, and more — from Carrie's and my annual birthday parties. It was exactly what you wanted to eat if you didn't win or get nominated. Even Barbra Streisand showed up.

She'd presented an award, then left the awards show and headed up the hill to my place. I loved seeing her walk through the door, looking comfortable and ready to have fun. She had been screwed over by the Academy, yet everyone knew she was a brilliant talent and, as far as I was concerned, a great gal who knew real satisfaction in life came from doing work you loved, not winning awards.

CHAPTER 39

Batter Up

Penny and Tom Hanks on the set of 1992's *A League of Their Own*

After *AWAKENINGS*, PETER GUBER and Jon Peters, who were running Sony Pictures, offered me a production deal. They said something like, "If you come with us we'll even let you do that girls movie." They were talking about *A League of Their Own.* Fox had pulled the plug on David Anspaugh seven weeks into pre-production, so the Lowell Ganz-Babaloo Mandel script was back on my desk when I resurfaced and began looking around for my next project.

I went to Barry and told him about Sony's offer. Unable to match it, he encouraged me to take it — and do the movie. So did Bob Greenhut, who called around the same time and said, "Let's do the baseball picture. Sets are already built and in storage somewhere."

I had already made up my mind after asking Tracy if she'd want to play Betty Spaghetti. She did — and that was enough for me. She started to practice and would come home happy. In a way, I saw in her what I wanted to capture in the movie: empowerment and pride. Don't be ashamed of your talent.

League chronicled the inception of an all-girls baseball league started by a clever team owner who needed a gimmick to keep the sport going and fill the stands while his star players were overseas fighting World War II. Top female players were recruited and organized into teams. The league got off to a rocky start, but the women eventually ended up in Cooperstown, proving greatness wasn't a men-only club.

I wanted my production team to include Anton Furst again. He had designed my offices at Sony, but declined the movie. "Let Bill do it," he said, referring to Bill Groom, the art director on *Awakenings*. Anton was suffering through a deep, deep depression. Whatever was going on in his life, he couldn't deal — or didn't want to — and that included work. His turned into a tragically sad story. In November, after we'd completed filming *Awakenings,* Anton committed suicide. As his doctor was checking him into Cedars-Sinai Medical Center, he went up to the parking lot roof to smoke a joint or something and jumped to his death. It was terrible.

Unlike Anton, Miroslav eagerly reupped with me. He didn't know anything about baseball. I took him to his first game. All he talked about was the food people ate. "Ah, it's an American picnic."

True enough. But baseball was also a sport, and as I put together a cast, I had an unusual requirement: The girls had to be able to play. I couldn't double them in the movie. They were going to be in little skirts. It wasn't like making a football movie where you could hide athletes inside a helmet and pads. Any girl I cast had to be able to throw, catch, hit, run, and slide. So I had longtime USC baseball coach Rod Dedeaux run the girls through the paces. It was probably the toughest tryout any of them had ever had for a movie. Some of the actual AAGPBL women who lived locally also judged them. I heard batting cages around the city were packed with actresses learning how to hit.

Anspaugh had wanted Sean Young in the lead. Demi Moore had been my first choice for Dottie. I had run into her prior to *Awakenings* and asked if she could play ball. It turned out she could. She was coordinated — and a strong actress. Perfect. But she was pregnant when the role came around again. She literally got fucked out of the part.

I was able to choose anyone in the world, but great actresses don't necessarily make for great athletes. One showed up in ballet slippers. Sorry, not right. Marisa Tomei sent me a tape of herself playing ball. I saw that Joe Pesci had been teaching her as they made *My Cousin Vinny.* As much as I loved Marisa, though, she wasn't a ballplayer. Farrah Fawcett, an excellent athlete, wanted in; unfortunately she was a little too old. Lori Singer was an excellent actress who could play, but she wanted a bigger part. The list of buts went on.

Finally, I gave the lead to Debra Winger, who signed up with a great deal of enthusiasm — and she could play. She was a tough girl. We were eager to work together, too. Nearly a decade had passed since we talked about *Peggy Sue.* Because of her, I cast Lori Petty as her sister, Kit Keller, a part that I was thinking about Moira Kelly for, until she hurt her ankle while making *The Cutting Edge.* Lori was perfect, though. Scrappy, athletic, confident, she was the only actress who stood up to Debra Winger when they read together.

It ain't easy to read with Debra, either. She'll fuck with you. She'll throw in extra lines or add asides. It flusters some people. Which is why she does it. You have to stay together, and Lori did. She was also a hell of a player.

Then Tom Hanks asked for that role of Jimmy Dugan, a former star player (based on slugger Jimmie Foxx) whose drinking problem had driven him out of the big leagues and into a last-chance job as manager of the Rockford Peaches. Tom had done a handful of not-so-hot pictures, which happens when you work as often as he did, and he was reading scripts, looking for a movie that would get him back on track. He wanted a part where he wasn't the lead, but audiences would be happy every time he came on screen. *League* was perfect.

"Can I have it?" he asked.

I thought he was wrong for the part. But he's a great guy and gets along with everyone. I just couldn't let him look the way he looks. He would seem like a distraction to the girls. They would be thinking he was cute. So I tried him in glasses, messed with his hair, and finally I said, "Eat! You've got to eat. Get fat." Tom ate his way through our locations in Chicago and Indiana. He lived on pork, "the *other* white meat," as numerous signs in Indiana claimed, and Dairy Queen.

Rosie O'Donnell was at the other end of the spectrum. I told her not to eat. To this day, she says that I'm the only director that ever told her to lose weight. Well, I say those things if they need to be said. Lindsay Frost, a tall, blond, pretty actress, was all set for the role of "All the Way" Mae, a character originally written as a California hottie. But then her TV pilot got picked up and all of a sudden I had to find another girl who could play ball *and* dance.

I went to Madonna after reading a magazine article in which she mentioned she wanted to act in more movies. When I met with her, she asked if I wanted to see her pitch. I said, "No, I already have a pitcher. But I do have to see if you can play." She was on her way to Cannes for a screening of her documentary *Truth or Dare*, but she stopped in New York and worked out for three hours with the coaches at St. John's University. They gave her a thumbs-up. She was trainable. And that's all I needed: trainable. So she was in.

But that pissed off Debra. "You're making an Elvis movie!" she said. I didn't understand what that meant, and I suppose my lack of understanding frustrated her even more because she dropped out of the picture. I wasn't going to look for another "All the Way" Mae. Lowell and Babaloo were rewriting the role to fit Madonna, turning Mae into a sassy, cigarette-smoking centerfielder. Rosie was enamored of the superstar singer. I knew their chemistry could work onscreen.

I helped that friendship along, too. At our first meeting, I began referring to them in a single breath as Ro and Mo (I couldn't get the word Madonna out), and I issued them marching orders: "You're going to be best friends. Mo, you teach her how to set her hair, and Ro, you teach her how to play ball."

Geena Davis slipped into the lead. She had read *League* but wanted to meet with Lowell and Babaloo about them writing another script for her. She ended up at my house. Her agent said not to play ball with her, but I took her out in the backyard anyway and discovered she was a natural. I had my new Dottie.

Obviously Geena and Lori Petty didn't look like sisters, but I wasn't going to recast Lori, who was a sensational player, one of the best natural athletes of all the girls. Instead, I matched their hair color. Suddenly they were sisters.

As for the rest of the cast, Megan Cavanagh, an actress, was waitressing at Ed Debevic's, a '50s-style hamburger joint, when she was cast as Marla; she learned to switch hit. Like her, Anne Ramsay and Bitty Schram could really play, and Freddie Simpson was so skilled, Tom joked that "she dipped Skoal." Renée Coleman and Annie Cusack were trainable. Robin Knight, another excellent athlete, showed up after we were already cast. However, she refused to take no for an answer. She got herself to Chicago, talked her way in, and slept in another girl's room every night. How do you say no to that kind of effort?

After some final workouts in L.A. with Rod Dedeaux's crew, we left for Chicago. When Jon Lovitz, who played the scout Ernie Capadino, heard that Madonna had checked into her hotel under a pseudonym, he registered under one, too: Edna Poop-a-dee-do. Rehearsals included daily workouts.

Garry flew in at the last minute to play team owner Walter Harvey after I couldn't afford my first choice, Christopher Walken. I had called him on a Friday and said I needed him on Monday. He was a good sport and a natural at playing the boss. He wasn't the only family member I pressed into service, though. In addition to Tracy, my niece Penny Lee worked in the editing room and my other niece Wendy was a PA in charge of getting the girls from their campers in hair and makeup to the field. Like my brother, I cast family out of loyalty.

It turned out Bobby De Niro was also in Chicago, researching one of his upcoming pictures, *Mad Dog and Glory*. Tracy got involved with his personal trainer, Dan, who she knew from *Awakenings*. Bobby corralled me into going to crime scenes with him. He knew the cops would talk to me while he wandered around and observed. After a couple field trips, though, I told him that I couldn't go with him every time a body turned up.

"I have to work," I said. "I have a movie to do. It's about baseball!"

As shooting began, I felt more like a coach than a director. The girls worked constantly on their throwing and catching, and took daily batting practice. Even Tom took his cuts. He didn't want to miss out on the fun. But I was a stickler for authenticity. I wanted them to throw like players. I also brought in a Slip 'N Slide so they could practice slides (and have fun at the same time). Working that hard, though, made injuries unavoidable. One day a ball sailed through Anne Ramsay's old-fashioned mitt and broke her nose. (In practice, they used larger, modern gloves with more webbing and padding.) Rosie broke her finger after we began shooting games. In the scene where Lori and Geena did a double slide into home plate, Lori turned her ankle after catching her cleat on the base.

Lori was much faster than Geena, and when we shot the scene where they were running for the train that took them to Chicago for tryouts, Lori kept passing Geena and she wasn't supposed to. She complained that Geena was too slow. I told her to stay behind anyway. If you watch the scene, Lori's feet are going faster than she is moving forward.

One of the most inadvertently funny moments was never seen on-screen. It happened as we shot the scene early in the movie when Jon Lovitz visited the girls at the farm after scouting them on the ball field. He walked into the barn as Dottie (Geena) and Kit (Lori) were milking cows and made his pitch about the league. However, as he said his lines, the cow next to him fell down and began to give birth.

Somehow Jon didn't even blink. He didn't even notice. He said his dialogue without interruption. But I couldn't ignore the drama — or the noise — happening directly behind him. I yelled cut.

"What?" he asked, upset.

"Didn't you notice the cow behind you just fell over?" I said.

He turned around and, as only Jon could, said, "Oh." The farmers named the calf Penny.

Later, we were outside and Jon was interrupted by a mooing cow. This time he heard and he stopped. I asked what he was doing. He said the cow kept mooing. I said, "Well, tell it to shut up." He did and it got a big laugh in the movie. One of his best ad libs came after he dropped Dottie and Kit off at tryouts. As he turned to leave, they asked what was next for him.

"I'm just going home to grab a shave and a shower and give the wife a pickle tickle," he said, "and then I'm on my way."

That was why I used Lovitz.

Tryouts were shot at the Cubs' stadium, Wrigley Field. I brought in more than a hundred girls on the field. Madonna cracked, "I was a star and you turned me into an extra." The other girls included Téa Leoni, who played first base for the Racine Bells, and Janet Jones, their pitcher. She was an excellent athlete, with a great look. My brother had used her in *The Flamingo Kid*. But she disappeared sometimes. Maybe she went to see her husband, hockey legend Wayne Gretzky, or her kids. I don't know — and didn't have time to worry about it.

We only had the stadium while the Cubs were away. To save me time, I spoke with directors who'd done baseball films, including Phil Alden Robinson (*Field of Dreams*), Barry Levinson (*The Natural*), and John Sayles (*Eight Men Out*). Their tips were invaluable: Run your cables on the dirt so they don't kill the grass (Barry); buy a ton of green paint in case you have to paint the grass (Phil); and don't yell "cut" each time they throw and catch and run — don't stop. Let them keep batting and throwing. Otherwise it will take for-fucking-ever. Keep the cameras running (John).

And John was right. I would scream at the makeup people as they ran into scenes to apply touchups. "Get the fuck out of there." I hated all the *patchkeying*. But there were lovely moments, like the day Miroslav turned to me and complimented Megan. "She has beautiful eyes, like a cow." There were also quick asides you wouldn't have heard anywhere else, such as when I told Madonna to stop her upper-body workouts. "Your arms are getting too cut," I said. "Your legs are fine. And keep the food out of Rosie's mouth."

After finishing the train scenes in the train station in Union, Illinois, we moved to Evansville, Indiana, a small town near the border of Illinois and Kentucky. We had found a great field there to shoot games as well as old-fashioned-looking diamonds in neighboring areas. We camped there for what seemed like forever. It didn't take long before I lost patience with the makeup people interrupting all the time to try to match the dirt on the uniforms. Finally I just had the girls roll in the dirt on the baseline. "Get some dirt on your arms and legs."

We had a whole season of games to film, though I can think of only one time when the girls actually played a full game. We were at the Rockford stadium, and while waiting for the fireworks, I said let them play. Some didn't know all the rules, like how to tag up on a fly ball. One of the best parts about being on a film full of girls, as opposed to guys, was that while waiting for the crew to set up the lighting, we went shopping. Tom's wife, Rita, was always willing to go on the hunt for quilts. I also got into collecting duck decoys. I furnished an entire house with all the cabinets and chairs I bought.

I knew Tom aced the "there's no crying in baseball" scene he had with Evelyn. His timing and delivery were impeccable throughout, like the gem when he gets booted from the game for asking the ump if "anyone's ever told you that you look like a penis with a little hat on?" He nailed the entire movie. The whole picture was full of riches — too full, in fact. I cut a hilarious monologue Lovitz had early in the movie about having once saved Babe Ruth's life. The scene with the team owners was shortened and turned into a newsreel. Marla's wedding was also cut down.

And those are just some of the examples. These characters took on lives of their own. As such, it seemed like we were in Evansville for much longer than we were. We were still shooting there over my birthday in October. I remember because my brother arranged for a plane to fly over the location trailing a sign that said Happy Birthday, Penny. The first time it was a fun surprise. On the third pass, I was like, *Okay, thank you, good-bye.* After fifteen minutes, I was yelling at him to get the fuck out of here. It was enough. I had to shoot.

And I still had to go to Cooperstown.

League ends with the women reuniting forty years later at the Baseball Hall of Fame. The Hall is located in Cooperstown, New York, a small, inviting town with an early-twentieth-century atmosphere and the perfect backdrop for a museum for America's pastime. None of us had been there before. We took tours and thought it was a fantastic memorial to the game's greatest players and epic moments.

But the tribute to the All-American Girls Professional Baseball League was disappointing. "Insignificant" is a better description. When it came to thinking in cinematic terms, Miroslav simply called it "ugly." As a result, we took over a room and decorated it ourselves, making it look more like a genuine shrine to the pioneering women who inspired the movie.

For the actual reunion, I asked our casting director, Ellen Lewis, to bring in a few professional actresses that looked similar to Geena, Rosie, and Mo. But I also used the real AAGPBL veterans. They were why we had made, and indeed were able to make, the movie in the first place. We all felt their spirit — and we heard about the fun they'd really had.

There wasn't a dry eye on the set when actor Mark Holton, playing Evelyn's grown-up son, Stilwell, said, "My mom always said it was the best time of her life." But what you don't see in that scene is how long everything took and how behind schedule we were. I had a contingent of AAGPBL ladies who were heading back to Florida early the next morning and I didn't want them to be delayed.

I called them together and explained they could go back to the hotel for the night and I'd shoot the rest without them, or they could stick around. It was their choice. But they had to know we were going to shoot late, possibly through the night. They exchanged looks. Then Pepper Davis stepped forward and, speaking for the group, said, "That's okay, Penny. We'll consider it a doubleheader."

That still gets me.

As usual, I had an extremely long first assemblage. I threw four teams of editors on it and showed a first cut to my brother, Randy Newman, and a few others I trusted. I hired Hans Zimmer to write the score. On paper, an English-German guy who didn't know shit about baseball was an odd choice. But he was a night person like me. From his work on *Driving Miss Daisy*, I knew he could do Americana, and he did a wonderful job.

I also had a song from Carole King for the end credits, but Madonna wanted to do her own song, "This Used to Be My Playground," which worked in that spot. I hadn't let Madonna start the singing in the Peaches song earlier in the movie. I didn't want to exploit her. So this gave fans something they had expected.

My finished cut failed to impress the studio president, Mark Canton. He asked why I ended on the old ladies.

"Why not end on Geena, Tom, and Lori?" he asked.

"Because that ain't the end of the movie," I said.

"Well, I don't know," he said. "These are old ladies."

Test screenings proved me right. The numbers kept going up as we snuck it in various theaters. When I complained to Mike Ovitz, he said, "You don't have to worry. You have final cut." Up till then, I didn't know that I wielded such power. Who had time to wield?

Confirmation that my instincts were right came from two authorities, two of the highest that I knew. The first was the public. Despite what I considered a terrible premiere screening at the Academy Theater (the theater has no vibe; Tom and I left the moment it finished, skipping the party), the movie opened in June 1992 to positive reviews and a box office that climbed through the summer. Tom and I were promoting it at the film festivals in Deauville and Venice. We were in Venice when it reached $100 million, my second film to hit that milestone. We celebrated with an enormous cake.

Steven Spielberg paid me the biggest compliment. He asked how I had composed the end of the movie. It's a pretty big deal when Steven asks, "How'd you do that?" He was intrigued when I said that I used the real women. "They're who I did the movie for," I said. "They're who I wanted to honor." He asked if I would mind if he used that type of ending in his next film, *Schindler's List*. I said, "Of course not. You're entitled."

And the truth was, it didn't belong to me. In the same way that the end of Steven's movie belonged to the survivors, mine belonged to all the women who had played the game.

CHAPTER 40
Adding Wood

Penny, Gregory Hines, and Mark Wahlberg on the set of 1994's
Renaissance Man

"Renaissance Man" © 1994 Cinergi Pictures Entertainment, Inc., & Cinergi Productions, N.V.

A T T H E E N D O F *League,* Tracy revealed some familiar-sounding news: She was pregnant and engaged. I handled the news and preparations well, and I thought I mediated well when the two of them began to fight about whether to live in New York, where he was from, or L.A., where she had her life. My solution? I bought a second apartment in New York. It was a floor below mine.

But they were in L.A. at the beginning of October when Tracy went into labor. She was in what I considered one of her hippie-dippy phases, insisting on a home birth, and so she was in the bedroom with her midwife when I arrived at night after getting a call that it was time. My ex-husband Mickey was in the living room with Dan, and we had a warm reunion. He was remarried for the third time and excited about becoming a grandparent.

He and Dan made small talk and were oblivious to the panic I saw on the midwife's face when we peeked into the room for an update. Her expression caused me to step straight into the action and hold Tracy down. "Look at me," I said. The problem was that the baby coming out of her, a boy they named Spencer, weighed eleven pounds, seven ounces. I told Tracy that he came out asking for the car keys.

Two weeks later I celebrated my fiftieth birthday. Carrie and I had one of our joint parties and the world showed up. After starting them in 1981, these parties had become major events. We alternated between our homes. No invitations went out; everyone received a phone call telling them the date and time. A few days later, we would receive calls from people asking if they could come.

Most guests were longtime friends like Jack Nicholson, Anjelica Huston, and Robin Williams. New people, like Ben Affleck and Nicole Kidman, were added every year. One year David Bowie and Iman crashed. The food was a big draw. Carrie's housekeeper, Gloria, and her mother's longtime housekeeper, Mary, made fried chicken, meatloaf, mac and cheese, and other Southern staples. Barbra Streisand wanted to hire them for a party. Carrie wouldn't let her.

Albert Brooks once cracked, "If a bomb went off at one of their parties, Anson Williams would have a career." That's what the scene looked like at my fiftieth. My brother's wife, Barbara, still talks about introducing herself to Al Pacino, De Niro, and Pesci, who were huddled in a corner. As soon as they found out she was a nurse, they began asking her about their aches and pains. Pesci raised his arm and said, "When I do this, it hurts. What does that mean?"

Jerry Belson had gone home early that night with ulcer pains. But he called around 3 a.m. I was still up, getting the stragglers to go home.

"Penny, I don't know how to tell you this," he said.

"What?"

"I don't even know if you should know."

"Jerry, what?"

"I saw Gregory Peck stealing *tchotchkes*," he said. "I didn't know if I should tell you."

I knew he was joking and had called to find out what he had missed. He also knew that I'd be up at that hour. Despite reaching middle age, I felt as energetic as I did twenty years earlier. If necessary, I could go all night, and sometimes I did. After fixing up a house for Tracy in L.A. — she and Dan split soon after — I went to New York where I now owned two apartments. It was December, and I made the rounds of friends getting ready for the holidays. One night I went to a play with Greenhut, and afterward we went to a party Ronald Perelman was having for his then-wife Claudia Cohen. It was her birthday, and he was celebrating at the Paramount Hotel. When Greenhut and I walked in, Marvin Hamlisch was playing the piano. As soon as he spotted me, Marvin switched songs midverse and sang, "We flew to the sky with tears in our eyes . . ."

It was a song he had written for my group in camp. I immediately joined in. The funny thing was, another woman at the party had also gone to camp with us and she began to sing, too. Ronald hadn't gone to camp, but he had grown up in Philadelphia and knew a number of the girls I knew from camp. It was a small world. We enjoyed comparing notes.

Ronald and I clicked. Like me, he was a little quirky, but fun, smart, and loyal. He liked to travel. I guess this was what I'd call my CEO period. I was friendly with Paul Allen, David Geffen, Barry Diller, and Ronald. All of them had private jets. It was nice. You just don't meet many people who call you up and say, "Come with me to Germany tomorrow. We'll go on the jet. I want to look at a yacht." Another time Ron invited me to London for a Paul McCartney concert. I took the Concorde, thinking we were going to a rock show. It turned out to be one of Sir Paul's early classical symphonies. We ate dinner with Sting and his wife, Trudie Styler. That's the way Ronald rolled.

In early 1993, I tried to develop various projects, including *The Nature of Enchantment,* a moving story about a traumatized child growing up. I also worked on a script called *The Boys of Neptune,* a portrait of four men in their mid- to late forties who return to the Jersey

Shore and take the same lifeguard jobs they'd had as teenagers. The studios weren't interested.

One day Sara Colleton, a producer I knew from Fox, sent me *Renaissance Man,* explaining it was based on a true story. Written by her friend Jim Burnstein, a professor at the University of Michigan, it was about an unemployed single dad named Bill Rago who gets a job with the Army teaching recruits struggling with their class work in basic training.

As the story had gone down in real life, the recruits had to pass their high school equivalency as part of basic training. But the new Army required a high school diploma. So the story sort of went in the crapper. But we made it about the accomplishment of learning, in particular discovering and performing Shakespeare. Rago loved the Bard; his students had never heard of him — or much of anything else that came from a book. They were known on the base as "double D's" — dumb as dog shit. As he said in the first classroom scene, "I've never taught before, and you've never thought before. So good luck to all of us."

I didn't think *Renaissance Man* was a blockbuster (and I didn't know about the blockbuster part of the business, anyway), but I liked its message. *Renaissance Man* was a nice story about a guy who turned his life around as he helped kids. I knew that if I did my job, people would leave the theater feeling a little better — or, in the words of my mother, they'd leave feeling entertained — and that's what I was into.

The first reading at my house was an A-list evening with Leo Di-Caprio, Keanu Reeves, the Wayans brothers, and Courtney Vance among those who traded their talents and a couple hours of their time to help me to explore the script in exchange for a nice dinner. Danny DeVito wanted the lead, and I liked the idea of working with him. I had once played myself in an episode of *Taxi* where Danny's character, Louie De Palma, and I both wanted the same apartment. After signing on, he said, "Put wood in the budget."

"What?" I said, like I knew how to make a budget.

"You'll need extra wood," he said.

"Why?"

"You'll see," he said.

It was because Danny is short and I had to put planks of wood under him to raise him up. When he was teaching, he was up on a platform, and when he walked between the desks we switched the actors into lower chairs. For those young soldiers, I wanted a mix of guys who would look like they needed the Army to give them a boost in life and also who would tackle Shakespeare like regular-sounding people. Leo had looked too young. Though Keanu read, he didn't relate to the Army. And I badly wanted Marlon Wayans, but his pilot got picked up.

As I searched Hollywood for fresh actors, I went to a fashion tribute to Calvin Klein at the Hollywood Bowl. I had known Calvin since junior high and reminded everyone that night that he was one of the few boys who could dance well. The last model to walk out on stage at the fashion show was its biggest star, a rapping pop star known as "Marky" Mark. The crowd went nuts, and he stood front and center and drove them into an even bigger frenzy.

"Who is he?" I asked. I had never heard of Marky Mark or the Funky Bunch. I did period movies and didn't keep up with popular music. However, before we had left the Bowl's crowded parking lot, I was on the phone to my assistant, telling her to bring the kid in.

I met Mark in New York. He walked in looking confused, like he had no idea why he was there. Between modeling, concerts, and personal appearances, he was probably on a schedule where he woke up and didn't know where he was. But he gave me a strong reading and impressed me even more as a person. He was tough, sweet, and intelligent. I liked him. Whatever it was that made people stars, he had it. After an hour together, he left the room with his first movie role.

"Hey," I said before he disappeared. "What do you want your credit to be? Marky Mark? Mark? Wahlberg?"

"Just Mark Wahlberg," he said.

The other actors who played privates with Mark included Lillo Brancato, Kadeem Hardison, Stacey Dash, Greg Sporleder, Peter Simmons, and Richard T. Jones. I wanted Tupac Shakur to play Hobbs, a street-smart soldier who rapped. He auditioned and was very good. He gave me props for pronouncing his name correctly, too. But he didn't think Hobbs would rap. As we talked, the real issue emerged: He didn't want to rap onscreen.

I liked him and didn't give up easily. I knew the rap in the script wasn't any good because it had been written by a white, Jewish professor in Michigan. I told Tupac that he could write his own rap. He still said no.

The role went to New York actor Khalil Kain, and Mark wrote a new rap. To balance James Remar as the good, understanding captain, I wanted Ving Rhames to play the tough drill sergeant. He said, "Penny, I'd love to do your movie. But this other guy wrote a part specifically for me in this movie called *Pulp Fiction,* and I said I'd do it."

Ving helped me out with some casting, but in his place I turned to Gregory Hines, a sweetheart who could do anything—act, sing, and dance—except play mean or tough. Even if he got angry, Gregory was nice. Everyone loved him. During breaks, the two of us would go off in a corner and tap. His ability as a dancer made him impressive at leading marching drills, which we shot alongside actual basic training graduates at Fort Jackson, in Columbia, South Carolina.

We shot there for six weeks. Fort Jackson was and still is the Army's largest training base. Kadeem and Richard missed their plane and arrived late, and Mark was this wide-eyed, inexperienced kid who told people that he was working with Laverne and the little guy from *Taxi.* All of these guys were young. Before every scene, I sounded like a drill sergeant myself: "Lillo, put on your glasses. Mark, pull up your pants."

Mark was a quick study and excellent improviser, a skill that I valued in my actors. He annoyed the shit out of the base's major by wearing his hat sideways. I was amused. His only complaint was the same as mine: boredom. We didn't find much to do outside of work. The big thing there was Rally Burgers and Krispy Kreme donuts. Danny had a private chef who passed out cloves of garlic every morning as if they were vitamins. They didn't prevent stir-craziness. One day Lillo said something insulting that made everyone want to beat the shit out of him, which happens sometimes when you're too on top of one another. Mark stepped in, spoke to Lillo, got him to apologize, and kept the peace.

He was poised even then when he didn't know much, and we've stayed friends ever since. I'm not surprised he became a mogul while staying a great guy. I like that he's credited me with getting him out of underwear and the Funky Bunch.

We finished production on the lot at Sony, where Mark and the others would steal the golf carts and race around the studio. I also brought in the La Jolla Playhouse's acclaimed artistic director Des McAnuff to oversee the production of Shakespeare's *Henry V* that Danny's character took the soldiers to see. It was a play within the movie, and I wanted it to be authentic.

As George Bowers and Battle Davis edited the movie, Danny asked a favor. He was on the lot making *Get Shorty,* a dark comedy about a mobster who goes to Hollywood, and he wanted to know if I would play myself as a movie director in the movie's final scene. I said sure. It was only one day of work.

Get Shorty director Barry Sonnenfeld welcomed me onto the set. We hadn't seen each other since we made *Big.* He had been my director of photography. After that movie wrapped, Barry, Robert Greenhut, the writers, and I had all sworn never to work with one another again. It was a joke. Greenhut was producing *Renaissance Man* and we had worked together on *League.*

On *Get Shorty,* I only had to say a few lines and then get in an SUV and drive away. It was the end of a movie — a wrap. As a stickler for detail, though, I explained that I didn't drive. I always had a driver.

Everyone knew that about me. If I was playing myself... As a result, my assistant Kristin ended up in the movie, too.

At that point, *Renaissance Man* was ready to test. I insisted on showing it at a theater in Oakland, California. It was in a rough neighborhood. Andy Vajna, one of our executive producers, asked, "What's going on? I test *Rambo* films there, not comedies." That was my point. I felt like the film was for inner-city kids who might be dropping out of school or having self-esteem issues because learning didn't come easily to them, and I wanted to see their reaction.

It seemed positive. They laughed at the beginning and applauded at the end. They also teared up when the soldiers are on a drill at night in the cold and pouring rain, facing challenging elements and considering giving up, and Lillo's Benitez character recites King Henry V's St. Crispin's Day speech. It was an emotional measure of how far they had all come, including their teacher, Rago. The only glitch at the screening came when my wallet was stolen from my purse as I helped get Danny out of the theater. I got it back later, minus the cash.

The real problem was that Sony opened *Renaissance Man* in June 1994, the start of summer. They told me it was *The Fugitive* spot. I suppose they thought that was good. Even though this was yet another movie where the studio executives changed between the time I started and finished the movie, they were the experts. But I thought a summer release killed its chances at the box office, and it turned out that I was right.

It went up against *The Lion King* and *Speed*. I think if the movie had opened when school was in session, teachers would have sent their students to see it. I tried to be philosophical, though. You can only do your best.

Danny, Mark, and I promoted the movie in Europe. We helicoptered into Brussels for a press conference and landed next to a theater where a bunch of reporters waited for us. But the rotors kicked up a storm of dust that drove them all away. When we returned to Paris, my brother and sister had left messages for me at the hotel. That was not a good sign. I reached Garry first. He said that my father had suffered a stroke.

"Do I call Lorne yet?" I said.

It was a roundabout way of asking if I needed to make arrangements to scatter some of his ashes over Broadway, too.

"Not yet," Garry said.

At eighty-eight, my father was unable to speak and had trouble walking without assistance, but he refused to go to therapy. He would shake his arm at people and give them the finger. He was content with that; maybe that's all he felt like saying or all he had to say. We got him a driver who took him every day to his country club in Toluca Lake, where he drank vodka and gave the finger to everyone. Whether he was saying hi, 'bye, or thanks, it all came out the same: Fuck you.

CHAPTER 41

The Gospel

Penny on the set of 1996's *The Preacher's Wife* with
Whitney Houston and Denzel Washington

"The Preacher's Wife" © 1996 Touchstone Pictures & Samuel Goldwyn Company

NOT LONG AFTER the movie opened, Ronald bought a gorgeous estate in the Hamptons on fifty-seven acres known as "The Creeks" and invited me to decompress in his four-bedroom pool house. He asked me to tell him if it needed anything to make it more comfortable. After a few days, I told him he should get some bathmats, wastebaskets, and hair dryers, stuff like that. I also bought him some magnifying mirrors for next to the sink. "You're friends aren't that young," I said. "I can't see over the sink to put on my makeup.

Ronald was the king of what I called speed partying — stay fifteen minutes at each place. That's all he needed to see those he wanted or needed to see, and to be seen in return. One night I went with him to three events. I had a sip or two of a drink, but no more, and the next morning I woke up feeling stiffness in my left arm. It didn't hurt as much as it felt weird. I paged Ronald, who couldn't answer the phone because it was the Sabbath. He prayed for three hours on Saturdays. But security rushed in and then the paramedics. "Hey, it's Laverne," one of them said.

After we got around to talking about my symptoms, they checked my vital signs and then loaded me into the ambulance, all while I was protesting that I was feeling better and didn't need to go to the hospital. I stopped protesting when I was wheeled into the ER and saw that the doctor waiting to examine me was an Andy Garcia look-alike. That was not an unpleasant way to spend a Saturday. After sunset, Ronald showed up with the head of the hospital in tow.

By this time, they had given me a nitroglycerin pill even though the tests they ran earlier hadn't indicated a heart attack. I was feeling strong and feisty and was ready to go back to Ronald's, but the doctor wanted to me stay in the hospital twenty-four hours so they could watch me. I thought that was unnecessary. I asked what they thought the chances were of me suffering another bout of this mysterious whatever-it-was. The doctor put the odds at 50-50. "I'll take that chance," I said.

Although Ronald offered to have all of the hospital equipment shipped to his house, I ended up spending the night at the hospital. Cell phones were now being used, and I borrowed one from one of Ronald's security guards who stayed in the room with me. I called my brother, sister, and daughter and let them know I was fine. I also canceled a trip to Houston the next day to visit my good friend and editor Battle Davis, who had been diagnosed with an aggressive form of lymphoma after working on *Renaissance Man*. That was the dark cloud in my life then. Battle and I were close. His prognosis didn't look good—and it didn't get better. He died a few months later, at age forty-one.

The next day, as I returned to Ronald's, I heard a report on the radio that I'd suffered a heart attack. No, I hadn't. I was fine. Despite all the tests, the problem had never been diagnosed. The doctors said I had Syndrome X or Prinzmetal's angina, which I thought meant I'm not supposed to listen to heavy-metal music. I still don't know what it means. But I do know I only get it when I'm totally relaxed. My remedy? I needed more stress. Yet as we turned onto Ronald's estate, I had one of those moments when the extraordinary beauty of his property, especially the trees, which had been there forever, made me appreciate all my good fortune. Life happened too quickly—except for Ronald's trees. I had to remember to take it in — and find a project.

Back home, I produced Harvey Miller's movie *Getting Away With Murder,* a comedy he wrote and directed with Danny Aykroyd, Jack Lemmon, and Lily Tomlin. I also acquired a spec script titled *Cinderella Man.* It was the story of James Braddock, an Irish-American boxer from Jersey who shocked the sports world and became a Depression-era symbol of hope when he left the loading docks and won the world's heavyweight title.

A friend of the Braddock family from North Carolina wrote the script and sent it to me. Even though I'm not crazy about boxing, I thought it was an excellent story and arranged a reading at my house. I called Mark Wahlberg, who I immediately saw in the lead. "Get over here," I said. "I need you." Paul Giamatti also came up and read the part of Braddock's friend. Jimmy Woods read the role of his agent. Certain parts needed to be built up, but I thought it had potential.

Then Harvey Weinstein got involved and wanted Ben Affleck for the lead. As much as I liked Ben, I didn't think he was right. I also had Russell Crowe up at my house wanting the part. But he had done only one U.S. movie at that point, and Harvey wasn't interested in him. Or in me.

It was one of the few times people were really shitty to me. But I didn't care. My deal on the movie was in place — it was still in place ten years later when they finally made *Cinderella Man* with Russell, at that time an Academy Award winner, in the lead, and Paul in a role that combined his friend and agent. In fact, when they sent the script to Paul, who received an Oscar nomination for his performance, he said, "I read this script at Penny's years ago."

My skin was thicker when Disney came to me with *The Preacher's Wife,* a script based on *The Bishop's Wife,* a 1947 Christmastime romantic comedy about a bishop whose prayers for help rebuilding his church are answered in the form of an angel who also seems to have a thing for his wife. It starred David Niven as the bishop, Loretta Young as his wife, and Cary Grant as the angel. I watched it and didn't think it made sense.

I met with Loretta Young, the only cast member from the original film still alive. She lived in Beverly Hills and was lovely. She agreed with me that her version of the movie didn't make any sense because in the end the angel wanted her to go with him. Where were they going to go?

"They never got it quite right," she said.

I thought the same was true with the script for *The Preacher's Wife*, which the studio wanted out for Christmas. I sent it back to the studio with notes explaining why and how the script didn't make sense. They wanted a love story between the angel and the preacher's wife, who was in the church choir and very religious (and Loretta wasn't in the choir in the original). It didn't any sense for the preacher's wife to get involved with the angel like that. To me, the real story was about the preacher losing his faith, not about his wife complaining that he was too busy.

I turned it down. But they kept sending the script back to me until finally it came together enough to change my mind. Then it kept getting delayed for one reason or another, but mostly because the studio wanted Denzel Washington as the angel, and he went off to make another movie.

In the interim, Kmart came to me and said they wanted Rosie O'Donnell to do a series of commercials for them, but she would only agree if I did them with her. They told her the same thing about me; that my yes was contingent on her being in the ads. They played it well. They signed both of us. We met up on weekends, got paid a lot of money, and became best of friends. We were allowed to take whatever we wanted from the stores. My nieces and nephews loved me.

When I finally met with Denzel, I confirmed my gut instinct: I wanted him as the preacher. I thought the movie was the preacher's story, and I could envision him filling out that role with depth and charm. But he wanted the Cary Grant part, and I understood. Courtney Vance, who'd read for me in *Renaissance Man,* came to my house for another reading and nailed the part of the preacher. He was fantastic.

That left the pivotal role of the preacher's wife.

"Should we use Whitney?" Denzel asked, with a note of hesitation in his voice.

"Who else?" I said.

Whitney Houston had starred in two major hits, *The Bodyguard* and *Waiting to Exhale,* and she had the biggest recording career in the music business. Although she was on the road, I'd heard she was interested in *The Preacher's Wife,* and of course I was intrigued. I had never met her, but after a meeting in New York, I left a fan. She was sweet and her passion for this world came through loud and clear as she described how she started to sing as a child in Newark's New Hope Baptist Church.

Her marriage to R&B star Bobby Brown a few years earlier had confused those who thought of her only as a wholesome churchgoing girl. He was a stereotypical bad boy, and no one had more of a good-girl image than she did. Tabloid headlines aside, there were rumors inside the industry. I'm sure Denzel had heard stories. I had heard stories, too. I had said one thing to Whitney: Be honest with me. I just want to know the truth.

She said okay and then let me know that she couldn't sing every day, just like baseball pitchers couldn't pitch every day. She needed some time between sessions. She also mentioned that her pitch changed a little when she had her period. I appreciated knowing all the little things she told me.

"Just let me know, and we'll adapt," I said.

I brought in Jennifer Lewis as Whitney's mother and Gregory Hines, both of whom had been in *Renaissance Man.* I was a fan of Loretta Devine, who played Courtney's secretary, and I still remember casting young Justin Pierre Edmund as Whitney and Courtney's son, Jeremiah Biggs. During the test, he sounded like his nose was stuffed. His mother said he had a cold. Well, it turned out he talked that way. So we wrote in a couple lines where Jennifer referred to his cold. Problem solved.

By this point, I knew making movies was an exercise in flexibility. Denzel missed a few days of rehearsal in New York because he got hung up on a movie. When he did show up, he was frustrated by the lack of reaction to his read. Even Whitney was getting laughs. Well, he pushed, and that's the worst thing you do in comedy. Then we couldn't find him the next day. I called and got nothing. Later, he gave me a story about having just come off another movie.

"What the fuck?" I said. "Apologize to your fellow actors. Every one of them is looking up to you because of who you are. It's not nice to skip out. Just tell me. Say 'Hey, I'm going to a party,' or 'I have to do something to switch gears.' I don't like it. It's on my time. But I understand."

Denzel understood, too. When we arrived on the set the next day he was the definition of a leading man in every way. Our first day of shooting was in a courthouse in Yonkers. Courtney, as Reverend Henry Biggs, gave a speech at the hearing for Billy Eldridge, a teen who'd been wrongly arrested for robbing a local mom-and-pop grocery store. It was freezing out. A heavy snowstorm had left six feet of snow on the ground, causing a daylong delay. We couldn't get the trucks in. Since we had the courtroom for only two days, we shot for twenty-four hours straight. The crew, who'd worked with me on *League,* started singing, "We are the members of the All-American League . . ."

Weather and logistics pose unexpected challenges on every shoot, but *The Preacher's Wife* tossed a few new ones at me. For instance, the Pope visited New York City and the Popemobile tied up traffic on a day when we were shooting the interiors of the reverend's house on a soundstage at the Chelsea Piers. The exteriors of the homes and the church were in Yonkers. And the interior of the church was in Newark. In other words, nothing was in one place.

So when people in the church are getting up to leave, they are in Newark, and when they exit they are in Yonkers. Makes sense, right? No. But that's how movies are made.

There was a man who lived in the apartment building across the street from the house we were using for exteriors in Yonkers, and he did not like our trucks clogging the streets and taking up all the parking spaces. He let us know his displeasure, too. Every time I yelled action, he cranked up his music. After a few frustrating times, I figured out that I could fool him by yelling the opposite: cut when we started a scene and action when we finished.

That was a small annoyance compared to the disaster that occurred a short time later. We were shooting the scene where Jennifer Lewis as Margueritte was taking food to Hakim's (Darvel Davis Jr.) grandmother, who lived across the street. Jennifer and Denzel had to walk and talk as they went to the building.

In the middle of the third or fourth take, Jennifer was about to reach the top step of the building, and I was about to ask for the cameras to go in close for coverage. Then I heard a loud explosion, a thundering boom. Everything stopped. Producer Tim Bourne was next to me, and I turned to him and said, "What happened?" Moments later, we found out. A home around the corner and two houses down had burst into flames. We could see the fire shooting through the roof and out the windows.

Our grips and crew dropped everything, grabbed some ladders and hoses from neighboring yards, and pulled a six-year-old child from the house. Later, we learned that two children had died inside. Two teenagers were later charged with second-degree murder and second-degree arson. All of us heard the whole thing as it unfolded, from the explosion to the roar of the teens speeding away in a car. Then the fire trucks arrived, as well as the cops, and they boxed us in all night.

Another time Whitney looked around one Newark neighborhood where we were shooting and said, "This is a crack neighborhood." I replied, "Do you think they're going to get high and come out and shoot the actors? I don't think that's what happens on crack." Of course, I had never done crack. At least I didn't think I had. I had to call Lorne and ask if we had ever done crack.

"No, it was after our time," he said.

"Good," I said. "Just checking."

But for all that, there were days on *Preacher's Wife* when I felt like the spirit was shining on us. Before production, I had searched for the right choir for the scenes inside the church when Whitney would be singing with the choir. I had gone to Whitney's church, The New Hope Baptist, where she had learned to sing. I could see it was a special environment. Her mother, Cissy, still worked there. I put her in the movie, too. I had also gone to Denzel's church in L.A., the First AME. Finally, I scouted the Georgia Mass Choir in Atlanta. They were perfect for the movie.

Although we only used part of the 150-member group, they sounded at full strength when we shot Whitney and the whole choir singing "I Love the Lord" and "Joy to the World" inside the Newark church. I'm a gospel music fan, but it wasn't necessary to be a fan to know these takes were extraordinary. Nor did you have to be religious to sense a special, powerful spirit fill the church. During "Joy," they sped up, the floor shook, and everyone from the crew to the choir members jumped, stomped, and swayed. Jesus was in the house. I could feel it. Miroslav could, too. He pushed the camera in closer.

Despite reports, I didn't have any problems with Whitney. Yes, she did have an entourage, and yes, there were a few times when she fought with her husband, Bobby Brown, on the phone, and yes, she did on occasion miss her call times. But her people always sent word that she was going to be late or unable to work and we altered the schedule. That's all I asked. Let me know what was going on.

I know years later she told Oprah Winfrey that her drug use was already such a problem that she was getting high every day. She qualified that by explaining that she only did them at night, after work, so that could explain why I didn't see her misbehaving or high. If she had been high, I would have noticed. We talked before, during, and after scenes. We pushed in close often enough that I would have seen a change in her eyes. Bobby only came to the set a couple times, but he stayed in her camper. He was never a problem. If she "wasn't happy," as she told Oprah, I didn't see it on the set.

I'll tell you what I did see: greatness. On the night we shot her singing in Jazzy's, the club where Whitney's character, Julia, had sung as a younger woman, she brought all the talent, charisma, and magic that made her a superstar. In the scene, she let her old pianist, Bristloe, played superbly by Lionel Richie, coax her back onstage. We were at the end of the shooting schedule. This was her solo, her big song, and we'd worked hard behind the scenes to simply pick a goddamn song for her to sing.

Given the massive successes of the soundtracks of her previous two movies, as well as her own recording career, she was being pressured from all sides on which song to choose. Everyone around her seemed to have an opinion. She was overwhelmed by submissions. She couldn't make a decision and went into shutdown mode.

About a month earlier I had asked what she wanted to sing at Jazzy's. I wanted to nail down a song. I went into her Winnebago which she kept at 120 fucking degrees. I was layered in winter clothes and dying. I had to talk real fast. She explained if she picked so-and-so's song they would get royalties. If she did a cover, like she did with Dolly Parton's "I Will Always Love You" on *The Bodyguard*, that person or group would get royalties. It was about money. Everyone wanted a cut.

I cut to the chase.

"Look, I don't get a cent either way," I said. "So let me ask you this: What do you *want* to sing?"

"There's a Four Tops song," she said. "It's called 'I Believe in You and Me.' That's what I want to sing."

She played it for me. I saw how it fit into the movie. I said fine, let's do that. I was dying from the heat.

We shot the scene in a club on 14th Street in Manhattan. Whitney and Denzel were seated at a table. Then Lionel came in and said a few lines that set Whitney up to get on the stage. Denzel clapped at the table as she stepped up to the microphone. It sounds simple, but these things take forever. As the scene wore on, I saw Denzel get a little cranky. Whitney said he had a case of suit fever, which was like cabin fever, except she was referring to the gray suit he wore throughout the movie. He had eighteen of them; they were exactly the same.

I let him go home, took his place at the table, and had Whitney sing to me. We did a number of takes and each time I got chills. Like everyone there that night, I knew these performances were special.

Then it got better. BeBe Winans, the award-winning gospel singer, had come to visit and even though I had what I needed for the movie, I also had Whitney onstage, Lionel Richie on piano, and the Grammy-winning producer-musician-arranger Mervyn Warren leading the band. So I said, "Why don't you go up and sing with her?"

It was 4 a.m., but after huddling with Mervyn for a few moments, BeBe and Whitney sang together, and it was unbelievable, one of those genuine you-had-to-be-there experiences where talent was on full display alongside the sheer joy of singing. I'll never forget it.

CHAPTER 42

The Last Bull Run

Dennis Rodman driving Penny away on a motorcycle after a 1997
Pacers-Bulls playoff game

Nunu Zomot

LOGIC WAS MY COMPASS. On- and off-screen, I tried to base everything I did on what I thought made the most sense. Was it logical? Most of the time things worked out, but *The Preacher's Wife* tested my faith. We had shot in one of the coldest winters on record, starting on a day that dropped record-breaking snowfall on the East Coast, and yet when we traveled up to Portland, Maine, to shoot the scene with Whitney and Denzel ice-skating, the weather changed.

It started to get warm. The ice melted. Things began to grow. We had to make fake snow and work fast. I went straight to Whitney and said, "Now I need you. I don't care what's going on. You've got to be here every day."

And she was.

I edited through the summer and was looping some of the actors that fall in New York when I heard that my close friend Ted Bessell had died unexpectedly at UCLA Medical Center of an aortic aneurysm. Ted was only fifty-seven. I knew that he'd gone to the doctor twice before, complaining of chest pains, and they'd said it was anxiety. He was directing *The Tracey Ullman Show*. He had also joined my production company and was preparing to direct *Bewitched*, the feature film that eventually got made with Nicole Kidman and Will Ferrell.

My jaw hit the table when I heard the news. I loved that man. I didn't want others who were close to him to also hear about it on TV. I called Louise Lasser, who had gone with Ted years earlier and lived in New York. Then I called Rob at home in L.A.. His wife said he was busy. "Just get him," I insisted. Rob hadn't heard yet. Like me, he gasped, "Oh, my God." It was a deep shock; Ted was a dear friend for thirty years. He was one of us.

At his funeral, the casket was open. MTM writer-producer Ed Weinberger's wife, Carlene, and I put rouge on Ted's cheeks. He looked too pale. Ted's wife had a high mass, but about a month later Ed Weinberger rented a room at the Beverly Hills Hotel so those of us who were Ted's friends could say a less formal good-bye. Wearing buttons that said "I'm a Ted Head," we reverted back to the people we'd been in our twenties. We laughed, we cried. It was a fantastic night, as much as such a night can be.

Then, as I worked on finishing the movie, the studio began talking to me about their marketing plan, and I didn't quite get it. *The Preacher's Wife* was a Christmas fable told through the eyes of a child who talked to an angel. It was a family movie for the holidays. But the studio wanted to sell a love story between Whitney and Denzel. The record label also couldn't make up its mind about which songs, and further, which versions of which songs, they wanted on the soundtrack. By the time the movie opened, the Christmas season was half over.

Too bad, too. Critics from the *New York Times* to the *Los Angeles Times* to Roger Ebert in the *Chicago Sun-Times* found plenty to recommend. But I knew it needed help. I went to New York to do press with Whitney, and while there, I called Lorne and said, "I think we need *Saturday Night Live*." He made it very easy. Even better, he arranged for Rosie O'Donnell to host.

Unfortunately I lost my voice at the end of the press junket and woke up Saturday morning barely able to make a sound. That had happened to me once before when I was playing Ado Annie in *Okla-homa!* I went to Ronald's doctor and told him about some red stuff that I had gargled with right before I needed my voice and it lasted for about two minutes.

Somehow he knew what I was talking about. I was impressed. As a result, I was able to participate in three sketches, including one where Rosie, Whitney, and I sang "I've Got You Babe."

Then I left the country, as I always did when one of my movies opened. This time the destinations were Laos and Cambodia. I went with Janie Wenner, the ex-wife of *Rolling Stone* founder Jann Wenner. Janie liked getting away over the holidays, I think because she and Jann had wed at Christmastime in 1967. With a private jet at her disposal, she asked if I wanted to join her and a couple friends. I signed on immediately.

After *SNL*, I went home and packed, and we left in the morning. We stopped in Turkey to refuel and let the pilots sleep. Then we arrived in Laos, a country of immense beauty and extreme poverty. The people were sweet. The children we saw had nothing. I gave them everything I could down to the pencils and pens in my bag.

We explored the capital, Vientiane, and boated on the Mekong River before heading into Cambodia, a rougher country where we needed guards. We went to Angkor Wat and Angkor Thom, both ancient temples, and I tried to take video but kept shooting my feet, underscoring how mechanically challenged I am. We went to Phnom Penh and saw parents pinch their kids to get them to cry while they were begging for money. It was a different, unsettling culture. As an antidote to all the terribleness and poverty, we bought shit from the locals like you wouldn't believe and gave it away.

We spent New Year's at our hotel, where we bumped into *60 Minutes* executive producer Don Hewitt and Atlantic Records founder Ahmet Ertegun and their wives. They were with a party coming from Vietnam. There's an immediate camaraderie when you're traveling abroad and see fellow Americans. We all ate together and listened to an all-girl band lip-sync to American pop songs. We may as well have been in a Hyatt in Detroit.

On the way back home, we stopped for a day in Hawaii so the pilots could sleep. My brother was still there with his family for their annual holiday trip. I was half out of my mind with jet lag when I saw him. He asked how my trip had been. I showed him a monk's outfit that I'd bought. Didn't that say it all?

In February 1997, the studio sent me to Europe to promote *The Preacher's Wife*. I wasn't against taking a trip, but what was the purpose? *The Preacher's Wife* was a Christmas movie. Did they celebrate Christmas later in Europe? I didn't think so. It just shows the challenges studios needlessly create for themselves. However, the movie turned out to be a warmly received moneymaker, as well as a tribute to Whitney's talents. I had no complaints.

Life was good. I went into my office every so often, read scripts, and surfaced occasionally on TV shows, like the episode of *Nash Bridges* I did at the end of the year so I could hang out with my friend Don Johnson, the show's star. I appreciated the freedom I had to play.

I embraced it, too. After shooting a Kmart commercial in Detroit, I flew to Chicago with my hairstylist, who wanted to see his family there. I wanted to go to a basketball game. The Chicago Bulls were in the Eastern Conference Finals against the Indiana Pacers, vying to win a third NBA championship in a row for the second time. I was able to get seats close enough to the action that I almost felt like I was in the game.

Sometimes I was. I knew Pacer forward Chris Mullin from when he played for the Golden State Warriors. At the Los Angeles Lakers games, he would dribble past me and say, "Hey, Bronx." He was from Brooklyn. He did the same thing at the Bulls game. We had gotten friendly, and then I became close friends with his wife, Liz. She was impressed with my intensity.

But what wasn't to like? These guys were gorgeous, and they

barely wore any clothes. Then, the Bulls won and moved on to the championships, and I celebrated that night at a Mexican restaurant with some of the players, including Steve Kerr, Ron Harper, Bill Wennnington, and Tony Kukoc. Later, I met up with the team's flamboyant rebounding and defensive specialist Dennis Rodman at the House of Blues. He put me on the back of his motorcycle and took me to a strip club. At that point, I said no, thank you. His idea of fun wasn't necessarily mine.

I was back in New York when the Bulls played the Utah Jazz for the NBA championship, and I was caught up in the excitement, the team's quest to make history. I watched the first two games on TV since they were in Utah; they each won one before returning to Chicago. Ronald's then-partner, Donald Drapkin, had the corporate jet, and we took it there for game three. I brought a friend from New York who liked the Bulls, and we ended up staying in Chicago for the next three games.

There were celebrities at every game, but I thought the athletes were the real stars. I was awed by Michael Jordan's ability and poise on the court; off it, he had an equally impressive knack of always saying the right thing, like when he told me not to pay attention to the fans' boos when they put me on the JumboTron. "They just know that you're from L.A.," he said. "But I know you're a basketball fan." Dennis and Scottie Pippen were great, too.

Led by Jordan, the Bulls won two games, but then they lost the third, ruining their chance of winning the title in front of their hometown fans. They had to go back to Salt Lake City, and we arranged to follow. How could you break away from the excitement and drama?

I couldn't — and game six turned out to be the best one of all. The Jazz held the lead late into the game, but Jordan made a crucial steal and then hit the game-winning shot with five seconds left on the clock. The Bulls owned the title for the third time in a row, the sixth time in eight years, and Jordan was named the MVP. Leonardo DiCaprio was there, and he wanted to meet Michael. After the game, I took him into the locker room. Actually, both of us followed Dennis's bodyguard, George T., who cut a path through the crowd. The whole scene was pretty remarkable.

Those of us looking to Chicago to fourpeat were disappointed. During the off-season, the team began a rebuilding phase. Michael Jordan retired and Scottie Pippen, Steve Kerr, and Luc Longley, all mainstays, were traded. With the Bulls' dynasty ended, the Los Angeles Lakers saw their opportunity to recapture some of the glory they had enjoyed in the Magic Johnson–led "Showtime" era. They had two young superstars in Shaquille O'Neal and Kobe Bryant, and the team put together a talented supporting cast that included veterans Robert Horry, Derek Fisher, Rick Fox, and Glen Rice.

The Lakers also wanted Dennis Rodman, who had not been offered a new contract with the Bulls. The team had run out of patience with his off-the-court antics. Wearing a wedding dress to promote his memoir didn't win him any fans in the front office. But the Lakers saw value in him, and they called me.

I guess word had spread that I knew the game's flamboyant bad boy. Why wouldn't I know him? I had radar to the insane. One day I got a call from the team's owner, Jerry Buss, asking if I would speak to Dennis about playing for the Lakers. They had spoken to his reps and felt they also needed someone who knew show business to pitch him on the benefits of playing in Hollywood.

Dennis was unconventional. He was scarred from a childhood spent in one of the poorest neighborhoods in Dallas. For most of his youth, his two sisters were considered better basketball players than him. Nothing about him was normal, including his work ethic. He may have had green hair, but he was one of the hardest-working athletes in the NBA. He practiced before games, played hard, and then worked out again *after* the game.

I understood my mission and spoke to him one day in the private club at the Forum. I said, "Look, you're doing your whole act. Why not do it in Hollywood?" The harder part, which wasn't my job, was keeping him with the team. He only played for twenty-three games.

Then he showed up once without his sneakers, and the team's general manager, basketball legend Jerry West — who was respected for his shrewdness as an executive even more than as a player (and he's a Hall of Famer) — fired Dennis's ass.

I fared better. In appreciation of the effort I made recruiting Dennis, Jerry Buss gave me a set of coveted floor seats for Lakers games at the L.A. Forum and then at the Staples Center where they moved the next season. I had to pay for the tickets, but they were fabulous. I was with notable Lakers diehards Jack Nicholson, producer Lou Adler, and Dyan Cannon; and best of all, I was next to the action. They spoiled me forever.

Even forever has its limits. In January 1999, Harvey Miller returned to L.A. from the Hamptons and died of a massive heart attack. I helped organize a memorial at my brother's theater, the Falcon, in Toluca Lake. It was the first of a few such gatherings we'd have there over the years. All of us who knew and adored Harvey were there, including Garry, Danny Aykroyd, Albert Brooks, and Rob, who looked around the theater and said it was like being back in our old living room on Hesby.

It felt like it, too. We reminisced, traded stories, and agreed that the previous year had been the happiest of Harvey's sixty-three years. We all watched a video of clips I put together from his recent one-man play, *A Cheap Date with Harvey Miller: The Comedic Life of a Legendary Unknown,* which had been backed by my basketball friends Dennis Rodman and sports agent Dwight Manley, and Harvey made us laugh again. If you want people to remember you for something, laughter ain't a bad thing to leave behind. Danny recalled his favorite Harvey joke ("A skeleton walks into a bar and orders a beer and a mop"), and Dick Gregory, who'd given Harvey his first break as a joke writer, sent a note that said, "Laughter is the best medicine and you've given us a big dose."

Seven months later, we dealt with another loss when my father passed away. Garry, Ronny, and I had been taking good care of him since his stroke. He didn't want for anything and had all the help he needed. He went to his country club every day and drank with his cronies. My sister went over to his place and paid his bills. When he saw me, he shook his fist. "You never come over!"

That summer he was diagnosed with cancer. Garry broke the news to him. "Pop, you have to go into the hospital and have surgery." He died the next day. "I wish we would've told him ten years earlier," I joked. "We could've saved a fortune." He was cremated and remembered at his country club where his friends, including Bob Hope, toasted him with a shot of vodka and a middle-finger salute.

"Here's to you, Tony," they said. "Fuck you!"

I called Lorne and asked if I could use his office again. Then I flew to New York and sprinkled my father's ashes out his window. "Be with Mommy again," I said. I'm sure that thrilled her. Unlike my mother, though, he didn't get a song.

But all was not heavy-hearted. After fifteen years of struggling in secret, David Lander revealed publicly that he had multiple sclerosis. I had known since the early '80s. He said he felt strange during the last year of *Laverne & Shirley*. Sometimes he fell down. Then he was diagnosed with MS. But he kept quiet about his condition for a long time so he'd still get work. He said he'd rather be thought of as an alcoholic; there was less stigma to that in Hollywood. I had used him in *League*. He was a huge baseball fan. A while later I spoke to Tom Sherrick, Fox's president of marketing, who was very involved in MS fundraising, who asked if David had MS. I said I didn't know. But I told David that he should speak to Tom about coming out if and when he was ever ready. In June 1999, he came out, and his wife, Kathy, told me that it changed his life. He wrote a book, *Fall Down Laughing*, started speaking to groups, and has continued to do fine.

About a year later, David called with news he knew I'd want to hear. He had spoken with Cindy Williams and learned that she had split with her husband, Bill Hudson, after 10 years of marriage and two children.

"You should call her," he said.

"Where is she?" I asked.

"She's doing a play in Kansas City."

I was eager to reconnect. I had seen Cindy once or twice over the years at TV Land specials, but these occasions were more professional than personal, always fleeting and in crowds. We never sat down and talked about the unfortunate way we had parted on *Laverne & Shirley*, or how much I had missed her over the years. I still considered her a friend. We had shared too much for me to consider her anything but a special person in my life.

So I called her as soon as I hung up with David, and the two of us had a good conversation. I told her that I'd heard the news, asked if she needed anything, and if she wanted to stay at my place. Everyone else did. I also told her to call Bill's first wife, Goldie Hawn. "Just call Goldie," I said. "It's the best advice I can give you."

After Cindy finished her play, we got together at my house and had the conversation I wished I'd been able to have fifteen years earlier. I told her of my frustration with the way the show had ended and that I'd called numerous times to get her back, but Bill never let me talk to her. The same thing happened in the years after we finished. I hadn't been able to get through to her. Naturally, she had her side of the story and remained unapologetic for leaving the show and forcing me to drive it solo through the last season. She was steadfast in her belief that we didn't want her. Of course, I reiterated how wrong she was, but in the end what could I do? We agreed to disagree. I didn't have to be right. Those things happen in life. You move on. Our friendship was more important.

CHAPTER 43

Riding in Cars

Penny directing Drew Barrymore in 2001's *Riding in Cars with Boys*

*J*IM BROOKS HAD gotten ahold of the rights to *Riding in Cars with Boys* from Sara Colleton, who had optioned Beverly Donofrio's memoir about getting pregnant at fifteen and overcoming numerous challenges on her way to getting a degree and becoming a writer. After reading the script, I didn't love it. But, as Jim probably knew would happen when he pushed the project in front of me, I identified with the character from my own experiences of having a kid and getting married. Even if a girl hasn't gone through that she's probably thought, *What if.*

My wheels began turning. I had people in New York read actresses for the part of Beverly and I read them like crazy at my house. I brought in Kate Hudson, Marisa Tomei (I didn't need her to play ball in this one), and Reese Witherspoon, who was pregnant and asked me not to videotape her. I said fine. So she read and did a good job. Hillary Swank and Angelina Jolie both came in. Anne Hathaway did, too. But she was too young. I sent her over to my brother, who used her in *The Princess Diaries* and said thank you to me.

I had readings for the other parts, too. I wasn't even through the list of actresses and actors being sent to me and I could have cut a whole movie together just from my readings. But then Jim came to me and suggested Drew Barrymore for the lead. He saw her in the role. I thought she was a terrific girl and very nice, but I had Marisa and Kate in mind.

It didn't matter. Amy Pascal, the studio president, informed me that Jim had already promised the part to Drew. I was furious. If that was the case, why not tell me? That's all I ever asked from anyone. Tell me the truth. I wouldn't have wasted so many people's time, including mine.

So I hired Brittany Murphy as her best friend, added Sara Gilbert, and got ready to go. Then suddenly we had to put everything on hold and wait for *Charlie's Angels* to wrap. Once we did start, nothing was smooth. Drew didn't think my Academy Award–winning cinematographer, Chris Menges, was lighting her properly. Chris explained why she was wrong. But Jim made me fire Chris, one of the nicest people in the business, and I had to bring Miroslav out of retirement.

I brought in Jimmy Woods to play Beverly's father, but he was on a movie with Denzel that went long, requiring me to shoot pieces of scenes as I waited for him. Lorraine Bracco, who played his wife, would say a line that should have had Jimmy there to respond to, but what could I do? The script also drove me crazy; there were no transitions. I'd call Steve Zahn in all the time to make them up as we went along. One time he said, "Can I bring my dog?" I said, 'Sure." I didn't care who or what was there as long as I could get from one part to the next. I mean we saw Beverly as a child, then as a teen, then raising her child, and then as an author needing permission from her ex before she could publish her book. There were no in-betweens. It just skipped years.

Plus Jim, who could normally be counted on for his share of brilliant ideas, was going through a divorce and producing *What About Joan,* a television series with Joan Cusack, so he was a little preoccupied. It all was a mess from the get-go. As a general rule, don't work with people who are getting divorced. They're thinking about other things.

We shot a bit on City Island, in New York, but spent the bulk of production in New Jersey. We built our own town on the campus of the defunct Upsala College, in East Orange. After we finished, the fire department set fire to the homes and storefronts we'd built and used them for practice. Meanwhile, I brought in people I knew, like Rosie Perez, who was funny, and David Moscow, who had been in *Big*. If he could understand me when he was twelve, I figured he could do even better now in his twenties, and he did.

Brittany Murphy was also a trouper. She would work through anything. She was sick as a dog when we shot a scene where Drew's kid fell in the pool. No problem. I also knew she could sing; I'd seen her test for the Janis Joplin movie that never got made. So I asked her to sing "Soldier Boy." She jumped into it. No problem. I appreciated that attitude. Drew required more finesse and patience. However, Miroslav was able to say whatever he wanted to her because he didn't speak any known language, so she always thought it was something nice.

This was the first of all the pictures I did where I felt less than fully in control of the challenges, and it was because I didn't I have any support. Even when Whoopi was angry on *Jumpin' Jack Flash,* I had Joel Silver and Larry Gordon backing me up. Jim was going through too much shit to pay attention, and his response when he did focus was usually a variation of "Well, cut to Drew." He wanted all Drew, all the time. That might have worked in another movie, but this wasn't one of them. There was too much other stuff going on.

We'd had several screenings for the studio and had sort of finished putting it together when 9/11 happened. The studio pushed all the violent movies back and asked if we could come out in October. I said sure. The movie wasn't going to get any better. It was what it was. The bigger problem was getting people into the theaters. The president of the United States was warning the public to stay away from malls. Where were we going to open?

I wanted a premiere in New York. Besides drawing attention to the movie, it would serve as a positive event for the city. It was shot in New York. We had a New York crew. Most of the actors were from the East. And as a New Yorker myself, I thought it was important to show the terrorists and the world that the United States was not going to be intimidated and New York City was not going to be stopped. But Jim said no. Like many others, he didn't want to come in from L.A. I was furious. I took it personally.

I called Lorne and said I needed a date for Drew to host *Saturday Night Live*. He said fine, no problem, and put her on the October 13 show. However, unbeknownst to me, she didn't get on the plane from Los Angeles to rehearse. I got the call from Lorne. "Guess what? She's not here." Eventually she showed up, but fled again when an envelope containing white powder and a note stating that it was anthrax was delivered to NBC's offices at 30 Rock.

I called Ronald Perelman and said I needed his security people, all ex-cops, to find Drew. They located her in the doorway of her hotel and took her to their doctor.

Rosie O'Donnell was ready to fill in. "Look, I'm already on Cipro," she said, referring to the antibiotic that was a treatment for those exposed to anthrax. But Drew resurfaced in time, summoned her courage, and did the show. Her monologue was an accurate account of what had happened.

"I was so afraid to fly here — so I canceled my trip," she said. "And then I saw Giuliani on television saying to be brave. So, the next day I got on an airplane. Then we started rehearsing, and I got calm, I got really excited. And then, yesterday, they discovered anthrax in the building! So, I immediately left. I went back to the hotel, and I thought again about being brave. So I came back, and I'm here, and *you're* here, and *you're* being brave, too! And I thank you for it! And

I want to thank my husband, because he's here and he's supporting me — Tom, thank you!"

They cut to comedian Tom Green, who was sitting in the front wearing a gas mask.

I flew into New York the next day, after Carrie and I had celebrated our birthdays, the last of our joint parties. We had done them for twenty years. They were like the *Vanity Fair* party after the Oscars. It was too much — and too expensive. When you see Shaquille O'Neal and Salman Rushdie waiting for their cars at the end of your driveway, you know things are out of control.

The day after arriving in New York, I attended Denis Leary's benefit for the Firefighters Foundation. It was at a club downtown, and everyone was there: James Gandolfini, Lorraine Bracco, Julianne Moore, Rosie Perez, Ronald Perelman and his then-wife, Ellen Barkin. I was going to read "Sitting," a poem my brother had written a few days after the attack. But I knew I couldn't make it through without breaking down. Ellen graciously read it for me and brought the place to tears.

Sitting

If you ever sat on a curb
Or on a park fence railing
Or a running board
Or on a red fire escape landing
It's time to stand up and stand together.

If you ever sat in Shea Stadium
Or bygone Ebbets Field
Or the stands of Yankee Stadium
Or in the shadows of the Polo Grounds
It's time to stand up and stand together.

If you ever sat under a low-lit lamppost
Or in an empty subway car
Or the dark balcony of a movie
Or on a gray cement stoop
It's time to stand up and stand together.

If you ever sat on a bridge chair in front of your building
On a roof of tar in the sun
Or on a snow bank piled by your sidewalk
Or on a pony in the aromatic Bronx Zoo
It's time to stand up and stand together.

If you ever sat at a table at the Automat
Or the stairwell of your public school
At a desk with a blue black ink well
Or on a spinning soda fountain stool
It's time to stand up and stand together.

If you ever sat on a fire hydrant
On a car fender
On an orange crate
Or on the seat of a three-wheeler or a Schwinn
It's time to stand up and stand together.

If you ever sat on a bench in Central Park
Or the Ferris wheel at Coney Island
On a blanket at Orchard Beach or Jones Beach
Or the deck of the Staten Island Ferry
If you ever sat in any of these places, you're probably from
New York City. They're burying people in New York these
days, but they'll never bury the New York spirit. It's time to
stand up and stand together . . . to make sure the spirit of
New York City shall go on forever.

The following evening I hosted a screening for the cast and crew. Before the film, I stood in the front of the theater and asked if there was any press in attendance. No hands went up. "Good," I said, and then let everyone there know exactly how I felt about the situation.

At the end of the week, I was in Cuba. As was my habit, I had made plans to get out of the country when the movie opened, and I stuck to them. I flew there with a guy I knew from Texas. I had a script that was partially set in Havana. We went to the Communist beach, which was a pain in the ass. So we changed to the public beach. The hotel where we stayed was beautiful, but I left all my clothes there for the people, who had nothing.

Five days later, I was back in New York, where I made it my job to attend every public event where I might be needed, seen, and photographed. I made it my mission to testify to the safety of New York City and the resiliency of being a New Yorker. I showed up at benefits for firefighters. Patty Smyth and I bought supplies, including new bed sheets and blankets, for our local firehouse, Engine 74. I went to benefits held downtown. I went to anything downtown. I went to the first basketball game at Madison Square Garden, the Knicks versus the Wizards, and while there I watched the clock because I wanted to get up to Yankee Stadium for the World Series game against the Arizona Diamondbacks.

Spike Lee saw me getting up. "Where you going?" he asked.

"Yankee Stadium," I said.

"It's only the second inning," he said.

"Yeah, but there's security galore because Bush is there," I said, referring to the president.

I went to all three of those home games. I also went to Ground Zero with the firemen from Engine 7, Ladder 1 and listened to their stories, though, as I think about it, they didn't say much. They kept most of the horrors they saw that day to themselves. I did a lot of hugging and saying thank you. They made me want to go every place I could to show that it was safe in New York, and I did, non-stop.

I would flash on my mother, me, and the other children from dance class doing our routines on the subway to entertain. I could hear her say everyone should know what it's like to entertain. In those weeks and months after 9/11, I felt like everyone should know what it was like to be in New York. It was a terrible thing that happened. We had to make it better. People were doing their part. I wanted to do mine.

It was a job that suited me. For the next eight years, I devoted my time and energy to charities and sports. I got involved in helping Blake Hunt, a teenager who was left a quadriplegic after getting injured playing football. I met him at Mount Sinai Hospital in New York and followed him on to Beth Abraham, where Dr. Sacks had once worked. I also got involved in helping his roommate, Jermaine Fairweather, a college-bound kid who'd been working at Macy's when he was shot and paralyzed. Charity work agreed with me. I supported food banks and inner-city kids. I arranged for athletes to visit children in hospitals. My brother had opened my eyes years earlier when he told me that I could give someone a life. It was true—and it didn't require much effort. If you can't always provide a new life, why not do little things that simply help improve someone's life? I know it's cliché, but after getting so much, it felt good to give back.

And after more than a decade of nonstop movie-making, I finally slowed down. Movies changed, and the kind of heart-warming human dramas that I liked to make were fewer and harder to find. Indie movies were on the rise, but I liked to get paid for my time—and it takes as much out of your life to make a low- or no-budget movie as it does a movie for $25 million. I ended up directing a handful of TV shows, including *According to Jim* and *United States of Tara,* and I made two basketball-related documentaries, one for former Lakers center Vlade Divac that was only shown in his native Serbia, and the other, titled *Crossover,* chronicling the new-school foreign invasion to the NBA. It was a Showtime project that got lost in one of the network's regime changes.

I was a fixture at the Lakers and Clippers games. My seats at the Staples Center became a second living room. Phil Jackson, the Lakers' coach starting in 2000, was more aloof than the previous coach and kept the team private. But I knew Kobe Bryant. Occasionally, we went out to dinner. He was too young to go out drinking with the other players. Unlike Jack Nicholson, who took advantage of his floor seats to let the refs know what he thought and sometimes ribbed opposing players, I went to enjoy games, not run them.

Okay, once I was at a Golden State Warriors playoff game and told Stephen Jackson to walk away from a player who got under his skin. "Do you want a technical?" I asked. "Or do you want to win?" Shaq, Vlade Divac, Robert Horry, and Rick Fox were among my favorite Lakers. Mitch Richmond will always be close to my heart for giving me a championship ring. One of the refs, Bob Delaney, also amused me. He once kicked Dennis Rodman out of a game after Dennis threw a ball at him. Later, Dennis apologized.

"You're a good guy, Bob," he said. "You just need to get in touch with your inner freak."

"I didn't even know I had an inner freak," Bob said.

I was in New Jersey when the Lakers won the 2001–2002 title against the Nets, their third NBA championship in a row. It was even sweeter than seeing the Bulls' threepeat. These were my guys.

In 2004, Tracy met and married Matthew Conlan. A year later, she gave birth to a daughter, Isabella. She wanted another home delivery. This time she set up a baby pool in her bedroom and had Lori Petty filling it with warm water from the bathroom. But after she began to bleed, she ended up having the baby at the hospital. A year later, she had another girl, a cutie named Viva. By this time, her hippie days were done, and she went straight to the hospital.

I stayed home both times. After Spencer, I didn't want to be involved in any more births. "Just call me with the news," I said.

A short time later, I was in Sacramento for a Kings game against the Lakers. I had gotten to know the Kings' owners, Joe and Gavin Maloof, whose father had gone to high school with Mickey in Albuquerque. I was sitting in floor seats that night next to baseball superstar Barry Bonds. During the game, he turned to me and said, "Did you ever think when you were growing up that one day you'd be who you are and sitting here in these seats?"

I paused before answering. I thought back on my life, starting with the Grand Concourse to those days in Albuquerque when I was pregnant and scared and getting married in a suit with a fur collar that I hated, and on to all the improbable things that happened to me after I moved to Hollywood and decided to give show business a shot.

"No," I said.

"Me neither," he said.

I guess that's the way it is for everyone. It's just how life turns out. It keeps things interesting.

You never know.

CHAPTER 44

Make It Funny, Honey

Penny with Jerry Belson at the 1982 roast of her brother, Garry

Nunu Zomot

*I*N MID-OCTOBER 2006, just a few days before my birthday, Jerry Belson died following a difficult battle with cancer. He was at his home in the hills, surrounded by his family, including his daughters and his wife of thirty-five years, JoAnn, who was remarkable throughout his illness and made sure that his last days and hours were as comfortable as humanly possible. My brother called me, trying to sound strong but breaking down as he delivered the news about his writing partner and friend of forty-five years. "Jerry's gone."

Even though Jerry had been sick for a while and, if you asked him, in poor health since shortly after he was born sixty-eight years prior, it was inconceivable to think that he was gone. Everyone felt that way. He was a fresh breath of cynicism and warmth. In a way, I had known him for as long as I had known my brother. I was eight when Garry left home for college, and when I reconnected with him upon moving to Los Angeles, he and Jerry were a team. Jerry was always in the picture, at Rob's and my house, on *The Odd Couple,* and at my birthday parties.

My brother arranged for a memorial on a Monday afternoon at his theater in Burbank, the Falcon, and everyone turned out. It was a packed house. Michael Eisner and Hector Elizondo had to watch on TVs in the lobby. It was *that* crowded. Garry told Jerry about it before he passed. "Please don't be candid," Jerry had told my brother a few days earlier. It was like them to have discussed what was basically their last show together.

"He thought it would be nice if we got together," my brother informed the roomful of people. "He didn't know about Monday, though. I said we had a show every other night. He said, 'What a shame it would be if I go and the Falcon loses money.'"

There wasn't a dry eye in the theater — and mostly that was from laughing so hard at the stories people told about Jerry. His brother, Gordon, and several longtime friends spoke about his growing up in El Centro, California. His first agent spoke about discovering this major talent who had only written comic books for his own amusement before trying his hand at a script. His daughter Kristine, the middle of his three children, also spoke on behalf of the family. His sister, Monica Johnson, sat with them, daubing her eyes with a tissue and deferring to others, starting with Lowell Ganz, who recalled being in awe of Jerry when he started at Paramount fresh out of college and with absolutely no experience.

"Not only hadn't I written a script before," he said, "I had never met anyone who had written."

Then, one day, as Lowell told it, he was eavesdropping on Jerry and several other writers, including Harvey Miller, and he felt his stomach sink into a pit of despair. "I thought if you had to be as funny as Jerry to be a sitcom writer I was doomed," he said. "But later I realized there was a large gap between Jerry and employable." He went on to praise my brother and Jerry as teachers. He said Garry was instructive and hands-on, whereas Jerry "had the attitude of 'why should they know what I know?'"

I went to the podium and read a message from Carol Kane and a longer remembrance from Paul Schrader, who recalled phoning Jerry one day, asking if he wanted to get together. Jerry said he was too depressed to get out of bed, but Paul was welcome to come over.

So he did, and once there he got into bed with Jerry. Then Albert Brooks dropped by, found them in bed, and climbed in with them. They talked and laughed for a couple hours, until Jerry was ready to get up. Paul called it one of the happiest days of his life.

"I don't want to read Paul's book," cracked Albert, who followed me up to the stage. Dressed in black, he let out a sigh that captured the way all of us were feeling at that moment. Like, really? "I spoke to him a few days before he died," Albert said. "He said, 'I have cancer.' I said, 'How's it going?' He said, 'If they give you a choice between che-motherapy and death, pick death.'" Albert told more stories that had everyone laughing hilariously. "He said he didn't know how much longer he had," Albert continued. "A day, a week, a year, fifteen years. He didn't know. I said, 'Isn't this exactly like our first conversation forty years ago?'"

Carl Reiner said a few words, as did Rob, who spoke about how all of us had always looked up to Jerry. Rob recalled a trip he and I had taken with Jerry and his wife, JoAnn, to the Dominican Republic. We had gone into town and were walking around when we saw a man with no legs on the corner. We all assumed he was a beggar. But as we stood there, Jerry quipped, "He's waiting for the sign to change from 'Don't Crawl' to 'Crawl.'"

Tracey Ullman and Jim Brooks added to the funny memories. My brother also reminded us of one of the best Jerry stories, which was how he proposed to JoAnn. Apparently she gave him an ultimatum: marry her or she'd go to Europe. Needing time to think, he drove her to the airport. There, she repeated the ultimatum. "What do you want? Should I take off? Or should I stay?" she asked. He rubbed his beard. "Can you take off and circle?"

I mentioned that Jerry always said, "I paid for your braces," a refer-ence to the braces I wore in the movie *How Sweet It Is,* and added, "So you have to give me drugs." He was a big pot smoker. "Then he'd call me up and say, 'I'm coming over so hide everything.' But then he'd show up and beg." I recalled he had made a guest appearance on one of the *Laverne & Shirley* talent show episodes, and he'd been incredibly nervous. But he was wonderful — and he was going to be missed.

At the end of the gathering, the memorial, whatever you want to call it, everyone sat still for a few moments. No one moved. We had been ushered into a special place. For many of us, it was a trip back to a special time. We didn't want to be reminded that it had ended. We wanted to hear Jerry pick up the phone one more time and say, as he always did, "Hey, babe." We wanted his advice one more time, even though he always said the same thing: "Make it funny, honey."

We tried. He succeeded. As we testified that afternoon, the many laughs he had created lived on, and would live on, continuing to do their job, providing people a temporary timeout from the harshness and hardship of life. For that grown-up kid from El Centro who had given me so much professionally and personally, that was very cool.

CHAPTER 45

Get Me Some White Castles

Garry, Penny, and Ronny at the 1992 American Comedy Awards,
where Penny received the Creative Achievement Award

Barbara Marshall / Tracy Reiner

GARRY AND I WERE at an event for AARP in Las Vegas. He was telling old jokes to an old audience, and I was trying to keep up with him, apparently cracking a few funny lines of my own. Actors John Amos and George Takei were also on the panel with us. In sport coats and ties, they looked appropriate for a discussion on the Golden Age of television, as opposed to me, in a navy sweatshirt and baseball cap. I seemed ready for a pickup ballgame at the park.

Garry said that I was hilarious, but I can't remember what I said. It was the end of October 2009, and something was wrong with me. I walked off the stage in a daze. Garry was concerned about me. Sensing something was wrong, he asked how I felt and suggested I go back to L.A. with him. It was only a forty-five-minute flight, he said, and maybe I should see my doctor. He should have been more insistent.

Assuring him that I was tired and would sleep on the plane, I gave him a hug at the airport before we went off to different terminals. I wanted to get to New York. God forbid I miss any fun. My friend Joanne worked for the New York Giants and had given me passes to the season's first home game and I was attending a fund-raiser for the

Brain Injury Association of New York State. But my never-ending quest for five more minutes of fun hit a snag at airport security. I couldn't find my ID and they wouldn't let me through.

Annoyed, I snapped, "Obviously it's me." The TSA folks did not respond well to my testiness. They escorted me to a private room where I waited a few moments until the head officer came in. He looked at me and declared, "She's Laverne. Let her go through."

After reaching New York, I spent the night in my apartment and woke up ready for the football game. My friend Diana picked me up. We spent the pre-game on the field, enjoying a close-up view of the festivities, celebrating the team's Super Bowl victory the previous season. A lot of former players came back for the game, and Michael Strahan was pushed onto the field in a fake trophy. I was enjoying myself when it was time to make our way toward the owner's seats. That required a walk up the stadium, halfway around, then back down to the front row on the 50-yard line.

After getting up the first set of stairs, I began to have difficulty. A security guy from the Nets basketball games recognized me and offered to get a cart. Diana sat me down. "You're walking funny," she said. I looked down at my feet. "I don't have on the right sneakers," I said.

"I don't think it's that," she said.

One thing I did know was that I was feeling off, different, and suddenly that frightened me.

"Let's go home and watch on TV," I said.

A surgeon friend named Rula, who worked for Ronald Perelman, came over and said I seemed okay and maybe needed some rest. I called a masseuse I had used on several movies, and she came over and gave me a massage. Then I must have taken a Xanax to put me to sleep because the rest of the night is a blur. Apparently I called a number of people, including my brother, my assistant, Terry in L.A., and Chris Mullin's wife, Liz. Later, they all told me the same story—that I had called but didn't make any sense.

I woke up in the morning in a semifog to find that Diana and my former assistant, Bonnie, had called Ronald, who had a car waiting downstairs to take me to the hospital. I must have been more out of it than I remember to have let them take me to the hospital without putting up a struggle. I'm too stubborn normally. After an exam and various tests in the emergency room, I was taken in a wheelchair back to the ER where Rula, Bonnie, and Diana were waiting for me.

"See, I'm fine," I said.

But I wasn't. Soon a sober-looking doctor came into the room holding my file with what I assume were the results of the preliminary tests. With a minimum of bedside manner, he got right to the point. I had lung cancer and a brain tumor. Bonnie ran out and threw up in the bushes. Rula and Diane, holding back tears, looked at me. I took a deep breath and let the news sink in. I was strangely, eerily calm, as I get in a crisis situation. It's the way I imagine Michael Jordon must have felt in the final seconds of a game. Maybe it has to do with being a pragmatist and problem solver, and accepting life for what it is, rather than dwelling on what it isn't. In any event, time slowed and my thinking grew sharper and clearer.

"All right," I said.

"All right what?" Diana said.

"Is the driver still here?" I asked.

"I think so," Diana said.

"Good," I said. "Can you send him to get me some White Castles?"

They rolled me into the biggest private room I'd ever seen in my life. Ronald called my brother, my sister, and my daughter and told them to come to New York. The next day everyone arrived. They were all flipping out; I stayed calm. I treated the news like everything else that popped up unexpectedly on my agenda. As Carrie Fisher later observed, I don't have a high enough voice to get crazy like everyone else. I was also impressed that there was a private chef on the floor. However, he only had a microwave oven, so he couldn't even make an English muffin. But I learned his mother had taken dancing lessons from my mother.

"Your mother was the Marjorie of Marjorie Marshall's Dance School?" he asked.

I nodded. "Yep."

"I grew up hearing all about it."

"Me too," I said.

It all came back to dance school.

The room kept filling up with people. I don't know how word spread, but family and friends came. My firemen friends came. Ronald was there, telling me to look at the view. The window looked out on New York. It was a stunning view, something you'd see in a Woody Allen movie. Just gorgeous. I couldn't have cared less. I am not a hospital person.

I had a benefit that night, the Brain Injury Association dinner. Lorraine Bracco and I, the honorary chairpersons for the event, got involved with the organization after a dear friend named Steve Green was injured in a hit-and-run accident in 2007. While visiting him at the hospital, we met Joanne Miller, who was heading the dinner. Her son, also named Steve, had been injured in a construction accident at the World Trade Center site. We all promised to support BIANYS. Once involved, I also learned about all the soldiers returning from the Gulf and Afghanistan with brain injuries of one kind or another. What I realized following 9/11 is that you can't just lie in bed and wait for other people to do something. It's up to you.

"No, you're not going," Ronald said, looking around the room for support from my brother and the doctors he'd brought in.

"Yes, I am," I said. "Lorraine is going with me. We're the goddamn chairpersons. I have Otis Anderson from the Giants going. He's a big guy. He has good hands. He'll catch me if I fall."

"That's not funny," Ronald said.

"I'm not in any pain," I said. "I'm going."

As Jim Brooks once said, there's no stopping me once I put my mind to something — even if my mind has a tumor. That night I got ready at my apartment and went to the event in a hydrogen-powered car that I had been asked to promote. I met Lorraine and Ronald and his wife, Anna, there. The event honored ABC reporter Bob Woodruff and Trisha Meili, the Central Park jogger, both of whom had overcome traumatic brain injuries. As the evening progressed, I went outside every once in a while for a cigarette. Each time, Ronald gave me a dirty look.

"What? I already have the cancer," I said.

I returned to my palatial hospital room — feeling fine, I might add — where my brain surgery was scheduled for Friday. I met the surgeon, who said he was in the midst of getting a shotgun divorce and would then head to Florida to hunt and fish. So he was in a wonderful mood. Just the guy I wanted drilling into my skull. I spent all day Thursday filling out forms. Each one seemed the same. I must have written out all my allergies to opiates, latex, rubber, etc. a thousand times. The surgeon explained they would put me out with propofol, which I love, and also give me a little morphine. I heard that and went ballistic.

"Do you not read the fucking forms?" I said. "I spent six hours writing down that I was allergic to opiates."

Ronald bent down and whispered in my ear: "You can't yell at him. He's doing me a favor."

"You yell at people," I said.

"That's different."

"But I'm allergic," I said.

"How about Dilantin?" the doctor said.

"Isn't that the same thing?" I asked.

"No," he said.

I ended up having Tylenol and feeling no pain. It was explained to me that there are no nerve endings up there. But I woke up with eighty-two IVs in one hand, which swelled to the size of a baseball mitt. Several nurses came in one after another and told me about the procedure I had just had and then they asked me to repeat it back to them. When the second nurse asked the same question, I snapped, "I already did that. I have it." I'm not a great patient.

"Just don't yell at everyone," Ronald said.

"I'm sorry," I said. "I get frustrated."

After three or four more hours in the recovery room, I began insisting on a change. I had woken up in the fetal position because they didn't know how to make the bed longer. The incompetence drove me nuts. Finally, they put me back in the big room, where my doctor visited me and said good-bye at the same time. He was on his way to Florida. That pissed me off, too. Later that night, I reached for my purse to light up a cigarette. My fireman friend Mikey, who was visiting, jumped out of his chair and grabbed the cigarette out of my hand.

"Holy mother of —," he said. "There are about to be eighty-five fire trucks here. Did you look behind you?"

"No," I said. "I'm too busy looking at the beautiful view."

"Well, look behind you," he said.

I did. There was a row of oxygen tanks.

"Oh," I said. "I didn't know."

"Yeah, you could've blown up the hospital — or at least this floor."

So I was back in my apartment on Saturday.

Ronald, bless him, had a twenty-four-hour driver and round-the-clock nurses for me. Friends brought groceries and sat in the kitchen while I dozed on and off. I kept my television on and set the air-conditioning so that my room was the temperature of a meat locker. Every four hours the poor nurses came into my bedroom to give me Tylenol and check my blood pressure. They dressed like they were braving a winter storm. The phone rang nonstop. There were fifty-two people in my apartment and everyone waited for me to answer.

"Can't someone pick up the fucking phone?" I growled at one nurse.

"No, Miss Penny," she said sweetly. "It's for you."

I hated answering the phone. My throat was irritated from the tube they had put down it during surgery. I sounded like I was at death's door. And everyone asked the same question: "Are you alive? I read you're dying." All the tabloids and gossip websites reported that I had liver cancer and only months to live. *Pray for her,* they said.

"I'm not fucking dying," I yelled into the phone countless times. "They make up shit."

After eight weeks, the stitches came out of my head, and I had the most enjoyable shower and shampoo of my life. Tracy took wonderful care of me — as did Ronald and the medical team he had arranged. Doctors, nurses, security, White Castles, and bagels . . . I was fortunate. I had the best care (and food) available. Did that make me the best patient? Probably not. One nurse kept trying to give me a Valium and take me for a walk. I thought she had it backward, and I wasn't shy about telling her so.

"Why don't we walk and *then* I'll take a Valium? Better yet, why don't you take a Valium and I'll keep watching TV? I can get to the kitchen just fine."

Now able to travel, I returned home, met with doctors, and set up a treatment plan. My surgeon was at Cedars-Sinai; I liked him. My radiologist was at UCLA; I liked him, too. My oncologist was also at UCLA; I didn't like him. We had a run-in at the end of my first exam. He wanted to put a "smart port" in my chest. He said my veins wouldn't be able to handle all the IVs I would need. That wasn't the problem.

The problem arose when he also said the port would be convenient at the end.

"Excuse me?" I said.

"Death with dignity," he said.

Obviously he had never seen *Laverne & Shirley.* Otherwise he would've known I was not concerned about dignity.

"You'll be able to have a morphine drip," he continued.

"Wait," I interrupted. "Didn't you read the forms I filled out? I'm allergic to morphine. That's not dignity. That's me throwing up all over."

I didn't plan on dying — not yet. As far as I was concerned, cancer was like my mother telling me it was getting dark outside and it was time to come in. But I could still see the ball. I wanted five more minutes — at least. I had 18 days of radiation for my head at UCLA. My friends Carlene Watkins Weinberger, Wendi Lasky, and my assistant Terry Trahan drove me every day. They made sure I didn't get lost and were nice to the nurses. I got a pass to use the handicapped parking spaces; that made me happy. I also liked seeing Ronald Perelman's name on the side of the hospital. It gave me a sense of comfort as I went through treatments. And as long as I was there, I saw a dentist at the David Geffen School of Dentistry.

The radiation cleared my head of cancer — and of everything else around it. My memory was gone. Then I had to deal with the cancer in my lungs. They told me it was a little spot; fine. I knew that was better than a big spot or a lot of spots. Since I wasn't fond of my "death with dignity" oncologist at UCLA, I changed to one at Cedars-Sinai. He headed the lung program. He and my surgeon knew that I was allergic to opiates, and they said I should have it zapped.

They felt radiation and chemotherapy could be as effective as surgery. I went for treatments several times a week, and after six months the tumor disappeared. They were right. Zapping was better than cutting. Afterward, I went for monthly scans where they injected me with so many radioactive isotopes I could have lived in Japan. Each time I got good news.

But there were side effects. I gained sixty pounds. Everyone else in the world on chemo and radiation loses weight. Somehow I got fat. Better fat than dead. At the Lakers and Clippers games, players on both teams and their opponents said they had me in their prayers. I had to constantly tell them that I wasn't dying — except when they put me up on the JumboTron. *Then* I died of embarrassment. I looked like a big, fat *South Park* kid. I complained to my oncologist.

"I'm depressed," I said.

"The reason you're depressed is that you gained weight," he said.

"Well, how do I lose weight?" I asked.

"How should I know?" he said. "I'm a lung doctor."

Great.

Fortunately, Carrie Fisher was the new celebrity spokeswoman for Jenny Craig. I called her and asked for some meals. Thirty years earlier we had dropped acid. Now we were microwaving our Jenny meals. What had we become?

Fat!

Food wasn't the only thing I gave up. I quit smoking cigarettes, too. A smoker since junior high school, I had read the warnings, heard the news reports, and knew the dangers. I had tried to quit numerous times before, including once while I was married to Rob (he begged me to start again), another time with Artie in Australia (we bet $10,000), and again in the early '80s when I visited director Miloš Forman in London—and he asked that question worth repeating, "Why don't you visit someone you hate?" I was a better smoker than not.

I knew I couldn't get off the nicotine alone. I brought in a guy from the Allen Carr's Easyway center. Allen Carr was a British guy who was a chain smoker like me and quit after coming up with a theory that smoking was connected to the fears and anxieties of not being able to smoke. They even let you smoke while they explained the rationale behind their program.

Kooky? Maybe. But it worked. I put out my last cigarette and didn't light up again, didn't miss it, didn't have any withdrawal, and stayed that way for eight months. Then, on November 1, 2010, my friend Monica Johnson died of esophageal cancer. She was at Cedars-Sinai, the same place I had been getting my treatments. She had spent the past few years living in Palm Springs. A few weeks before her death she posted her own obit on her website:

> She went to the desert to find her health, her spiritual needs, herself, and to write a book. She wound up in Palm Springs across the street from the Spa Casino. The spiritual aspect of the desert renewal faded like everything else left in the sun.

Monica's sister-in-law, JoAnn Belson, hosted a memorial for her. I was among those who spoke. I was very emotional and thought a cocktail might help me through a tough afternoon, but I wasn't a drinker. I didn't like it. What I did like were cigarettes, and as I chatted with people afterward I said to myself, "I'll just have one." But I couldn't smoke just one. I can't have just one of anything. Lamps. Tomato plants. Hummingbird feeders. Autographed baseballs. And most certainly cigarettes. Within a day I was back to my same habit.

Fuck.

There went my chance at achieving perfection.

I still smoke. I know I should quit. I think the reason I haven't tried to quit again is that I'm bad at prioritizing my problems. Take today: I asked myself, should I quit smoking or try to finally figure out how to use my DVR?

I feel like I have a better chance with the TV, but I don't know. I've been struggling with the fucking remote for two years. The frustration might kill me before the cigarettes.

CHAPTER 46

Five More Minutes

Penny on Santa's lap in 1948

Marshall personal collection

Penny with her daughter, Tracy; Tracy's husband, Matt; and their
children, Spencer, Bella, and Viva, in 2011

Marshall personal collection

S O THEN WHAT? Like anyone, after hearing the words *cancer, malignant,* and *metastasized* all in one sentence, I wondered not only how much time I had left but what I was going to do with that time. (As you know, I sent for White Castle burgers.) A year later, after I began to hear the words *remission* and *cure* and *we'll check you once a year,* I found myself asking similar questions. What was I going to do with the rest of my life?

Bucket list time, right?

Wrong.

I had every kind of list you can imagine—to-do lists, lists of calls I needed to return, lists of thank-you notes I needed to write, lists of books I wanted to read and movies I wanted to watch, lists of invitations requiring a response, lists of things in the garage I wanted to get rid of. I had lists coming out of my ass. But none of them were bucket lists.

Were you supposed to have one? Apparently that memo never got to me. My bucket list, if you can call it that, had started and stopped fifty-seven years earlier when I got my own bedroom. Mission accomplished. Everything that came afterward had been gravy. My own phone? Check. Marriage? Double check. Motherhood? Check. Grandmotherhood? Check. Three times over. Good, lasting friendships? Check. Work I love? Check. Floor seats at Lakers and Clippers games? Check. Motorcycle through Europe? Check. Giving back to others less fortunate? Check. Losing weight? I was down thirty pounds, so mostly a check. Jumping out of an airplane? No thanks, I don't like heights so much.

I worked a day on my brother's movie, *New Year's Eve,* and then guested on the IFC comedy *Portlandia* with Portland Trailblazer LaMarcus Aldridge playing my boyfriend. I hosted Thanksgiving dinner for Garry's, Ronny's, and my family. Joe Pesci arrived late, as always, and played guitar and sang. I read movie scripts, watched TV series that inquired about me either directing or acting, and cheered the Lakers and Clippers through disappointing efforts in the 2012 playoffs. There's always next year, guys.

I've also enjoyed being a grandmother to my three grandchildren, who range in ages from 20 to 6. Surprisingly, it's a role I like. Not surprisingly, I go about it in my own way. I'm not blind like my grandmother was, but their school performances usually start a little early for me. They send videotapes, we talk on the phone, and Tracy brings them to see me. They're good kids, and Tracy is a terrific mother — much better than I ever was.

But I would ask myself, is this enough? Should I be doing more with my life?

I didn't know. One day I got on my computer and searched for "What do people do with their lives after surviving cancer?" Nothing came up. Apparently people didn't do anything. I guessed they either dropped dead from trying to pay their medical bills or they went back to whatever they had been doing before, because what the fuck else is there to do when, as in my case, you like your life?

Indeed, one day Dennis Rodman called and asked me to make a documentary about his life. He said I could talk to all of his family, friends, ex-wives, girlfriends, teammates, and opponents. No door would be closed, he insisted. He had already written three books, though, and given God knows how many interviews. What was there left to say?

Well, we had a long talk about what he was doing and why he wanted me to undertake such a project and it boiled down to him knowing that he was fucked up. He drank and had money problems. I think he was scared. He wanted to have his story told. He wanted others to tell it. I think he knew it would come out sounding like the character he had created if he told it himself, while others would talk about the real Dennis. That Dennis had been in the NBA for years before he had his first drink, was pathologically shy, worked incredibly hard, did many nice things for people without needing to publicize them, and ended up in the Hall of Fame.

Dennis came to my house, where I sat him in front of a camera and did the first of three in-depth interviews. In between, I interviewed his family, his former teammates, opponents, coaches, referees, announcers, and writers. I interviewed everyone, and along the way Dennis would check in. I came to realize that he had enlisted me to help him figure out his life.

It was ingenious of him. Somewhere along the way, we all want to — or at least try to — figure out why we're here and what all the fuck it means, you know? I was doing it for him, but also confirming a few things for myself, starting with the fact that I didn't have to figure out what to do with my life.

I was doing it.

When my mother was little, her mother showered her with praise and told her she was incredible. She hated it. It made her nuts. She swore that she wouldn't make the same mistake with her children. Well, it worked. I thought being rag monitor in eleventh grade was pretty good, so I guess I surpassed expectations, hers and mine. When I look back, I see that I did it by sticking to the rules I learned when I was a kid and trying to make each day a good one, whether

I was sneaking off to the Parkway to be with friends or directing a movie. People call me a trailblazer, but as far as I'm concerned, the only Trailblazers I know play basketball in Portland. I don't think about the awards I haven't won or been nominated for. I don't get that stuff. Neither does my brother. We aren't that kind of family. We just do our best to entertain people.

My mother knew that was important. Maybe she wasn't as nuts as we thought. I don't know. What I do know after living sixty-eight years is that one way or another everything works out. How else does a girl whose life was about hating dancing school and hanging out on the Parkway fence end up with a star on the Hollywood Walk of Fame? Or even better. Jermaine, the paralyzed kid I met a few years ago in New York and helped out, recently came to my apartment and fixed my Wi-Fi. In a small way, that's also an example of things working out.

Oh, I also know something else to be true.

Perky is overrated.

A few years ago I did a *Vanity Fair* magazine "Proust Questionnaire." Among the questions they asked was what I disliked most about my appearance. "You name it, I hate it," I said. They asked what my greatest regret was. "That when I was a size 0 there was no 0," I said. They also asked what or who was the greatest love of my life. "Pizza and my daughter," I said.

As you can see, I haven't changed much over the years. My friends are still my most treasured possessions, just as they were when I was a kid. If you were to ask my greatest accomplishment, I would start naming names — and it would take a long time, too, because I keep up with everyone from NBA players to the kids I grew up with in my building in the Bronx. The only thing that has changed about me is that I don't worry as much about getting asked to the dances.

I've been given my five minutes . . . and then some.

Acknowledgments

M Y BROTHER, SISTER and I are 110 years old, but we still refer to our parents as Mommy and Daddy, and I want to put them at the front of the thank-you portion of this book. Although I was an accident, it worked out good for me, and so to my mother, who was nuts, and my father, who was my father, thank you. I also want to thank my brother, Garry, my sister, Ronny, and my extended family, all twenty-four of them, especially my daughter Tracy, my son-in-law Matt, and their three children, Spencer, Bella, and Viva, who have given me immense pleasure in life while having to put up with . . . well, I don't want to know. There are probably more times than I want to know about when Tracy has sounded like me and said, "My mother is nuts." Like my mother, though, I choose to ignore it. At least we've had a lot of laughs, and continue to have a lot of laughs.

· · ·

I want to thank Carrie Fisher, my friend and partner in crime for more than 30 years. We've lasted longer than all of our marriages combined. Our crazy lives have meshed perfectly. We've always said it's because we never liked the same drugs or men, but I know there's more to it. I want to thank my two ex-husbands and my boyfriends: Mickey was and always remained a very good guy, and without him I wouldn't have my daughter or grandchildren. Rob was a lot of fun and like me recognized when it wasn't, and yet we still remain friends. How could we be anything but friends after having gone through those extraordinary years together? It should be known that when I called him up to talk about this book he reminded me of stories and asked, "Did you write about when Tracy burned my new Mercedes with the cigarette lighter?" More proof that it's always better to laugh.

I want to thank Art Garfunkel, who showed me the world and was still himself just the other day when we spoke. I thanked him yet again for never letting me do heroin, and he worried that I was going to make it seem as if he based that off his own prior experience. He didn't. He was just smart.

I want to thank my assistants over the years, Amy and Bonnie, both of whom became producers, Nicole, Kristin, Jon-Michael, and Terry, who is the best. I want to thank all my doctors, who helped me dodge a bullet, the nurses who helped me recuperate, and Ronald Perelman, who has made sure I have received the best care because he just knows those kind of things. He is the friend everyone wishes they had. And also thanks to his family and staff.

I want to thank Cindy for being there with me back in the '70s and still being with me in our 60s. I recently (as of this writing) went to David Lander's 65th birthday party and had a great time, seeing him and his wife, as well as Carl Gottlieb and Larry Hankin and others from The Committee. I also saw Fred Willard, Ed Begley Jr., and Peter Elbling. They are all people who appeared on *Laverne & Shirley*.

I want to thank all of them and everyone else who made me laugh. There are a lot of dead people I still like, and I want to thank them, too. They include John, Ted, Jerry, Harvey, Britney, and Monica.

I need to thank my friends Carlene W., Wendi L., Paula H., Sheila J., Joann L., Jimmy and Mark W., Chris D., Big Al, the Mullins, Christopher G., Joe S., Joe P., Beverly D., Dwight M., Lorraine B., Sara C., Ken R., Chico B., Valorie A., Jane W., Patti S-M., Jimmy R., Michi, E, Jon L., Tom H., Paula R-S., Caren G., Robert A, Joel P., Steve G., George P., and Kori B.

I also want to thank everyone in my old building on the Grand Concourse and my neighborhood, all of my friends from JHS 80, Walton High School, UNM, and everyone I knew at Camps Odetah, Onibar-Geneva and Diana-Dalmaqua. Then there is everyone from my mother's dancing school. Even though I complained, those were good times — and I hope all of you are doing well. I haven't mentioned a few guys that I slept with over the years, but thank you, too. I have to thank the casts and crews of the movies I directed and produced. I want to thank Dick Clark for *American Bandstand*. Ringo Starr once recognized me at an airport. That was cool. So thank you. Dennis — thank you for being crazy. Rosie, love you, and thanks. Marcia, get well and stop driving people to airports. And to those I left out, I'm sorry. I have to thank my two dogs, Larry Bird and Magic. But they should thank me for not sending them "to the country." They have it so much better at my house.

Last but not least, I want to thank my manager Alan Iezman of Shelter Entertainment Group and my literary agent Dan Strone at Trident Media Group for creating the opportunity for me to do this book. I also want to thank my assistant Susan Yi at Parkway Productions, and Dan's assistant Kseniya Zaslavskaya at Trident, and Alan's assistant Martha Sanchez for facilitating so much. Then a special thanks to the talented team at Amazon Publishing led by publisher Larry Kirshbaum, editorial director Julia Cheiffetz, publicity director Katie Finch, marketing director Kiwa Iyobe, and also Carly Hoffmann and Katie Salisbury.

Finally I want to thank my collaborator Todd Gold, who let me blow smoke in his face but never up his . . . Thank you very much.